A LIFE INSIDE BRITISH CLIMBING'S GOLDEN AGE

HANGING ON

A LIFE INSIDE BRITISH CLIMBING'S GOLDEN AGE

HANGING ON

MARTIN BOYSEN

Vertebrate Publishing, Sheffield
www.v-publishing.co.uk

ACKNOWLEDGEMENTS

I should like to thank the many friends and members of my family who have encouraged me to complete my book. I am particularly grateful to those who so generously offered the photographs for the book. In particular I owe my gratitude to Susan Czerski who managed to transform my scrawl into legible print and to all of the publishing team at Vertebrate.

HANGING ON
Martin Boysen

First published in 2014 by Vertebrate Publishing.
This paperback edition first published in 2017 by Vertebrate Publishing.

 Vertebrate Publishing
Crescent House, 228 Psalter Lane, Sheffield S11 8UT.
www.v-publishing.co.uk

This book is a work of non-fiction based on the life of Martin Boysen. The author has stated to the publishers that, except in such minor respects not affecting the substantial accuracy of the work, the contents of the book are true.

A CIP catalogue record for this book is available from the British Library.

ISBN: 978-1-911342-31-1 (Paperback)
ISBN: 978-1-910240-01-4 (eBook)

Design and production by Jane Beagley. Cover design by Nathan Ryder.

 Vertebrate Publishing
www.v-publishing.co.uk

Vertebrate Publishing is committed to printing on paper from sustainable sources.

Printed and bound in Scotland by Bell & Bain Ltd.

CONTENTS

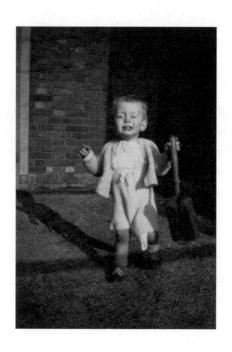

ONE
BEGINNINGS

My earliest memories are the wailing of air-raid sirens followed by the droning of Lancaster bombers and the distant thump of high explosives. I was always the first to wake and initiate the rush to the cellars with my mother, older sister and brother, Lorna and Bill. It was our misfortune to be living in Germany in the small mining town of Alsdorf close to Aachen. I was four years old and the war was drawing to its bitter end.

Why we were 'on the wrong side', stuck in Germany, perhaps needs to be explained. My mother was English, but my father was German. They had met each other when my father was a student on an exchange visit to England as part of his degree in English and music at Cologne University. He lodged at my grandmother's house in the village of Pembury near Tunbridge Wells in Kent. My parents fell in love and my mother became pregnant out of wedlock. This caused a dreadful stir in the village where my grandmother was a pillar of the community and my grandfather the owner of the village grocer's.

The relationship between my grandma and my father, somewhat sarcastically referred to as 'dear Jens', was never going to be easy and at the time of Lorna's birth it was understandably at an all-time low. After a quiet wedding in the old village church they fled to Germany where my father began his teaching career and the young newly-weds established their first home. We became a comfortably-off, middle-class family with three young children and my father starting in his first good job. Unfortunately my parents, along with most other intellectuals, were unconcerned or unaware of the stealthy advance of the Nazi party. Hitler had been a figure of amusement before he held the reins of power. Germany advanced on its nightmarish course.

I was born in 1941, when the Allies might so easily have lost the war. It must have been a nerve-wracking time for my mother. Contemporary photos and letters reveal the desperation of events; the increasing frequency of bombing raids, the lack of food, the struggle to stay alive. My father was enlisted in the Wehrmacht at a late stage and sent to the Eastern Front. I have no memory of him from this time. Indeed, I would not see him until five years after the war had finished.

We survived as a family hunkered down in our cellar, wisely refusing to uproot ourselves to a supposedly safer location. During the last desperate days before all communication from the outside world ceased the fateful black-rimmed letter arrived. My father had 'died heroically' for the Fatherland. My mother was strangely unconvinced by this terrible news, perhaps because my father had intimated his intention of staying alive and surrendering to the Russians at the first opportunity. His chance came in 1943 as the German offensive into the Kursk salient collapsed and the Soviet Union seized the initiative on the Eastern Front.

He was lucky to survive the first harrowing forced marches to prison camp in the Ukraine but once he arrived he was treated surprisingly well considering the atrocities committed by the German forces on the Russians. He was soon segregated from the hardened Nazis, given the task of forming a camp orchestra, and subjected to 're-education', a gentle form of brainwashing, which worked extremely well. My father had been politically naive before the war, but like many other unworldly intellectuals, he became a devoted Communist and remained so until his death. For many years after his return from prison camp we received Soviet newsletters and magazines warmly glorifying the happy workers presided over by smiling 'Uncle Joe'.

As the war finally drew to a close, it seemed a miracle that the whole family had survived – then tragedy struck. Aachen and the surrounding area was one of the first parts of Germany to be liberated by British troops. It was hugely exciting. Hungry children besieged the young 'Tommies', pestering them for sweets and any spare rations. My eight-year-old sister Lorna somehow caught the attention of a playful 18-year-old soldier, who teased her and pretended to steal her shoe. She demanded it back, advanced to get it and he aimed his rifle and 'pretended' to shoot. Only the gun was not unloaded, as he thought and claimed later at his court martial, and she was shot dead – with a bullet through her head.

I was – luckily – too young to realise exactly what had happened. To me it was just another inexplicable disappearance at a time full of strange happenings. But it was a shattering blow to my mother who had been so strong, resourceful and brave throughout these terrible times. When the Allies took over the administration of the area she was enlisted to help translate and act as co-ordinator. During the course of her duties, she discovered she was on the final list of persons to be sent to concentration camps for punishment in the last desperate days of Nazi bloodletting.

Germany was in a terrible state of ruin. Hardly a building remained undamaged. The roads were potholed with bomb craters. Unexploded shells and grenades were frequently found, and we children played soldiers amongst the ruins, collecting shrapnel as a hobby. Food was scarce but, due to the foresight of local miners, some milk was available; they had hidden the local herd of cows in the mine to prevent their seizure by the retreating army.

It was time for our broken family to return to the relative calm of England, to re-establish itself and await the return of my father from Russia. Passage was quickly arranged. A jeep and driver were made available, and the trip to Ostend began. It was an exciting journey and I particularly remember man-oeuvring around countless burnt-out tanks in the narrow forested valleys of the Ardennes – remnants of the last-ditch German assault on the advancing Allies. We reached Ostend in the evening and embarked on a troop ship filled with soldiers and sailors happy to have survived the war. I remember being spoiled by the soldiers and offered chocolate, an unknown luxury.

We arrived at Tilbury where my grandfather and his brother, Uncle Arthur, the grocery van driver, awaited in his Austin 7. We were too late for the Dartford ferry so our route was extended through the Blackwall Tunnel and then through the North Downs to Pembury. It was a strange arrival to a house with open fires, my unknown grandma and our 'odd' auntie – Aunt Margaret – who kept an injured green woodpecker in a cardboard box.

From my earliest days in England I rejoiced in the beauty of the coun-tryside. The house, 'Valeside', was situated on top of a hill with wide views of the Weald framed by huge silver birch trees. There were forests nearby and almost every day I walked or was pushed by my 'mad' auntie Margaret along sunken lanes and woodland paths where we collected wild fruits, mushrooms, chestnuts and sticks for the fire to heat the freezing house. My mother taught me the names of all the wild flowers and where to look for lizards and slowworms on the sunny roadside banks below our house. The winter of 1947 was extremely harsh; fuel was almost unobtainable, food was rationed and life was not easy. Fortunately my grandfather had a large garden where we kept chickens and rabbits and his allotment provided welcome fruit and vegetables.

My mother took up teaching again and started work in Germany with the children of army families of the British forces stationed there. It was not a happy time for me; I missed my mother badly. I had started school in the village barely able to speak English and not surprisingly the whole school seemed to gang up on me as I took on the role of 'the German' in the games of war, which children endlessly pursued.

An incident that still rankles with me happened on St George's Day. I slipped on some steps and had a greenstick fracture of my arm. All afternoon I was in agony and could barely hold my crayons to draw the required Union Jack. At the end of school a teacher walked me the two miles to the local hospital where the break was diagnosed on X-ray. The matron was most unsympathetic. When asked how I had done it I was accused of being 'a little liar'. According to the official account I had done it breaking school rules, swinging on the toilet door.

Most of the time, our grandparents looked after my brother Bill and me. My grandmother seemed a stern and rather remote guardian but my grandfather was a kind man who taught me a lot; I happily accompanied him to his allotment where we grew all manner of crops and he could retreat to his shed and enjoy his 'stinking' pipe in peace. With growing excitement, Bill and I would wait for the school holidays when our mother would return from Germany.

My mother was still there when it was decided we needed a change of school, and we moved to Michael Hall, a Steiner school set on the edge of the Ashdown Forest in Forest Row some 15 miles from our house in Pembury. It was a lovely place, set in an old country house, with extensive gardens, rhododendron jungles and the Kid stream flowing through the grounds. Education at Michael Hall was progressive; learning happened by osmosis rather than rote, art was encouraged, as was freedom of expression. It suited me; there was a huge oak tree in the playground with a ladder giving access to its lowest branches. At playtime, half the school swarmed all over the oak and all manner of ascents and branch traverses were known and attempted. I fell once and was knocked out for an hour or two. This was long before the culture of health and safety had been invented to blight childhood adventure.

For a period, when my mother expected my father's release from the prisoner of war camp in the Soviet Union, we returned to Germany and lived on the outskirts of Essen in a splendid mansion called Hohe Buchen, which had been requisitioned by the Allies from the Nazi mayor. Several large rooms had been converted into classrooms but the main attraction for me was the large swimming pool, huge garden and the way I was spoiled by the large and lovable resident cook Frau Sauermann and her daughter Katie.

In 1950 when we were back in England again after my father's release had been once more delayed, my brother Bill and I were woken up with the exciting news that he was home. We rushed into the sunlit garden where I enjoyed my first embrace with my father, who until that moment had been a stranger. He looked surprisingly well and even spoke fondly of his long sojourn as a prisoner of war. The Russians had soon sorted out the prisoners who were sympathetic to Communism and they were treated fairly. The hardened Nazis were less well treated and it became a concern that several of these recalcitrant types had promised retribution for 'turncoats' like my father when they were eventually released.

He spoke little of his war experiences. I recall him talking of the frightening shriek of 'Stalin's organs', the nickname for the deadly Katyusha rockets. And he liked to tell of the one shot he fired during his time at the front – an accidental discharge of his rifle, which narrowly missed the backside of the old horse dragging his sled.

My parents now decided to make a break with all things German, to start anew as a family living in England. The still discernible animosity between my father and grandmother ensured we quickly moved to a small house in Tonbridge. Although the house itself was poky and unprepossessing, it had a garden, which tumbled down to the River Medway in a series of terraces, and on the largest grew a huge Bramley apple tree. The back of the house had a big ramshackle veranda with a lovely view over playing fields and water meadows which flooded each winter when the normally placid Medway swelled to a turbid rush of water, leaving a fine deposit of brown silt on the garden's lower terraces when it subsided.

My father soon resumed his teaching life with night school classes and violin lessons at the Kent Music School in Maidstone. After the initial warmth and intimacy prompted by his return, he retreated somewhat into his world of music and adopted the traditional role of the stern Teutonic father figure. Piano music became the constant and melodious background to family life and to this day Chopin's Études, Beethoven sonatas and Schubert's Impromptus are engrained in my subconscious.

Our first years in Tonbridge living as a family were full of happiness. Bill had sailed through his 11-plus and was doing well at the grammar school. I attended the local primary school across the water meadows and close to Tonbridge Castle. My progress was less certain and with my dislocated schooling I struggled to make the expected progress. This did not worry me in the slightest as I immersed myself in outdoor activities largely centred on the river: fishing, swimming and natural history. I would leave the house as soon as I could, cycling along the towpaths, camping in the meadows with friends, listening to nightingales at night and the cooing of turtle doves.

We enjoyed our first holiday as a complete family touring Kent on our bicycles and staying in youth hostels. This was followed by a walking holiday in the Trossachs of Scotland, the first moment when I became aware of the enchantment of mountains. It was slightly frustrating, because my parents were content to do easy walks through wooded glens and visit romantic waterfalls rather than scale the heights. I was allowed once to scramble up a low summit, revelling in the physical effort and the liberating expanse of rugged mountaintops.

A year later, at the age of 15, I was old enough to go off by myself and I decided on a walking and bird watching tour of the Cairngorms. I reached the mountains by train from Aberdeen and Braemar and then walked to the tiny youth hostel at the head of the valley. The weather was hot and cloudless and I enjoyed several days in the hills, watching absurdly tame dotterels on the summit of Cairngorm, and eagles soaring over Loch Avon. In the old Caledonian pine forests I watched crested tits chattering away, flocks of crossbills and blundering capercaillies.

My mountain idyll was rudely shattered, however, when I discovered the loss of my wallet containing all my cash, Youth Hostel Association card and train ticket. My parents had gone to Germany and reaching them was impossible. I was downhearted at the thought of prematurely ending my first real adventure but fortunately a whip round by my sympathetic hostel companions produced a ten shilling note, which I was determined would keep me for another week or so.

I walked across the Lairig Ghru and camped out at Corrour bothy, sleeping in my sheet sleeping bag and living on a diet of porridge and tea. Climbing the surrounding hills, I became lean and fit, intoxicated by the surrounding scenery, the smell of heather and cold stone, the dark corries with their nestling snow patches and the clear green lochans into which I plunged thirsty and hot.

Aviemore was no more than a sleepy little railway village at the time. I spent my last few days in the youth hostel, surviving on the leftover food in other people's pigeonholes. I visited Loch an Eilein, gorged myself on a wild cherry tree and finally acknowledged it was time to go home.

With only a few pennies left I set off home and for the first time experienced the joys and frustrations of hitchhiking. I reached Edinburgh starving, a fact which must have been self-evident for as I sat exhausted on a public bench an old lady pressed a half crown into my hand and told me to go buy something to eat. I was astonished at this uncalled for generosity from ordinary people. When I tried to pay for the loaf the baker brushed aside the money and waved me on my way.

It was in my last youth hostel that night that I encountered a rock climber for the first time. He was a stout, bearded man who was addressing the surrounding walkers and cyclists with his feats of daring, extolling the arts of his craft in a slightly patronising manner. I would have left unimpressed had he not mentioned climbing on the sandstone rocks of the Weald. By strange coincidence as I flicked through old YHA magazines that night I came across an article about climbing on these very rocks. It showed a picture of a climber clad in old clothes and plimsolls bridged across a pocketed nose of rock at Eridge. I hadn't realised that rock climbing existed away from the mountains let alone so close to my home. It was something I would have to investigate.

Our family's initial contentment, which followed the move to Tonbridge, soon began to fall apart as Bill and my father moved more and more into conflict with one another. Bill, on whom my parents had pinned such great hopes, with his intelligence and excellent facility for languages and music, began to stand up against my father, became an ardent jazz fan and was all too keen to haunt the few local bohemian dives. He went up to London to a concert by Louis Armstrong and returned in a state of high excitement. This was the prelude to a dreadful outbreak of schizophrenia. For several years he endured awful medicines, which made him deeply depressed. Once more, our lives were in a turmoil of uncertainty and angst, only kept together by my mother's enduring love.

I escaped. I retreated still further into my own resources and after joining the Tunbridge Wells Natural History and Philosophy Society I would spend each weekend on trips to local sites of interest accompanied by many older naturalists, each an expert in their own field. I would learn a vast amount about the fauna and flora of the Weald. My favourite guide was a gracious, white-haired lady called Miss Graseman, an expert on fungi and I would often invite myself to a dainty tea after school and we would chat and reminisce. I have fond memories of treading over soft down-land turf in search of rare orchids, tramping over the shingle wastes of Dungeness and Rye seeking passage migrants and waders. My most ambitious adventure was a spring trip with my friend and fellow naturalist, Kerry, when we cycled through Suffolk bivouacking in a beach hut before taking the ferry to Havergate Island with its then rare breeding avocets. We continued to Minsmere where a kind couple temporarily adopted us and installed us in a cheap room at a local inn. In midwinter I combed the cold and desolate North Kent marshes; in spring I searched for bird nests and climbed the tallest trees, once reaching the top of an enormous beech to peer into a heron's pile of sticks holding two huge eggs of the palest blue. For many years this passion for nature satisfied all my needs.

The Pillar   5c   ★★

Start on the right-hand side and move up to the ledge; continue up the front face, and then move delicately left to the edge. Finish straight up. A good route on excellent clean rock.
FA M. Boysen, 1960

TWO
TO LEARN TO CLIMB

After arriving home from Scotland there were many changes in my life. The most worrying was an imminent transfer to the local grammar school. Having failed my 11-plus comprehensively and been placed in a secondary modern school, I was perfectly happy not to have to work hard and I positively enjoyed the wood and metalwork, art and gardening which filled a large part of each day. From four o'clock the day was my own and I relished the freedom of being able to go fishing or bird watching whilst my intellectual brother toiled over homework. I was a late starter and my mother became increasingly concerned about my prospects. So after badgering the grammar school head I was at last reluctantly accepted as a late entrant. The reluctance was very much mutual.

It was a typical small-town grammar school, built at the turn of the century in the conventional and uncomfortable neo-Gothic style. It was, of course, far too small to accommodate the post-war population bulge and at the back of the building lay a huddle of damp and squalid huts, one of which became my third-year form room. I hated my first few weeks but the chief objects of my loathing were Saturday morning school and the uniform. We were dressed in beribboned blazers complete with rampant leopards and Latin motto. The headwear was particularly irksome; a silly cap in winter and an even more ridiculous straw boater in summer. To be seen without the proper apparel seemed to be the worst sin possible and we were continually harassed with spot checks to ensure conformity. The only way to vent our spleen was through ridicule and to this end tiny caps were perched on massed hair, boaters were steamed and curled into ludicrous cowboy Stetsons.

If the uniform was tiresome Saturday morning school was intolerable as it severely curtailed my freedom to get out and about. As if this was not enough, Thursday afternoons were entirely devoted to playing soldiers. Despite the end of conscription, the whole school, bar a few boy scouts, despised conscientious objectors and assorted weaklings paraded up and down to bellowed commands. I was excused the cadet corps and instead enjoyed the privilege along with a handful of others of doing extra maths in the coldest room of the school.

Despite these grievances I soon began to enjoy my work. I had dropped down a year to start my O-Level course and because of my lack of Latin I was given my own private course of study, which included a mixture of arts and science. Surprisingly, I coped fairly well and by dint of hard work and extra study I soon made up for lost ground. The subject I most looked forward to was biology. Then I discovered my teacher was a ferocious and menacingly unpredictable Welshman known and dreaded as 'Oscar'. The tool with which he sharpened our wits was fear and his boast was that no one had failed O-Level – yet. I quaked at the thought of the years of exposure to him, which my devotion to biology ensured.

At first I was so preoccupied with schoolwork, homework and copying up missed notes that I had no time to pursue my hobbies. I resented this deeply and more and more I desired an escape. Even my beloved bird watching now seemed too tame a pursuit; I craved stronger excitement and strenuous effort. It was time to investigate the local rocks and perhaps learn to climb.

One Sunday towards the end of September, as the trees were showing the first golden flush of autumn, I set off walking across Tunbridge Wells common to nearby High Rocks. I had been before on childhood outings with my mother, days full of excitement with a maze of passages and bridges through the jumbled rocks and a teahouse wedged between two huge boulders. The rocks now appeared deserted, neglected and vastly overgrown. The tea shed was a mouldering ruin, the bridges had collapsed and the maze had long since vanished.

For an hour or so I wandered disconsolately along the rocks, scuffling through drifts of autumn leaves and surveying without enthusiasm the green repulsive overhangs. I retraced my childhood steps, scrambled up a few boulders, thumped the ever-disappointing Bell Rock, read a few carved inscriptions and prepared to return home disappointed. I was just about to leave High Rocks valley altogether when on the opposite side I heard voices.

I crashed into the coppiced wood, penetrated the deep gloom of some ancient yew trees and there were two climbers. I watched at first from a polite distance but edged nearer as they draped a rope round a tree at the top of the rocks and started to climb. It looked easy enough. Surely I could get up these myself? When the climbers moved on I tentatively tried the first moves until with a cheery shout I was told if I wanted to climb why not tie on to their rope? I was only too pleased to accept their offer, and rushed over to be taught the intricacies of bowlines, belays, stalactites, jug holds and mantelshelf moves. I kicked off my shoes and prepared to climb in stocking feet, aware of an enormous sense of occasion as I first laid hands on the rock and stepped up on the first rounded hold. My hands slipped easily into the correct combination of pocket holds, my feet slotted neatly into the horizontal breaks and I climbed upwards in relaxed and easy movements.

It was not a hard climb but that was unimportant. I felt instinctively at home on rock and at the finish experienced such a surge of happy elation that I knew then I was committed to climbing. I bounded back down with the joy of achievement and basked in the congratulations of my new friends. Life had suddenly opened up a new exciting horizon, a whole new world of undiscovered pleasures. I savoured each new sensation and was greedy for more. The sharp smell of leaf mould, sandstone and damp hemp became part of me, a timeless evocation of excitement. Darkness soon curtailed climbing but before we departed my newfound acquaintances invited me to join them the following Saturday at Harrison's Rocks if I wished. I could hardly wait.

I returned home exultant and with the cares of school forgotten. The week trickled slowly by in a fever of anticipation, desperate for Saturday to arrive. On Wednesday we played games and I flung all my pent-up energy and new zest for life into a game of rugby. As with all ball games I had little or no natural ability. I had only just started playing and to this day only have a dim understanding of the rules, but I was a fair size and aggressive. With my nose streaming blood, my arms and legs flailing around, I presented a moderately ferocious spectacle. I obviously impressed someone for next day came the stunning news that I was picked to play for the third XV that Saturday afternoon. I was not at all pleased to be so honoured and presented my excuse of a prior commitment. This was received with sarcastic incomprehension. The clichés were rolled out: it was simply not good enough; I was letting the side down; if I wanted to be part of the school it was time to participate in school activities. I felt miserable and misunderstood. I quite enjoyed sport but how could I explain my newfound passion? I did not even try and was released with bad grace and marked down as a shirker. I resolved to try less hard on the rugby field in future.

Finally, Saturday arrived and as the final bell signalled release from classes I was clattering down the stone steps and through the iron gates into the bright autumn air. I caught the first train to Groombridge and walked alongside the railway to where I knew the rocks began. Passing through a hop field full of scented flowers ready for picking, I entered a birch wood and emerged quite suddenly on top of some low rocks overlooking fields and oast houses and a railway line. There was no one about and the rocks were unimpressive but as I walked along the escarpment they grew taller and suddenly at the first sizeable crag I found dozens of jostling climbers fixing top ropes and climbing, sitting and chatting in convivial groups. There were shouts of encouragement, screams for tight rope, conflicting advice from all sides and good-natured derision. Everyone seemed to be dressed in the oldest of clothes; baggy trousers, sweaters with huge ragged elbow holes and the khaki and olive of ex-War Department stores seemed an almost universal uniform bar a few elderly gentlemen in smart alpine breeches.

It was obvious already that Harrison's Rocks were quite different from High Rocks. The place thronged with climbers, the rocks were dry and south-facing with pocketed routes rather than the sombre overhangs split by cracks. The tops of the climbs were deeply cut into a fretwork of rope-worn grooves; it was obviously a popular place. I moved slowly along seeking out my new acquaintances.

I found them below an imposing square block, which looked very hard. They had already had the best part of the morning to warm up and they were now prepared to attempt a famous testpiece called *Niblick*. I could see it was too hard for me but I settled down to watch them struggle to get from one horizontal crack to the next by a series of so-called 'Harrison's moves' which involved cocking your leg up high, pulling with one hand and pushing down with the other. They didn't make much progress on the first attempts but eventually after several rests on the rope one of the climbers managed it.

Before they removed the top rope it occurred to them that I might like to have a go but I was warned that I could hardly expect to get up it as it was graded 5c – just about the hardest grade then current. I decided to give it a good go; at least I now possessed a new pair of tightfitting pumps and could tie my own bowline. The first moves were supposed to be the hardest and involved finger jamming in a tiny vertical crack. I stuffed my fingers in, pulled and to my surprise was able to step up and reach the first crack. Another strenuous heave and I had gained the next. My companions were shouting encouragement and after clawing and pawing at tiny hand and footholds I was able to recover my breath and rest below the last over-hang split by a wide crack.

My final struggles up this were desperate; I lost composure, as my strength drained away from my arms. But so determined was I not to fail that I finally crawled over the top utterly spent. I was immensely pleased with myself. To have done such a hard route, virtually as a first climb, was a minor coup. My friends were impressed and told me I showed great talent. I had made a good start but for the rest of the day I was too fatigued to accomplish much else. I floundered often and was lowered to the floor ignominiously, the top rope nearly cutting me in two. My technique was raw and undeveloped, my strength was limited and my stamina non-existent, but I had a certain natural ability and with effort and application I knew I would be a good climber.

Weekend climbing now became the focus of my life. As soon as Saturday school finished I would dash eagerly through the wooded common to snatch the few hours of winter daylight climbing on High Rocks. On Sundays I would go to Harrison's. Initially my main problem was one of shyness. I had no one to climb with and I disliked imposing myself on others. I would wander along the rocks, loiter on the fringe of groups and hope to be invited to share a top rope. When this occurred I was happy but often I was ignored and on these occasions I suffered agonies of frustration. I longed to be attached to some club but all the climbers seemed to be London-based and they were all so much older than myself. I must have seemed insufferably young and pathetically keen and many people did not welcome the attention I paid them. Indeed some were positively hostile to the lanky pale youth who would watch them with such intensity and then, as often as not, go and solo the route they were trying. It must have seemed like arrogance but it was not. I just wanted to climb as much as possible and the best way of doing this was to watch others first.

As my visits to the rocks accumulated, I began to recognise more and more climbers and it became easier to find someone willing to share a rope. One decent old gentleman, known as Ossie, could always be relied on. He was a great theoretical expert, with knowledge of every hold and subtle technique. Unfortunately old age and arthritis prevented him from actually performing himself but he was happy to expound endlessly to anyone prepared to listen. It was in his company that I met another young climber clad in a striped rugby shirt grappling on a hard overhanging arête. His name was Nick Estcourt. Nick came from Eastbourne, and like me suffered Saturday school with the additional horror of a Sunday chapel parade. Needless to say he missed his devotions often, for which he was regularly and soundly thrashed by the padre.

Another climber to show me great kindness was known to everyone as Henry. On Sunday mornings he performed an athletic ritual of climbing each route on Birchden Wall – a series of hard fingery problems, which he bounced up with superb aplomb. It was a case of practise making perfect;

each move was known and rehearsed but when Henry attempted an unfamiliar climb he struggled as much as anyone else.

If I could find no companions to climb with I would tour the rocks, soloing everything I could and watching and learning from the best climbers. There were several recognised stars to watch; Chris Bonington was one of the most conspicuous and his braying Sandhurst-trained voice could be heard ringing around the rocks. He was not particularly strong or acrobatic but he climbed with the delicate assurance of a master craftsman. Geoff Francis was perhaps an even finer climber and I would watch in wonder as he smoothly demolished fierce climbs with an effortlessness concealing great strength.

Around this time I first ran into the Sandstone Club, a band of outcrop addicts based at High Rocks. They periodically visited Harrison's and I well remember two brilliant climbers, Billy Maxwell and Phil Gordon, racing each other blindfold up a route called *Stupid Effort*, which I had only just managed to do at all.

Studying the guidebook, the name of Nea Morin was prominent; she had first developed the rocks in the 1920s with her husband and over the years introduced all manner of climbing celebrities to High Rocks, like Menlove Edwards and Eric Shipton – and many new routes had been put up as a result. My first meeting with her occurred as I was making my first attempt at a very difficult route called *South West Corner* with Henry. I was coming unstuck on the last difficult moves, as usual, in full view of large numbers of climbers. There was a party at lunch on top of the rocks and I was startled when a slender, elderly lady announced from its midst in a loud clear voice 'he's doing it wrong – poor boy'. She graciously revealed the secret hold combination, advice I was grateful to follow, and I succeeded in finishing the climb. After this she invited us over to share a cup of coffee and a sandwich. Later she introduced me to many other routes, which she first demonstrated with devastatingly sinuous grace. I followed her up *Slim Finger Crack*, which I only managed after a tenacious struggle and frenzied encouragement. In style her ascent was like a well-practised ballet movement compared to my own unco-ordinated highland fling.

I was to meet Nea often over the next few years and these meetings had a great influence on me. She was a delightful companion, full of gay enthusiasm and encouragement. At the end of a hard day she would invite a group of friends back to her elegant Georgian terraced house in Tunbridge Wells. After scrubbing off the layers of ingrained dirt we would enjoy a refined and leisurely tea of lapsang souchong and toast and honey from exquisite china. Many of her companions were distinguished mountaineers with tales of desperate climbs both at home and abroad. At Nea's, I first heard of Joe Brown and Don Whillans, of the great Alpine north faces and of Himalayan expeditions. I listened with awed fascination, aware of my own lowly status as the great names were discussed and gossip shared. Nea seemed to know just about everyone in the climbing world. She was herself an exceptional climber with new routes in the Alps to her credit. She had married one of the finest French climbers of the pre-war years, a hero of the resistance movement who had tragically been killed during the war. It was through Nea that I became aware of the vast extent of climbing. I loved nothing better than hearing her talk, of browsing through her library where I thumbed through *La Montagne* magazine and read about Giusto Gervasutti and the exploits of Lionel Terray and Hermann Buhl. Already in my imagination I climbed upon airy rock walls and trod distant snows. In reality my efforts were as yet confined to a few ridiculous small sandstone boulders tucked away in the gentle folds of the Weald. It wasn't much but it was a start.

As the days grew shorter and winter approached I only found time to go to High Rocks each Saturday afternoon. I did not favour High Rocks as much as Harrison's initially for they were bigger, darker and damp with huge overhangs split by cracks and chimneys. Often the rocks were deserted and even if the Sandstone Club was camped there I was shy of imposing myself on such a tight-knit group. I contented myself with boulder problems, learnt the secret of a few easier routes and on occasion steeled myself for an epic grunt up one of the slimy constrictor chimneys.

Adjoining the rocks was the High Rocks Hotel, which, in sympathy with the grounds, was in a state of mouldering splendour. It was run by an amiable if disorganised landlord called Doug. Climbers were welcome and felt much at home, over-running the bars and being allowed to camp and climb at will. I longed to camp out myself for, in the evening, when I set off home, campfires glowed and flickered invitingly under overhangs in the same old Stone Age sites, and the pub thronged with cheerful noise. I didn't have to wait long. My birthday and Christmas soon came and armed with some money I scoured the war surplus stores and equipped myself with a sleeping bag, mess tins and bivouac tent which were to serve me for many years to come.

Now, as soon as Saturday school finished, I would dash home, pick up the parcelled food my mother prepared, stuff all my kit into my rucksack and head off for the rocks. As soon as I started to camp out I was drawn into the company of all the other bivouacking climbers, for all were welcome around a blazing fire and friendships were easily established in the convivial High Rocks Inn. A tough-looking band dressed in camouflaged smocks and driving a jeep soon took me in. They looked like a small private army and in fact the two principal characters, Terry Tullis and Max Smart, had just been demobbed after a stint in Malaya where they had first met. By pure chance they had met again at High Rocks. Both were keen to start climbing and they became the nucleus of their group.

They were a free and easy pair, happy to befriend anyone and without the rather insular attitude of the Sandstone Club. Terry was generous and friendly, outgoing in temperament with a Londoner's sharp wit. Max was quite different; he was a countryman, both reserved and thoughtful. With his immensely strong body, wild mane of hair and deep penetrating gaze his physical presence was powerful. I was immediately attracted to him, particularly as he shared my love of nature and had a profound understanding of living in the wild. Max worked for himself felling trees, landscape gardening and turning his hand to anything. He was capable of prodigious work and was so scrupulously honest and trusting by nature that he was often cheated of his proper rewards. On one occasion he laboured all hours to dig a ditch but because he finished so soon the owner refused to pay the agreed price. Max returned in the night and dug once more, this time to fill it all in again.

Terry worked at this time in a butter warehouse but was shortly after employed by Blacks climbing shop on the Gray's Inn Road. He had a restless spirit and was too talented to stay there long, for amongst other things, he had been a successful photographer.

Almost every weekend Terry would hurtle down to the rocks with his girlfriend Julie and others such as the livewire Roger Cole, the diminutive Griffiths brothers and another group, the Maher brothers, who came up from Brighton. Our base was High Rocks but we ventured frequently to the other outcrops, which often were strictly private and required a stealthy approach. We often visited at night under a full moon and the ghostly shadows and fear of discovery all added spice to the adventure. Once at Penns House Rocks a huge Irish wolfhound crashing through the rhododendron thicket startled us. It picked up our scent and approached me, snuffling and sniffing, as I stood stock still against a rock. I watched helpless in horror as it came within inches of my leg softly growling until it suddenly looked up, gave a howl of pure panic, somersaulted backwards and went baying off into the night. I was relieved a similar thing didn't happen at Chiddinglye Wood Rocks, reputedly haunted by a man-hunting black hound called Gytrack. We could joke about such things in daylight but at night the tree-shrouded rocks with their weird and fantastic forms could become infinitely menacing. Perhaps it was an evocation of the ancient past, when Stone Age men camped out as we did. Perhaps it was just my fertile imagination conjuring with the druid stone and sacrificial altar. One thing was certain. I would never sleep out alone in the Eridge amphitheatre and I was even uneasy at High Rocks, if alone.

Of all the rocks, Eridge was by far the most beautiful, set among tall trees and thick rhododendron. It was the site where the Tunbridge filmy fern was first discovered by Victorian botanists. The rocks ramble for half a mile or so as a series of buttresses and prows of distinctive shape shrouded in moss and ferns. We camped there on many weekends and climbed a whole series of excellent new routes including *The Pillar* and various overhanging cracks and walls in the amphitheatre. Climbing and camping were strictly forbidden but we were discreet and inconspicuous and for a while were even tolerated by the Marquess of Abergavenny himself, who often rode by in the mornings as we cooked breakfast. Once he addressed us telling us that he 'did not mind too much our climbing but to make sure we did not harm his trees'. We had no reason to do otherwise and continued to enjoy the rocks for some time, witnessing the full Eridge Hunt gallop by on several occasions. We continued to climb and explore Eridge until others started to camp there. Litter was left and disturbance was caused.

In the course of our wanderings we visited just about every bit of rock mentioned in the guidebook from collapsing Rockrobin Quarry to Eastbourne chalk. Many of the outcrops we found were very fine – particularly Bowles Rocks, spoiled rather by the stench and clamour of squealing pigs housed at their base. Even with this disadvantage and the threat from the gun barrel of the owner's half-mad son, we would sneak the odd surreptitious climb. These included the spectacular *Sloth*, a route swinging over a large overhang on a horizontal birch tree which was later cut down and the route destroyed. It was a crag with immense potential but we were going to have to wait a few years before we got the chance to climb on it. Another favourite outing was to Stone Farm Rocks, delightfully situated at the top of a hill overlooking the huge Weir Wood reservoir. We would usually walk there at night from High Rocks and camp there when we arrived.

The camping and walking around the outcrops was in many ways as enjoyable as the climbing we did when we got there. We had our routine: a light tarpaulin was rapidly strung up between trees, wood and water was collected and a fire started. We cooked on smoke-blackened pans late into the night and in the warm glow of the fire we talked and reminisced till we finally stretched out in our sleeping bags and fell asleep.

In winter we would often go for longer walks to the south coast. Although there was little climbing apart from the occasional sea level traverse, these walks made a powerful impression on me. There was a tremendous sense of freedom about midnight walking. We could go where we wanted, through fields and woods, slip quietly through farmyards and private estates. Particularly memorable were the hard, frosty nights under a moonlit sky with only the wild barking of foxes to break the enveloping silence. I remember a shooting star streaking through the sky like a giant rocket before disappearing into the earth.

It was on these walks that Max would show his immense stamina. He could have walked all night but I tired all too rapidly. My feet blistered painfully and I remember fixing my eyes on the all too distant line of the South Downs and willing them to approach. The tired relief when we finally crunched over the shingle beach and sniffed the sea air was delicious because now we could finally lie down and warm ourselves round the tar-smelling driftwood fire. In the morning we would take a ritual swim in the freezing sea, before rushing back to our fire and wander along the cliffs scrambling and beachcombing till it was time to go home.

Whether I was walking or climbing I would return home late and exhausted with the scars of battle. My hands were invariably black with grime, my knees permanently grazed, my hair full of sand and my clothes reeking of earth and wood smoke. I was often so tired from the effort of climbing that I could not close my hands to manipulate the knife and fork on my dried-up Sunday dinner which lay waiting in the oven. I couldn't have cared less. I was happy with my new way of life and as I gained strength and experience I began to dream of more ambitious adventures.

I was now 17, but for the first year of my climbing I was hampered by lack of money, equipment and climbing partners. I longed to visit the climbing grounds of North Wales about which I had heard and read so much but I had no rope and no one to climb with if and when I got there. At Easter I had the chance of a lift to Cornwall. I knew there was climbing there having just read the delightful book *Commando Climber* by Mike Banks so I prepared myself for a walking holiday, hopeful that I could do some easy scrambles and maybe meet up with some climbers.

I arrived at Land's End and thankfully escaped the jostling tourists along the north coast towards St Ives. After a mile I was on my own among thickly perfumed gorse, bramble and bright spring flowers. The walking was rough and magnificent; the coast path was for the most part non-existent and I threaded my way around headlands and up sea-slashed zawns, past ruined and desolate tin mines with their concealed shafts and iron-rung ladders leading nowhere. I passed Pendeen Lighthouse and arrived at the bay of Bosigran with its saw-toothed ridges and noble headland catching the last golden glow of the setting sun. It seemed like an earthly paradise. I was enraptured by the beauty and decided there and then to linger for a few days. I climbed the rough granite ridges and the delicate cathedral spires of Porthmoina Island, swam in the clear cold water and watched with delight the aerial antics of ravens and peregrine falcons.

No climbers came, so reluctantly I set off to continue my walk. I had only gone a few miles when I fell and cracked my ankle so painfully that I was reduced to crawling to the nearest road. It took me all day to get there and then hitch a lift to Hayle youth hostel where I stayed for two days. I hobbled around and after some therapeutic barefoot wanderings in the vast sand dunes and paddling in the sea I started the long hitchhike back home a day late for the new school term.

At Whitsun, Terry, Max and some other lads arranged a short visit to Fontainebleau, the Parisian equivalent of Harrison's Rocks. In fact, as I soon discovered, their rocks are much finer and more fun, a chaotic jumble of boulders scattered amongst idyllic pine forests. It was a bit of a busman's holiday for the climbing was on sandstone similar to our own. We arrived at night, settled down in a cave and immediately horrified the locals by lighting a small fire, which was definitely 'interdit'. They took pity on us, however, when we explained we had no stove, but later when Terry arrived with a Primus our problems were solved.

We spent a delightful few days climbing innumerable short climbs and boulder problems, following marked courses, until it was time to go back. In Paris we made a pilgrimage to Pierre Allain's famous shop, appropriately located among reliquary shops in the shadow of the mighty church of Saint-Sulpice, to buy 'PAs', his eponymous rubber and canvas climbing footwear, which played such a large part in improving climbing standards. Fitted with extreme care, they cost less than £2.

By the time the summer holidays arrived I was still uncertain about my plans. I wanted very much to go to Wales but I had no one to climb with. Then much to my annoyance I was pressed into accompanying two German youths, sons of my parents' friends, on a grand tour of Scotland and Wales. I set off with them on the first leg of the journey to Scotland but at Glasgow we split up and arranged to meet in a fortnight's time when we would hitchhike to North Wales.

I set off immediately to the Isle of Arran intending to walk its spiky granite ridges and perhaps manage a climb or two. I had hoped to camp and bivouac out under boulders high up among the mountains but I was emphatically flushed out of Glen Rosa on the first night and forced to seek refuge in youth hostels where I sat and watched the torrential rain and gales sweeping in from the south-west. In desperation I once tried to cross the mountains in thick mist but my compass needle became stuck and after staggering about lost I emerged in the same valley I had left. In a fortnight I enjoyed three good days of limpidly clear weather squeezed in between successive depressions. Still, I traversed the complete ridge, scrambled up easy rocks and tested my new PAs. They seemed to work like magic. I could hardly wait to try them on the sterner rocks of North Wales.

I met my friends as arranged in Glasgow and they led me to an unbelievably hospitable farmer they had met. He fed us like prodigal sons for a few days then drove us to the start of the Carlisle Road where he seemed reluctant to see us go.

Hitching to North Wales, we competed to get there first. I won the toss and claimed prime hitching spot while the others walked on. To my delight a car stopped at once and an elderly white-haired American asked me if I wanted to go as far as Manchester. Smugly I jumped into his Volkswagen and waved triumphantly as we shot away rather jerkily south. It was a left-hand drive car and he needed me to assist him in overtaking. My nerve soon started to fail me. Not only did the driver look and sound like Mr Magoo, he drove in the same blithe but deadly style.

We barely avoided several lethal accidents in a matter of moments and my attempts at conversation dried up along with my throat as I watched the road with a growing sense of terror. The grand finale almost came as we rocketed up the wrong side of a dual carriageway. A Jaguar came tearing towards us and with tyres squealing skidded round our car. As the last tattered remnants of my composure left me I screamed hysterically into his hearing aid. He seemed mesmerised for a moment then with a quick pull on the wheel accompanied by a call to his maker we crashed over the central reservation, through a thin hedge and into the path of a giant lorry. We sped away to a cacophony of screeching brakes, honking horns and flashing lights. At Carlisle I climbed out grateful to be alive and fled. The rest of the journey was tediously slow but gratifyingly safe. I crossed over the Mersey ferry to Birkenhead, slept soundly in the station waiting room among a crowd of assorted vagrants and was 'moved on' nice and early next morning. I continued hitchhiking through ancient Chester and then along the coast road, skirting the mountains, to Bangor.

Crossing to the Anglesey side of the Menai Straits I arrived at a huge mansion where an aunt of one of my German friends worked as a private nurse. My friends had already arrived and we camped on the shaved lawn under a spreading cedar and for two days lazed about, plundering the huge greenhouses and swimming amidst countless jellyfish to the huge ocean-racing yacht moored off the shore. At last the weather was fine but I was not happy to bask in the sun; in front of me lay the mountains of Snowdonia. I was restless to be in them and, when I could wait no longer, set off for Ogwen. I could hardly contain my excitement as I was driven up the Nant Ffrancon valley, broad and gently contoured at first but becoming more and more rocky and enclosed until suddenly Tryfan, the Carneddau and Cwm Idwal came into view. The names and images were already familiar but now I was experiencing them for real.

It rained heavily towards evening and I was turned away from the full youth hostel so I sheltered on the slate slabs of a nearby chapel porch. Even here I was asked to go so I waited till dark and returned to sleep. Next morning the skies cleared after early rain so I set out to walk up to Idwal Slabs. Before I got there I saw climbers at the foot of a small crag on the left and ran up towards them with such eagerness that I was immediately invited to join a father and son team who had only recently taken up the sport. The route we climbed was not hard or long – a well-worn classic. But how I enjoyed feeling the rough volcanic rock with its profusion of sharp holds and the giddy plunge of exposure. When they found out about my inadequate lodgings I was invited back to their cottage, driven there in a fine old Riley saloon to a remote farmhouse high on the moors of Merionethshire.

Next day we drove out to Tryfan and climbed on the east face, up *Pinnacle Ridge* in bright breezy weather. I led all the tricky bits and found it satisfyingly easy but it was an exhilarating excursion, which finished on the topmost crags of the mountain. It was the last climb I made with my kind hosts. They realised I was technically much more advanced, that I would be frustrated to be taken up easy routes I could lead with ease. It was better that I found someone of comparable standard with whom to climb. Once more I returned to the uncomfortably cold slabs at the chapel.

The following day I set off for Llanberis, walking over the Devil's Kitchen and then down the close-cropped grass on the other side to be confronted by a wildly gesticulating purple-faced farmer who tried to force me back the way I had come. Instead, I wandered down to the dreary village of Llanberis overshadowed by the immense slate quarries, which gashed the mountainside opposite. The youth hostel was once again full and the surly warden so unhelpful that I vowed there and then not to bother with hostels again. I walked back up the Llanberis Pass, scoured the boulders and found a dry cave well away from the soiled rock shelters lying close to the road.

I awoke next morning to glorious bright sunshine. It was September already, the heather was bright purple, the bracken was turning gold whilst above me hung the ripe red berries of a rowan tree. I felt relaxed and happy for the first time in weeks. I had no one to care for but myself; I had arrived. I cooked a leisurely breakfast, climbed all over my boulder home and then got ready to investigate the crags. To my surprise they were nearer than I thought and already there were dozens of climbers on them.

Walking up to the bottom of the nearest cliff, I discovered it was Clogwyn y Grochan, put on my PAs and waited hopefully. The climbers all knew one another and it transpired they were from Sheffield University Mountaineering Club. There were two obvious stars and with much preparation they set off to climb a vertical pitch called *Kaisergebirge Wall*. The leader was Dave Gregory and he moved neatly and quickly, commenting and chatting almost continually in a curious high-pitched voice, which contrasted strangely to his well-set frame. His second, Jack Soper, was dark and supple. He followed with ease, bounding upwards in long loping strides like a climbing Groucho Marx. I was too impressed to even contemplate asking to have a go although I longed passionately to test myself on such a difficult looking climb.

Later in the day another tall and easy-going climber in the same group called Mike James invited me to join him on a pleasant girdle of the crag. The last climb of the day was to be *Shadow Wall* on Carreg Wastad. It was graded Very Severe, the hardest I had yet attempted in the mountains, but all did not go well; the second on the rope became stuck, night fell and I still sat shivering and angry at the bottom. The next day, I teamed up with another climber and we climbed *The Cracks* on Dinas Mot. I didn't enjoy the experience much as I was treated as an absolute beginner. I was not allowed to lead and had to watch in frustration as he climbed slowly and clumsily, knowing I was far better than he was. The showdown came the day after when he failed on *Pharaoh's Passage* on Dinas Cromlech. For two hours I sat holding the rope as he made futile efforts. I could see exactly what to do and began to show my pent-up frustration and impatient scorn.

Eventually he gave up and angrily offered me a try, no doubt hoping I would fail miserably. I did it with a speed and ease that did not endear me to him but the next day he left anyway with the Sheffield team.

For the last two days of my holiday I mooched about in search of someone – anyone – to climb with and managed just one route: an easy VS on Carreg Wastad called *Trilon*. It was time to go home. But on the morning of my departure two Scottish climbers came bounding up the scree slopes to the Grochan. The older climber casually asked if I fancied a climb. He said his name was Jimmy Marshall and his partner, a tall and bony youth about my own age who twitched nervously, was Dougal Haston. They flashed up *Brant* at breakneck speed, untying the rope as soon as it got easy and soloing to the top. I followed, amazed at the nonchalant ease of their climbing. They had no sooner finished *Brant* than they were leaping down the descent gully like goats and were all set to climb up *Slape*. I hardly had time to catch my breath but I was exhilarated by the sheer speed of our movement. At last I was climbing hard rock on equal terms with experts. I had the ability. All I needed was experience and I could only gain that by climbing in steady partnership with friends. That became my goal.

I felt old enough now to start shaping my own future. I wanted to go to university and study biology so I worked hard midweek at school to pass the necessary exams. The weekends were devoted entirely to my great passion for climbing. I continued to roam and climb throughout the south-east with Max and Terry but increasingly I was drawn to the more developed outcrops of High Rocks and Harrison's where I tested my skill and strength in readiness for the next summer holiday in Wales. I felt sure I could make my mark.

High Rocks was my favourite crag and it was also the nearest, a forbidding place of great overhanging buttresses cleaved by cracks and chimneys and deeply shaded by trees. There were luckily several large isolated boulders with fine dry face routes and nearby was the Continuation Wall and High Rocks Annexe which also had many excellent routes. Added attractions were the hospitable pub and the fact that camping was allowed. At each visit I would try fresh routes, puzzle at the mysteries of hand jamming on *Coronation Crack*, learn to loathe squeeze chimneys after struggling on *Anaconda* and *Boa-Constrictor* and to abseil at breakneck speed from the Isolated Boulder. In the evenings we would choose a secluded campsite amidst the bracken and trees at the top of the rocks, or if it was raining huddle under the shelter of an overhang. We lit great fires, cooked up and retired to the pub for a game of darts, talk and a few pints of beer.

Suddenly this free and easy existence changed. Doug, the charmingly lackadaisical landlord who had allowed the hotel and rocks to moulder so pleasantly, sold up and moved to Worcester. We helped him pack and cleared vast amounts of accumulated rubbish and waited anxiously for the new owner, Charles Gibson Cowan, who had recently returned to Britain from the Far East. He was an ill-looking man with the dark jaundiced skin of someone who suffered with his liver and kidneys. He was an excellent chef, perhaps unsurprisingly, since the one-time author and actor had famously been the boyfriend of the cookery writer Elizabeth David. They had sailed around the Mediterranean before the Second World War and wound up in Alexandria in 1941. At first he was friendly, conspicuously so, and out of goodwill we helped him clear a good deal of junk from the hotel, including some grotesque stuffed vultures which we placed on a suitable ledge above the scenic walk. Soon, however, we grew fed up of acting as unpaid workmen, the friendliness wore off and we learned the shape of things to come.

The hotel was tarted up and turned into an exclusive and very fine restaurant. Climbers were now directed to a small dingy room renamed the 'Climbers' Bar'. Ugly tangles of barbed wire appeared around the rocks, campers were ejected and there was muttering about 'the difficulty of insuring accidents'. Climbers, if not actually unwelcome, were obviously an inconvenience. They were too scruffy to be hanging about the hotel and clearly didn't spend enough money.

Only the Sandstone Club, the group from London who had converted a tea shack conveniently sandwiched between two boulders into a club hut, were allowed the privilege of camping among the rocks. In return they were expected to act as unofficial guardians. Our group of climbers, while not actually belonging to the Sandstone Club at the time, were sufficiently friendly with them to gain the same privileges. Yet Max was so disgusted with the new regime that he no longer visited. I was sad about this because I loved High Rocks dearly but if I wanted to climb there it would have to be with others.

Gradually I got to know the Sandstone Club members better. At first I thought them aloof and standoffish. In fact they were merely a close-knit group, mostly London-based, no doubt suspicious of the shy gangling youth who hung around so disconcertingly to watch them climb. I longed to be accepted for they included so many accomplished and stylish climbers and appeared to have such fun together. With time I gained acceptance. I too became more relaxed and self-confident, my ability was noted and eventually I was all but an official member of the club.

It was the golden era of High Rocks exploration. Each weekend the best climbers would clean and investigate new possibilities up the bulging uncompromising rock. Billy Maxwell was the finest of the older climbers with several hard routes to his name, like the layback arête of *Henry the Ninth* to his credit. He was a tidy person who climbed with impeccable grace, moving his tiny body from hold to hold so neatly that he remained immaculate where others became soiled with grime.

Of the younger group, who were mainly students, Phil Gordon was one of the most delightful. He was hugely strong with a build that earned him the nickname of 'Man Mountain'. He climbed with incredible daring, soloing many hard routes and seemingly quite happy to jump off from a great height and thunder into the ground. He, more than anyone else, had made a name for himself in Wales, at a young age making effortless ascents of some of the hardest and, as yet, rarely repeated routes of Brown and Whillans – such as *Cenotaph Corner, Erosion Groove Direct* and *The Grooves*. His finest effort had been to climb *Surplomb* unaided by slings, a first which even impressed Joe Brown. He also had some long falls on Clogwyn Du'r Arddu, that most forbidding of Welsh crags, when he had attempted *Vember* in the rain. He also hauled a huge rock onto his head as he was halfway up the then unrepeated Whillans's route *Taurus*. The rock shattered.

The other gifted climbers were the Smoker brothers, John and Paul. They presented a bizarre contrast in style and temperament; the only similarity was their scruffiness. They vied in this as in everything else. Paul was the likable one, being relaxed and humorous. With his shaggy black hair, long beard and ragged appearance he looked like a prophet emerged from the wilderness. John was not far behind, with a moth-eaten ginger goatee and a wardrobe of torn sweaters and ex-army fatigues. Paul was the climbing natural; he was built like an ape with immensely long and strong arms and an otherwise puny lower body. He drifted up steep rock with languorous grace. John was anything but relaxed. His movements were jerky and he was a spiky individual. He delighted in being rude. After a choice cutting phrase he would stand back grinning owlishly through his glasses to observe the effects. As a climber he was exceptional in that he appeared to be constantly out of control and about to fall off. He was described by Joe Brown as the 'cycling window cleaner' as his legs pedaled furiously and his arms lashed about. Despite his appalling technique, he possessed a wiry strength and fierce determination, which got him up hard routes and in fact made him the major new route contributor at the rocks.

Just as my association with the Sandstone Club began there was an explosion of new route activity. We would comb the rocks for possibilities, clear out earth-filled cracks, spy out holds on a rope and assemble for a group assault. It was immensely enjoyable and with a top rope from above we would throw ourselves wholeheartedly at the problem without fear. The routes were often so hard and devoid of good holds that the ascent would take all day. Everyone would have a go to a background of light-hearted banter and ribald shouts of encouragement and derision, each attempting their own method. The trick was to learn from each other and husband sufficient strength so that when the approved technique had evolved by trial and error one could climb fast and win the race against fatigue. When an ascent had been made we would retire gleefully to the pub, drink a pint of shandy while we dreamed up a name for the route and entered it in a logbook. Many happy exhausting days were spent in this way and many of the routes are now hard classics. *Lobster*, *The Sphinx*, *Sputnik* and *Graveyard Groove* were John's efforts, while my best routes were first free ascents of *The Dragon*, *Tilley Lamp Crack* and *Bludgeon*.

Climbing *Lobster* was perhaps the most fun and occupied us for a couple of days. It had just received its first ascent by a North London team using pitons and drilled-out rawl bolts. The Sandstone Club sensibilities were enraged. John Smoker finally worked out the solution; a combination of hand jamming and laybacking up an overhanging flake led to a last good undercut. Using this to its utmost, you could just reach a rounded, green and damp hold, your feet would shoot off the tiny holds and a desperate one-arm swing brought a tiny tree-root within reach. We were tremendously proud to climb past the boltholes and climb such an unlikely route free.

By the time the summer term drew to a close I was fit and ready for my next trip to Wales. More importantly, John Smoker, George Clarke and several others would be there and I would not have to search for climbing partners. I hitchhiked once more up to Ogwen full of anticipation, and arrived in a shower of rain. I immediately set out to find the Sandstone Club encampment but without success. I was close to despair; time was slipping away, the crags were all around me and yet I was once more alone. I wandered along the road to the Milestone Buttress and immediately bumped into a middle-aged climber who had once given me a lift from Harrison's Rocks. He was a kindly enough person but a little predatory, which put me on my guard. Even so I was delighted when he suggested a climb and on reaching the top my joy and relief bubbled over when I saw John Smoker. I detached myself from my companion and later that evening pitched my old ex-US Army bivouac tent in some sheep pens at the edge of Cwm Idwal. It was a lovely still evening, the Devil's Kitchen crags glowed orange and the damp smell of turf rising from the ground was rich and exciting. I could hardly wait for the next day to come.

In the morning we walked up past Clogwyn Bochlwyd to the high crag of Glyder Fach. First we climbed the *Direct Route* – a highly enjoyable excursion with several testing cracks highly polished by the scraping of nailed boots. Then we climbed *Lot's Wife*, a short but perfectly formed climb of rough volcanic rock. John then announced I ought to do *Lot's Groove*, an imposing little test for my first lead of the day. I attacked the climb in an excited rush, not really thinking how to place my feet to the best advantage. I was also clueless in the safe placement of runners, which were anyway just a few thin line slings, which I draped over spikes. Most of them dropped off and slid down the rope as soon as I continued upwards. The last few moves up the groove were steep and strenuous but I emerged at the top tired and satisfied. It was the hardest route I had yet led.

The following day John took me to the steep East Wall of Idwal Slabs. He had already spent a day attempting *Suicide Groove*, his high point marked by a dangling sling gently waving in the breeze. I was impressed. He lashed me firmly to the belay and set out, quickly climbing back up to his lone runner hanging around an inadequate spike. He then began a prolonged and exhausting struggle with the overhang above. Eventually, he shouted a warning and came back down in a flurry of thrashing arms and legs. Having rested awhile, John set off further left up a black greasy crack until he finally pulled over the top with a joyful shout. I followed and was impressed with his bold unprotected lead. John was elated with success, bubbling with enthusiasm and decided he was going to crown this achievement with a trip to Llanberis Pass to climb the mighty *Cenotaph Corner*. I was excited at the prospect. At last I would find out how hard this famous route of Joe Brown's really was.

British rock climbing was at this time overshadowed by the mythology of the Rock and Ice Club. In the early 1950s this small group of tough working-class climbers emerged from the industrial towns of the north-west and shattered the leisurely rock climbing scene, which had up to then largely been a pastime for the upper-middle classes. Spearheaded by Joe Brown and Don Whillans, this group set new standards with a glut of intimidatingly hard routes on the gritstone of Derbyshire and the mountain crags of North Wales. Their main centre of activities was the Llanberis Pass and the imposing high crag of Clogwyn Du'r Arddu. Such was the impact of these routes, that they remained unrepeated and often untried for years, which only added to their reputation.

As the years passed the legends grew: Brown and Whillans had inex-haustible strength; they had developed techniques unknown to everyone else; they were super men. This mythology was compounded by an almost total lack of reliable information. There were no route descriptions, just a list with the occasional cryptic comment such as 'second unable to follow' in the back of the out-of-date Llanberis guide written by Peter Harding. In this guide older hard routes like *Spectre* and *Ivy Sepulchre* were described almost in terms of horror as being 'excessively difficult, strenuous, loose, awe inspiringly steep', so what could the new and much harder routes be like? It seemed likely they must be too hard for mere mortals, an impression confirmed by Geoff Sutton in *Snowdon Biography* where he theorised that only small, light and exceedingly muscular climbers – preferably plumbers – could hope to follow. As a gangling, six-foot, willowy youth, I found it depressing reading.

The Brown and Whillans creations were indeed harder than the old routes but the most decisive factor was that they looked so much harder. They tackled glaringly obvious lines up smooth vertical walls, like *Cemetery Gates* and *Shrike*, soaring cracks such as *Octo* and *Diglyph* and great open grooves, the most imposing of which was *Cenotaph Corner*. By 1959 a handful of climbers were beginning the assault on the Rock and Ice routes. Hugh Banner, a small wiry climber from Liverpool who trained on the sandstone crags of Helsby, made many early repeat ascents, but often so slowly that it only seemed to confirm the enormous difficulty. Allan Austin and Eric 'Matey' Metcalf from Yorkshire and Patsy Walsh, a myopic Glaswegian, were also in the forefront, while Phil Gordon also played his part with impressive ascents in the Llanberis Pass.

John and I hurtled across to the Pass on his fast black Velocette bike until we reached its crest then coasted gently down. I looked with wonder at the great, dark-streaked, open-book corner set high on the dome shaped crag of Dinas Cromlech. It had been climbed at least a dozen times by this stage but still enjoyed a reputation for great difficulty. I had first heard it spoken of – in hushed tones – from climbers I encountered at Harrison's. Apart from Phil Gordon, the only person I had met who had done it was Robin Smith – the extremely gifted Scottish climber who had immense reserves of strength. He was working at a Kentish canning factory shovelling peas all night and had come to the rocks for some exercise prior to his trip to the Alps. He smiled wryly and admitted it was 'tricky'; he had spent all day bridged across it. I took this to mean it was very hard indeed.

We arrived at its foot and John set off. He was climbing remarkably well but the first really hard moves where you need to swing out on the wall slowed him down for a while. He continued bridging widely across the corner to the crux and after a frantic move or two gained an exiguous niche 20 feet from the top where he could rest a little. A final straining layback manoeuvre followed and then he disappeared into the trees. After a while the ropes went tight; it was now my turn. I followed, tense with anticipation, but to my surprise the holds appeared regularly, they were sharp and good, and slowly I was able to relax a little and enjoy my surroundings. The most unexpected feature was the abundance of natural protection in the form of chockstones, threads and jammed knots. John put in 10 runners. It seemed an amazing number – far more than most people carried at the time. I found the route strenuous and hard but I was certain that I too could lead it. Indeed I was determined I would, and soon.

John stayed for another day but he was content to rest on his laurels and let me lead some climbs. I first led *Brant Direct* and later *Ochre Groove* on the Grochan, where a young Manchester climber, Alan 'Richard' McHardy, joined us. He was a stocky, tousle-headed youth of my own age, with an open, friendly face and warm generous nature. Richard's enthusiasm for climbing was infectious and if he was not actually doing it, he did the next best thing, and talked about it over a succession of leisurely brews of tea. It was impossible not to like him.

There were many young climbers that summer in Wales; some like me were still at school, others like Richard were apprentices taking their annual fortnight holiday. There were also many older climbers – students and tradesmen all mixed together in a friendly huddle of tents and gleaming motorbikes on the Grochan field. There was no problem of finding climbing partners; in the free and easy melee everyone drifted from tent to tent, sharing tea, talk and laughter. Motorbikes were lovingly cared for, 'burn ups' along the Llanberis Pass frequently shattered the calm. Another favourite pastime was lazing back on the grass and critiquing climbers on the crags above.

With Richard as my host I was quickly integrated into his group of Manchester lads who were soon to form the Alpha Club. There was Al 'Festy' Parker lounging in the sun, oiling his body, a cigarette drooping in the corner of his mouth, forever delaying the moment of action. Platty, who was soon to disappear from the scene, had the permanently grease-grey complexion of a motorbike fanatic. The two best climbers were the 'ginger giants' – Paul Nunn and Bob Brayshaw. Paul was the rising star; just 17, he was already huge with thick long legs, a shock of ginger hair and a great grinning face covered in a thick red down which earned him the nickname Angus McFungus. He was immensely energetic and courteous with a booming, infectious laugh. Paul had already climbed *Cenotaph Corner* and various other hard routes. His other claim to fame was a small but potent motorbike, a gift from his granny on which he rocketed up and down the valley at breakneck speed, sometimes demolishing walls in the process. He was, like me, still at school, which in his case was a Catholic grammar, Xaverian College in Manchester, and he formed the nucleus of a group of lads from the same school that included John Peck and John

Moss. Every Sunday they would go off, three up, down to the village for mass.

For a week or so the weather was bad and I knocked about with Richard and Festy, sitting in Wendy's Cafe watching the rain, listening over pots of tea to involved tales of gritstone climbs, of Richard soloing *Right Unconquerable* in a fit of pique, of Bob Brayshaw leaping for pebbles on *Count's Buttress*, of Ma Thomas's Cafe, of the rivalries between the Alpha lads. After a week I felt as if I had known the Peak District for years. On the final day of Richard's holiday the rain continued unabated and just about every disconsolate climber in the Pass assembled at the Llanberis 'flea pit' to watch the matinee of *The Vikings* with Kirk Douglas. The noise was tremendous, cheering and jeering, the stamping of boots, and several times the projectionist threatened to stop the film. We identified too closely with the hairy sea bandits and revelled vicariously in the epic's lawless excitement.

With the departure of Richard and Festy I moved in with the Liverpool contingent and immediately we were enthusing over our respective sandstone outcrops. They included many fine climbers: Hugh Banner, Jimmy O'Neill, and Bob Beasley. Unfortunately they also had a high accident rate – mainly on motorbikes for it was the fashion to race each other at all times. I soon established a friendship with Roger Heywood, a swashbuckling character who was a bold and dashing climber. He was tremendous fun – vital and funny – an enthusiast who would throw himself wholeheartedly into any activity whether it was drinking, womanising or climbing. At the moment it was climbing for he was unemployed and in no hurry to get back to Liverpool to take up another menial job. He was practically penniless, his clothing was falling to pieces, his *kletterschuhe* were tied together with string but his PAs were brand new. Together we had just enough money for a daily half pint of beer, fish and chips and a loaf of bread. It was all we needed, although on Sunday night we could rely on a sausage or two, a half tin of beans and a rasher of bacon courtesy of departing weekenders.

We started our campaign with a series of hard routes in the Llanberis Pass. I climbed *Spectre, Hangover, Subsidiary Grooves, Kaisergebirge* and many more routes until I was relaxed and moving easily on steep rock. I was now ready to prove myself on *Cenotaph Corner*. To second it was one thing, to lead it quite another. It was the Pass testpiece – the gateway to the hardest climbing. I put aside my niggling doubts, assembled 10 slings and karbiners and set off ready for the hard struggle. I succeeded, not without difficulty, especially on the strenuous top moves, which have seen many a fall, but as I pulled over the top I was thrilled to have accomplished my first serious climbing ambition. I was now ready for sterner stuff.

The weather had slowly improved and was now set fair. It was time to tackle Cloggy; the Black Cliff was now surely dry. We toiled up the steep scree slopes direct from the Pass in sweltering heat to emerge suddenly onto the railway line at the crest of the ridge, cooling our faces against the refreshing breeze. As we descended the immense and shadowy crag came suddenly into sight. I had never seen anything look so vast and impressive and sat down to absorb this new wonder. The towering Pinnacle Walls split by cracks and brilliantly lit in the morning sun, the steep, sweeping mass of the East Buttress and the great curve of overlapping slabs of the West Buttress; so big and varied a structure, yet such a visually satisfying whole.

We bounded down to Halfway House and sat in the delicious cool of the flimsy tin structure, slaking our thirst on homebrewed lemonade made by the white-haired and kindly Mrs Williams. She knew all the climbers. Did we know that nice Joe Brown? It seemed that not many had climbed there in the recent past and she was surprisingly well-informed as to the activity of the Rock and Ice stalwarts.

We finished our drinks and walked back into the sun until we entered the shade of the crag. Too overawed to attempt anything hard, we chose *Chimney Route* and *East Gully Groove* and had no problem on the climbs. It was the grandeur of the surroundings that impressed. The rich peaty smell of bilberry ledges, the desolate 'cronk' of the ravens, even the chuffing and puffing of the Snowdon railway echoing noisily between the walls of the East Gully held their own peculiar charm.

We were completely in Clogwyn Du'r Arddu's thrall and simply had to return next day and the next – there was so much to do. All we lacked was route descriptions to the Rock and Ice climbs but as luck would have it we obtained some that night. Word went round that someone had arrived with a notebook of full descriptions. We located the source – a small grey van – and found we were not alone, for already seated inside was an intense, white-haired youth furiously scribbling copies from the treasured 'black book' of Allan Austin. We joined the queue, made our notes and departed with a description of *Llithrig* – an Exceptionally Severe on the East Buttress.

We approached it with trepidation and after a first easy pitch Roger set out on the hard climbing. He climbed in impeccable style, moving gracefully up the small holds to a spike from which he tensioned right on the rope to a small airy ledge in the middle of the sheer wall. I soon joined him and we earnestly consulted our description, which seemed to indicate the next pitch was the crux. I set out cautiously, sliding my body from one good hand and foothold to another. I was suspicious – somewhere it had to get hard – yet amazingly the holds and spikes kept on coming. Roger kept up a steady monologue of encouragement and suddenly I was unmistakably on a belay ledge. What had happened? How had I got there so easily? Was the rock easy or was I climbing brilliantly? I didn't care. I was up. Roger bounded up after me and soon shattered any illusions of grandeur when he pronounced my lead to be just mild VS. The next pitch, which hardly rated any description turned out to be much harder, with an awkward and unexpected move up shallow cracks. We reached the top pleased and happy. It was a marvellous route. We had climbed it with ease.

Next day we concentrated on The Pinnacle where I was determined to test my hand-jamming ability on the steep, smooth cracks. First we climbed *East Gully Wall* and then we dropped back down to climb *Octo*. I had just reached the top and was bringing Roger up when a large panting figure appeared and approached us, hesitated for a moment looking a little baffled and finally asked if one of us would like to second Joe Brown on a new route he was halfway up on the Far East Buttress. Joe Brown! It was a visitation from the gods. We dashed swiftly over the top of the crag and descended a dark loose gully until we saw a rope swinging out from the rock disappearing into a high, vegetated recess. Roger and I looked at each other meaningfully. There followed an awkward silence, and then, with typical generosity he waved me on and even insisted I exchange my disintegrating PAs for his new ones. It was an act of kindness I shall never forget.

The rope drew tight. I took a deep breath and began to climb as fast as I could, feeling quite lightheaded. I could still barely believe my luck – to be climbing with the greatest of all climbers! I flew across a steep traverse, negotiated a greasy groove, and before I knew it the crux was behind me and I was pulling onto the large stance, face to face with my hero. He was seated, comfortably bundled, at the back of the ledge. Grinning shyly, Joe said 'Hi,' and offered me a sandwich. I waited politely to be filled in about the climb and the present strange circumstances, and slowly, in clipped sentences, he explained that his partner Doug Verity had failed repeatedly to follow the first pitch and, as he weighed 16 stones, every fall had been rather a trial. Eventually, they were about to give in when Joe spotted me climbing *Octo*. For some reason, he thought I must be an acquaintance of his: Patsy Walsh. This explained Doug Verity's confused approach.

The pitch ahead followed an undercut flake of rock split by a wide and dirty crack. It looked hard and I waited with rapt attention and bated breath for Joe to start on it. His technique was a revelation; he skipped up each move after a quick appraisal, crouched and contorted his small body into resting positions in which he appeared utterly relaxed. But the main revelation was the cunning placement of runners he found, delving deep in the crack to find threads and chockstones. He also manufactured a couple of chockstones by placing rounded pebbles he had brought with him into constrictions in the crack. Around these he threaded frayed and dirty bits of line and thus safeguarded his progress to the next stance. He positioned himself on the edge of the ledge so he could watch my progress and the rope went very tight. It was time for me to start climbing. I followed up rather less elegantly, the resting places turning out to be nothing of the sort. The crack was hard to use; the runners were awkward to dislodge.

The first short exit groove looked very blank indeed. 'I hope we can get up it,' he said. 'The ropes will never reach the deck from here.' It was only then that I really appreciated the incredible exposure of our position, sat on a small ledge with overhangs on every side. I longed to be asked if I fancied a go at the top pitch but I realised the presumption this entailed. Instead I was securely lashed on to the longest of spike belays and with a growing sense of urgency Joe started to climb. He was late for dinner, evening was approaching and we would have to hurry. He threaded a sling, then bridging boldly, he made a move but his foot scuffled and grabbing his runner he leapt back down. His next attempt was equally abortive and I could feel his growing impatience. Finally, he swore softly, pulled out a ring piton and hammered it in. He then used it as a hold, cleaned out some more, and moved up on them in a wide, insecure bridging position, which he held for some moments. Placing another piton, he jerked the rope out quickly and lunged up and over the top. I untied my belay and with feverish haste started climbing myself. I took out the second piton and when the rope went taught I just had to climb it. I reached the top feeling slightly annoyed at the unnecessary assistance, indeed thought it might even go free. My silent criticism was anticipated; Joe announced he had made a muck of it. It should go free but there was just not time. I coiled the rope thoughtfully. I had served my purpose and my climbing companion was once more the unapproachable Joe Brown. The others joined us, we made an inadequate farewell and they walked off into the misty September evening.

I was still walking on air for weeks afterwards. I had climbed with Joe Brown. I could still hardly believe it. Much more important, I had learned a lot: about the placement of runners, the importance of resting, the subtleties of hand and fist jamming. Joe Brown was after all mortal. He had climbed the top groove in less than perfect style – there was hope for me. My confidence was enormously boosted. The world of hard rock climbing seemed at my feet.

Next day we idled in Llanberis Pass, waiting for the bus to take us to the shops. Roger saw it first, stepped out to stop it and was suddenly – and horrifyingly – cartwheeling through the air. A car, hidden behind the high stonewall, thumped into him. He was semi-conscious as we got him to hospital and kept insisting he was okay and couldn't let me down. We held him down gently and consoled him. Later that night we learned he had a fractured skull. It was a sad end to our happy partnership, and it was almost an end to his active climbing. A year later he suffered an appalling motorbike accident which crushed his leg.

I thought for a time I should pack up and go home but my morose mood soon evaporated with the clear blue skies and bright sun. The Indian summer had turned into a tropical heatwave, the streams had dried to a trickle and there was a national drought emergency. Roger was not forgotten. But the memory of his accident was put aside and replaced by my burning ambition. Such is the callousness of youth, I suppose.

As September drew to its end a trickle of out-of-work climbers arrived back from the storm-soaked Alps. Among them were Dennis Gray and Eric Beard, and Phil Gordon, grinning in his goggles astride a huge rusty Norton, soon joined us. Dennis was sharp as a needle and in his element as storyteller, camp ringmaster and general factotum of the Rock and Ice. Beardie was a strange-looking individual with short-cropped hair and a barrel chest from which his etiolated limbs stuck out. He was the proverbial happy camper, forever cheerful and singing and never so happy as when he was doling out honey butties and brews. As a climber he was a novice; his forte was fellrunning which he did morning till night, covering immense distances with his loose, loping strides.

Phil was raring to go. He had just finished a long series of exams, which he found extremely irksome, while toning up his fingers on sandstone. He was now ready for revenge on *Vember* from which he had been so recently and so rudely repulsed. Relying on Dennis's van and Phil's bike, we now approached Cloggy by way of the railway and flogged easily upwards from sleeper to sleeper while Beardie shot off into the blue.

We arrived at the foot of *Vember* and spied Hugh Banner just to our left on the steep crack of *November*. He was to be on it all day. It was Phil's lead and he shot up the first bone-dry cracks with barely a pause. The second pitch went with equal ease and I had the top pitch. I did not enjoy seconding but there was all day to play with so we bounded down the Western Terrace to the forbidding slabs of the West Buttress to attempt our next route – *Bloody Slab*. This was a delicate and unprotected climb breaking through the guarding overhangs onto iron-stained rock. The angle was easy but the rock lacked holds. As Phil had led his climb it was now my turn. We exchanged footwear. My PAs were almost useless with my toes poking out while Phil's *kletterschuhe* were brand new. I tiptoed delicately up for a long, long way until I reached a tiny stance with a great iron spike incongruously driven in as a belay. Phil followed at speed despite his footwear; our blood was up and we finished the day by storming up *Left Edge*.

The next day we sauntered across *The East Buttress Girdle* and, spying some tents at the side of the dark Llyn Arddu, descended to see who was there. It was Jack Soper, who I had previously seen on *Kaisergebirge Wall*, and with him was the fair-haired youth I had seen copying out route descriptions. His name was Pete Crew, and he was just making his mark as a climber. He was keen to know what we had 'done' and responded guardedly with a list of his own routes. We were far too unsubtle to hide our competitiveness. Pete was intense, humming with pent-up energy, which he released in a machine-gun rattle of words in a thick Yorkshire accent. He was reputedly a boy-wonder mathematician and had won an open scholarship to Oxford. But it was obvious climbing was his present obsession. He had camped here to snatch as many routes as possible, determined to 'smash the Joe Brown myth' by repeating all his routes and then supersede him by climbing the 'last great problems'. His plan of action was ready and he was to be largely successful. I was staggered by his detailed plans, which contrasted so starkly with my own less predictable course. Jack playfully suggested 'you two tyros' climb a route together and as it was late we rushed up to the foot of the classic *Longland's Climb*. Pete led out at breakneck speed. I, not to be outdone, followed equally fast, and catapulted into the lead. In a matter of minutes we were at the top and back at the tents. We had tested each other's mettle and were both impressed.

Our holiday had now reached its close. We had time for a few last routes in the Pass, which included the impressive vertical *Left Wall* of Cenotaph and then it was time to go. Dennis suggested we pop quickly to Derbyshire gritstone and although I was due back at school I accepted the invitation with glee. I had heard so much about the wonders of grit from Richard and Festy that I was prepared to be truant.

We set off in convoy through a hot and dusty Manchester swathed in a brown fog, then over the Pennines to Leeds. Having stayed the night with Dennis's parents, we quickly visited Almscliff to do *Great Western* and *Demon Wall* then set off for Froggatt Edge in Derbyshire. We arrived at night with a great harvest moon lighting the buttresses peppering the skyline. The weather was set so fine we did not bother with tents and simply lay on the grass at the campsite. The morning mist soon lifted to reveal the golden edges of Froggatt and Curbar. Dennis took us on a connoisseur's conducted tour showing us the routes to do, while selecting some for himself. The most exciting moment came when he was soloing *Great Slab* convinced he was about to fall. His body juddered with strain but the reassuring mass of Phil at the bottom combined with our rousing encouragements saw him successfully to the top. Phil and I climbed *Three Pebble Slab* and *Valkyrie* and Phil leapt from the top of its pinnacle to the other side, twisting his ankle. He hobbled about painfully and we just about managed *Beech Nut* and *Chequers Direct* before moving on to Curbar. We struggled up *Birthday Crack* and I led *Peapod*. To finish the day, Dennis tried a recently climbed thin crack called *Insanity*. He selected it because with his small hands he thought it was possible to jam. After placing a grit-stone chock he tried and failed. I looked at it afresh and was sure it would be more straightforward to layback, which I managed in a few dynamic moves; Dennis followed suit.

These last few days in Derbyshire made a perfect end to the holiday. I was reeling with happiness. I had climbed more than I could have dreamed and met so many friendly people in the process that I had already resolved to move up north where Wales, the Lake District and Derbyshire were all at hand. The idyll had to end, and I packed up my sack reluctantly and threw away my now useless PAs. I was aware for the first time of my ragged appearance. My jeans were in tatters, my shirt was unwashed and my hair was shoulder length. As I hitchhiked home through the misty valleys with barely a penny to rub together I reflected on the most wonderful days of my life. The structured existence of school was about to begin again and I faced trouble for arriving back late, but I didn't care. I had made it.

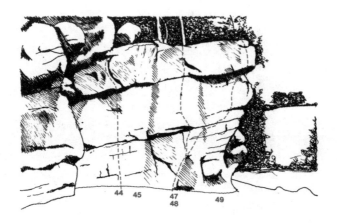

44   45   47   49
              48

48 **Digitalis**   6a   ★★★

An airy and heart-quickening route. From the pedestal go up and right on
good holds until a fingertip layback is reached (crux). Move right onto the
sloping ledge and mantelshelf over the nose as for Inspiration. An undercut
direct start is possible to the right.
FA M. Boysen, 1960

I returned home and to school basking in the memories of a glorious summer. I had moved into the sixth form and at last was able to pursue those subjects – zoology, botany and chemistry – I most enjoyed. The following Easter, I took part in my first Aldermaston march, the big annual gathering of the Campaign for Nuclear Disarmament, and afterwards met up with Paul Smoker in the Llanberis Pass where we climbed *The Grooves* on Cyrn Las, losing our way at the top and finishing up *The Overhanging Arête*. I continued climbing actively on sandstone, became a full Sandstone Club member, put up many new routes and extended my range of activity to neglected and still private outcrops. I managed to work hard, climb hard and begin laying plans and saving funds for my first trip to the Alps.

As a sixth former I enjoyed more freedom and gradually school life became less irksome. We were even treated as responsible young adults by some enlightened masters. Most of the time I spent in the tiny sixth form biology laboratory – a snug little sanctuary tucked away at the top of the school. It was a cosy room, crammed with specimen jars and microscopes, pervaded by strong aromas of formalin, alcohol, cedar-wood oil and tobacco. The last of these emanated from the still-menacing figure of Oscar Shaw. He had mellowed only slightly with time and my exposure to him. His dictatorial methods and unpredictable rages still filled us with fear but with less than 10 of us we were able to form an effective underground resistance group better able to withstand his bad temper. One thing was certain – he would drive us to exam success and for this we respected him and in time even felt a slightly nervous affection for him. He was dedicated to his task, was often a stimulating teacher and went out of his way to push us to our limits. Later on in our studies we were invited one evening a week to his house and, after tea and delicately prepared sandwiches, underwent the exquisite ordeal of discussing biological topics. We watched with amazement as this ogre tenderly kissed his small daughter; perhaps his stern temper was simply an act?

Back at school he did not betray any sign of weakness and towards the end of the long and trying Christmas term became so unreasonable and bad tempered that I rose in rebellion. Jumping to my feet, I blazed with anger, told him I had had just about enough of his bullying behaviour. An awful quiet followed, no more was said and we all watched the clock creep round to our break. At the end of the lesson my fellow pupils clamoured around and congratulated me. Any feeling of triumph at my classroom heroics was short-lived and hollow. Next day Oscar was taken seriously ill and I felt only remorse; his foul temper must have been a product of his ill health.

In my other life an event of great significance took place; Bowles Rocks was opened to climbers. In the course of my sandstone explorations I had already visited them and been amazed at their tremendous potential. Unfortunately they were very private and worse, formed the back wall of an extensive and highly offensive pig farm. I had visited with Max one evening and, to a background accompaniment of grunting pigs, climbed two of the finest routes in the area: *Pig's Nose* and the spectacular *Sloth*. The last route overcame a tall buttress capped by an eight-foot roof around which grew a gnarled birch. It was a simple matter to use this tree to swing out hand over hand under this huge overhang with feet tucked up round the horizontal trunk and so reach the top.

The local blacksmith, 'Old Jack' Fenner, owned Bowles. He ran an ancient village forge manufacturing scythes, sickles, and billhooks of the finest quality. When the pig market slumped the rocks were of no use to him and being a wily old character he approached the Sandstone Club one night in the High Rocks Tavern. His asking price started at 2,000 pounds, but as the evening progressed and the strong Merrydown cider began to take effect he hinted that he was open to offers and in the meantime we were welcome to inspect the rocks at will.

We were delighted to take up his offer and began immediately to clear the incredible accumulation of junk littering the rocks. Apart from the numerous pig sties there were ancient engines, troughs full of decomposing entrails and a vast hoard of empty snuff tins. We camped out under a large overhang situated in the Amphitheatre, a site used by Stone Age hunters; the sandy floor contained many smoke-blackened stones and flint chippings. The vegetation was dense and the rocks were a sanctuary for wildlife. Badgers romped undisturbed, a ghostly white barn owl roosted above us and a dapper nuthatch nested in an artfully cemented crack.

For several months we had the place to ourselves. We would arrive at night, get a fire going and cook supper before retiring to the local pub where we would be entertained by Jack Fenner telling tales of the rocks: how they had been used to hide smuggled brandy, of the huntsman who had galloped over Sloth Buttress in thick fog, and many more. The finale to the evening would come, after sufficient cider, with Jack singing some local bawdy ballad at the top of his voice.

In the mornings, after a leisurely breakfast, we would carry out some cleaning-up operations before setting off on the main business of climbing new routes. Unlike forbidding High Rocks, Bowles faced south and was a perfect suntrap. There was plenty for everyone but with Max, Paul and John Smoker, I climbed the lion's share. Many of the routes were very hard and all of them on perfect hard grey rock, including classics like *Inspiration, Hate, Digitalis, Fandango* and *Banana*.

The problem of what we should do with Bowles was not clear initially; we could in no way raise the necessary funds to buy them ourselves, so we approached various people and bodies in the hope that they could do it for us. Mrs Morin was interested but then a local Crowborough businessman made an approach to the Sandstone Club. Although in his mid-forties he had become converted to climbing after a visit to the Alps. This left him with a fixation with the Matterhorn and a desire to open a climbing gymnasium. He was a 'muscular Christian' type, energetic and with a fanatical gleam in his eyes. He had access to money, the purchase went ahead and Jack was delighted. I was deeply suspicious; a suspicion later confirmed when the rocks were 'landscaped', a clubhouse built and holds chipped on some of the best climbs. Last but not least an exact stone replica of the Matterhorn Chapel appeared. We no longer enjoyed free access to the rocks but by this time we had climbed practically all the routes. The badgers and owls had left and so did we.

The other momentous happening in my life was falling in love with Max's sister Viv. She was a tiny vivacious woman with a dazzling cascade of pale blonde hair. I had seen and admired her from afar, but she was older than me, had flashy boyfriends with cars and seemed utterly unavailable. Suddenly all this changed; she was at home every evening looking sad and depressed. Her boyfriend had left her and in an effort to cheer Viv up Max took her out one balmy summer evening. I joined them and we ambled through forested country to Eridge Green. In the wildly romantic setting of Eridge Rocks, darkness pressed us together, our hands touched and held. As night birds sang and the green sparks of glow-worms punctured the blackness, we clung to each other with desperate passion.

We shared a short glorious summer interlude of hopeless first love. I had sensed it would come; I was eager for the experience, yet when it arrived I was unprepared for its sweet powerful shock. For weeks I could think of nothing else and waited impatiently for the evenings when we could walk out into the scented air through sunken lanes and thick woods, to dark reedy lakes where we bathed in the moonlight.

In the early hours of the morning as the street lights switched themselves off I would walk back home with a buoyant stride, creep into the house, eat a long-cold supper and listen to the low, lush sound of Duke Ellington's band playing *Careless Love* and *Embraceable You* on the radiogram.

That our love could not last did not occur to me at first. True our ages and backgrounds were markedly different; I was still at school, she had long worked for a living. My life was just opening up, she was looking to settle down and with university coming our separation was inevitable. Viv must have realised this early; for her, the relationship had no future. The parting came when my holidays arrived. I had already decided on my trip to the Alps; I had saved 20 pounds, bought my first pair of Lawrie's alpine boots, acquired my first ice-axe. I just had to go. We kissed each other tenderly goodbye, I boarded the train, waved till it entered the tunnel and was at last alone with my thoughts on my way to Newhaven and the ferry to France.

My journey through France was pleasantly slow. The hitching was bad but the weather good. I seemed to spend most of my days lounging in thick flowery verges listening to the chirruping of crickets with one ear cocked for the sound of approaching cars. At last northern France was behind me, the gentle wooded hills of the Jura slowly rose in front and suddenly there were white gleaming tops, high and distant, extending for mile upon mile across the valley of Geneva. It was an exciting vision. The end of my pilgrimage was in sight. The last part of the journey went rapidly. I was picked up by a cheerful bunch of French climbers, bundled into the back of their car and driven flat out up the gloomy defile of the Arve valley until the gleaming mountains appeared, floating above the cloud. There was the immense dome of Mont Blanc, the jagged teeth of the Aiguilles, vast contorted glacier streams plunging into the pine forests. I had arrived and could hardly believe it.

I made my way to the Biolay campsite close to Chamonix and was heartened to see a host of climbers, mostly British and German, camped under an amazing variety of tents, tarpaulins and plastic sheeting strung between the trees. I had no trouble finding a partner and a couple of days later set off heavily laden with equipment and provisions to walk up to Montenvers with a young Nottingham climber. As we staggered up through the trees, hot and sweaty, the air began to freshen. We could 'smell' the ice, the trees began to thin and the most fantastic views opened up on all sides. Above us the West Face of the Dru towered in a perfect vertical shaft of tawny granite; beyond, at the head of the sinuous Mer de Glace, was the magnificent icy rampart of the Grandes Jorasses. The scale of everything was immense; I could not relate to it. How small and cosy the British hills and crags seemed in comparison.

We made our way to the Chalet Austria, a small free hut below the Aiguilles, and next morning climbed the West Face of the Pointe Albert, a short rock route on the smallest of the nearby peaks. It was a start but it was hardly an Alpine route for it involved no snow and ice, and it was grossly overshadowed by even the smallest of the neighbouring Aiguilles. All further plans were thwarted by the onset of stormy weather. For days we lay in our pits eating meagre provisions while a trickle of climbers arrived and departed, including two sunburned Austrians. They had just climbed the Bonatti Pillar on the Dru – heroes indeed. Later, the same pair became famous by making the first winter ascent of the Eiger North Face.

A huge youth with a crew cut arrived one night and introduced himself as Doug Scott. He had just come from a trip to the High Atlas where he had contracted hepatitis. A thin bespectacled Londoner called Barry Brewster also passed by. It was his first Alpine season but already he was talking of doing the West Face of Dru, the Walker Spur on the Jorasses and even more incredibly the Eiger's North Face. I wondered at such ambition. For my part I would have been satisfied with a few classics and even this modest aspiration seemed in doubt as my partner grew disenchanted in the continuing storms.

At the end of the first bad period, word reached me that an experienced climber from the north-east needed someone to climb with; his partner had twisted his knee. Jeff Allison arrived at the Chalet Austria in the afternoon, keen to do some rock routes at the back of the Aiguilles. I was to come with him quickly to the Envers des Aiguilles Hut for he was sure the weather was about to improve. We left immediately. He had food and provisions at the hut; all I needed was to get there. We set off up the Mer de Glace gleaming and polished from the recent torrential rain. I skidded about alarmingly and became quite nervous when a thick damp mist descended. We lost our way and were forced to put on crampons to negotiate the maze of crevasses and narrow ice bridges. It was a relief to climb off the glacier onto grass and rock for the final traverse to the hut, perched like a castle, austere and empty on a rocky ridge.

We arrived as darkness fell and I was delighted to meet up with Richard McHardy, John Cheesmond and Frank Carroll. They too had been sitting out the weather, hoping to snatch the Mer de Glace Face of the Grépon as soon as things improved. It was not to be the next day. Jeff rose at two but it was drizzling so we turned over thankfully in our beds and returned to sleep.

There followed a couple of cheerless days. It was bitterly cold and we were banished to the freezing cellar to do all our cooking. There was anyway precious little to cook; Jeff seemed to flourish on a diet of stale bread and thin ex-WD powdered oxtail soups. I was perpetually hungry and Richard – a noted trencherman – suffered similar pangs. Jeff was eternally optimistic, much to the derision of John Cheesmond, but after two days it did look much better. The clouds dispersed and we were treated to a clear, star-studded evening.

Jeff announced our intended route – the Dent du Crocodile by its East Ridge. The others got ready for the Grépon. In the early hours of the morning we stumbled out of the hut into the pre-dawn darkness, switched on our torches, started up the glacier and were soon wading up knee-deep snow. A serac barrier delayed us further and we were hours behind guide-book time before we reached the first rocks. Apparently we were supposed to be on easy scrambling but it didn't seem that way. Every ledge was banked with thick powder snow and so every move was a struggle. The hard climbing above seemed to get no nearer. We came to a couloir and Jeff waded across it before anxiously shouting that I should be careful and quick. I understood why as I reached the other side. In a thunderous rumble, a powder-snow avalanche shot past, leaving us covered and soaked in fine white dust. We climbed up a few hundred feet more till we could look into the first chimneys; they were encrusted in ice and we were obviously not going to get up them that day. Jeff called retreat and I was profoundly thankful. I had had enough, I was cold and wet, utterly tired and feeling the altitude. I did not feel ready for such a serious undertaking.

The descent proved tricky. We rushed panting and fearful across the couloir and then, while Jeff belayed me, I went down first. On an awkward traverse a large flake broke off and I went swinging across on the rope, crashed into a rock and cut my head and ear. I arrived back at the hut covered in blood and disheartened only to meet the others similarly disconsolate. It was obviously a waste of time staying at the hut. Even the optimist Jeff agreed and next day we trekked down to the Chalet Austria.

We stayed there for a couple of nights and were joined by Geoff Oliver, a delightful friendly Geordie who talked enthusiastically of climbing in the Lake District. That was all there was to talk about for by now everyone was thoroughly disheartened by the appalling weather and bad conditions. One night we went for a glass of wine at the bleakly empty Montenvers Hotel. As can so easily happen in good company, one glass followed another, my head began to reel and the next thing I remember was John Cheesmond hurling glasses at the wall. A large threatening figure materialised and pointed at the door. John collapsed and we carried him in a state of unconsciousness up the exposed track to the chalet. Next morning my boots were filled neatly with vomit. John denied any knowledge of it or of the entire evening but he thought it best not to collect an anorak, which he had carelessly left behind at the hotel.

This last binge marked the end of the holiday. Jeff and I climbed one last route on the Aiguille de l'M in teeming rain and then we decided to pack it in and return home. Descending to Chamonix, the snow line dropped to the tree-level, the Biolay campsite emptied and climbers drifted homewards. I wandered round looking for a lift and met up with a haggard Robin Smith and Dougal Haston. They had been trying the Central Pillar of Frêney. With them was a giant of a man with thick black hair and swarthy good looks. This was James Moriarty, or more familiarly Big Ely. He was also going home with a group of fellow Edinburgh climbers. 'Sure there was room for a little one,' he said. Compared with Big Ely everyone was small and if he said there was room, then room there was. I squashed into the already crowded Volkswagen van and we rattled back home as Big Ely recommended I 'come and try a few wee problems' like *Shibboleth* and *Carnivore* on his native crags, among the hardest routes anywhere. His mischievous smile warned me what to expect.

I could not wait to get back and find consolation following my first disastrous Alpine season with Viv. I rushed up to the department store where she worked with a pounding heart. Had she received my mushy postcards? How did she feel about me now? I spotted her in the shop window arranging an autumn display of leaves, tapped on the glass and watched her look up. She gave a sad little smile and I knew all I needed. It was amazing that I expected it to be otherwise. She was going out with a friend of mine; it was a hard blow to bear.

I could not stand to hang around so I borrowed a few pounds from my mother and hitched off up to the Lake District. I knew Geoff Oliver would be there and he had painted such a glowing picture of autumn in the Lakes that I was keen to see it for myself. I reached Penrith the first day and after a night under a hedge caught the first bus to Keswick in the morning. I walked up Borrowdale to Shepherd's Crag and to my delight

Geoff Oliver was already there. I was directed immediately to the local testpieces; since I was regarded as a 'Welsh climber' it was his duty; the Wales and Lake District rivalry was very much a tradition. I climbed *Conclusion* and one or two other routes and Geoff promised me that the following day I would be pitted against something much harder: *Triermain Eliminate* on Castle Rock of Triermain. Next day we approached the lovely wooded cliff and he pointed out the route to me – a thin crack going up a vertical wall. Geoff had tried it several times and failed; the problem was that it was both unprotected and strenuous. I took it at a dash, laybacking up a few moves, and to shouts of encouragement, arrived at a shallow groove. A tiny spikelet provided the only protection I could see but a couple of moves higher I could reach a good jug and with this swing to the top. The pitch was short but fierce – a typical product of Don Whillans.

The following day I met up with Jeff Allison and he drove me round to Langdale for a marvellous day climbing *Do Knot* and the classic *Kipling Groove* on Gimmer Crag. I was enjoying myself immensely climbing superb routes every day and when the Newcastle lads set off for home I straightaway made contact with Oliver Woolcott, a Workington climber who was a research student in chemistry at Sheffield University. He was a sound climber, a friend of Jack Soper, easy going and pleasant company. Together we climbed every day despite showery weather and on one memorable day at Castle Rock did *Thirlmere Eliminate* and *Rigor Mortis* without aid. As we accomplished this latter climb its progenitor Paul Ross arrived and watched us. He was a playful, impish figure, incapacitated by a bad back but keen to direct us to one or two more of his inventions. He pointed us onto Upper Falcon Buttress the next day and I was very careful not to fall off where so many others had done.

A few days later the Sheffield climbers Dave Gregory and Pat Fearne-hough turned up in their Dormobile van. They were going to Scotland to meet up with Jack Soper. We asked if we could join them and they gladly agreed despite the fact that we had no money to help out with petrol costs. We drove through Glencoe in sheeting rain, arrived at Fort William that night and next morning set off in welcome sunshine to flog up through the bogs to the Inglis Clark Hut under the North Face of Ben Nevis. We were carrying food to stay there for several days; it was much like an Alpine trip.

It was a snug little hut with a great coal stove at its centre. If the weather held we had ambitious plans to climb the long hard routes on Carn Dearg Buttress. It was not to be, the rain signalled its arrival in the night by rattling on the panes. A day passed and we killed time doing boulder problems while Jack the expert geologist pointed out volcanic ashes, tuffs and lava flows. The following day dawned watery clear, so Jack and I set off to try *Sassenach*, an impressive groove chimney line. The rock was still streaming, however, and when we got to the crux overhang it was pouring all over us. I tried rather half-heartedly, grabbed a sling hanging from a huge chockstone and next moment found myself swinging in space with the useless sling clutched in my arms. Jack had a go but agreed it was not on. We abseiled down and set off rather late to do the longest rock climb on the mountain, appropriately enough called *Long Climb* on Orion Face. As fast as we were able, we climbed up an apparently endless succession of damp mossy slabs and before we realised it, were totally lost in the gathering darkness. We knew only that to our right was Zero Gully; if we could traverse into it we could feel our way up. The traverse began, more dangerous than difficult; we could hardly see at all but made it eventually, crept up the comforting recess and emerged onto the open summit plateau. Jack thought he knew the way down so I followed him wearily until he stopped and asked me to guess which way a stream was flowing. 'I thought so,' he said, and announced we were going down the wrong side of the mountain. We plodded up once more and after an interminable descent through a boulder field arrived back at dawn to be met by our anxious friends.

We had had quite enough by now and as if to emphasise our thoughts it began to rain again. Dave decided to head south, this time to Wales, and, after dropping 'Wooly' off at Workington, we headed down the A6. Wales was dreary and rain-sodden; our spirits were low. I climbed *Surplomb* with Neville Drasdo and then at the weekend hitched a lift to London and then home.

It had been a year of mixed fortunes. It was the end of my summer's climbing and freedom. I had to return to my last year of A-level study – a year in which I would have to work hard for a place at university. It had been an unsatisfactory year; emotionally I was in turmoil, the Alps had been a disaster and in Britain it seemed to have rained unceasingly.

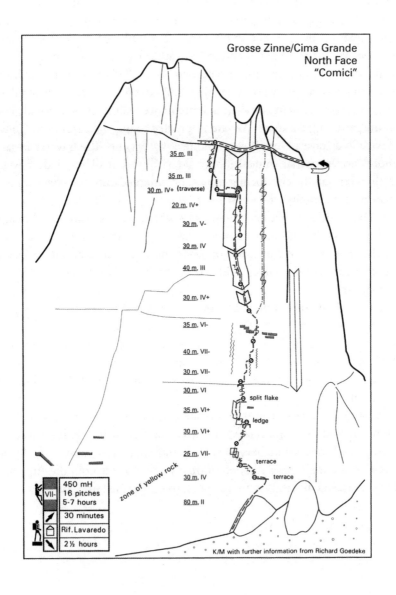

Grosse Zinne/Cima Grande
North Face
"Comici"

35 m, III

35 m, III

30 m, IV+ (traverse)

20 m, IV+

30 m, V-

30 m, IV

40 m, III

30 m, IV+

35 m, VI-

40 m, VII-

30 m, VII-

30 m, VI

split flake

35 m, VI+

ledge

30 m, VI+

25 m, VII-

terrace

30 m, IV

terrace

80 m, II

zone of yellow rock

VII-	450 mH 16 pitches 5-7 hours
	30 minutes
	Rif. Lavaredo
	2 ½ hours

K/M with further information from Richard Goedeke

FIVE
THE DOLOMITES

The train hooted, startling me from an uncomfortable sleep as it plunged into a tunnel. We were in the mountains at last. Suddenly in dazzling sunshine again, we rattled downhill, through meadows and dark pine forests. Far below the glacial-grey River Inn raced over its stony bed. We were approaching Innsbruck, the starting point for our Dolomite holiday.

The Dolomites had seemed a natural choice for my second Alpine adventure. In my first season in the Western Alps, I had discovered I wasn't ready for them. I had no experience of ice climbing, had inadequate equipment and no climbing partner. This year I was determined to overcome some of these disadvantages. The Dolomites, with their lower altitude, lack of snow and glorious expanses of rock, seemed an ideal starting point for someone who was essentially still only a rock climber. I approached Max as a potential partner. He was keen, but had already made tentative plans for a walking tour of the Tyrol with his work-mate Ernie. I was a little disappointed at first, but after a while could see no reason why we shouldn't combine a climbing and walking trip. Max was happy with the plan, Ernie had no objections and so, on a warm morning in July, we stepped off the train at Innsbruck, shouldered our packs and set off through the outskirts of the city towards Italy and the Brenner Pass.

Although I had never seen Ernie before our train journey, I took to him immediately. He was tall and lean, apparently made entirely of sinew and bone. Well into his forties, he was fit and tanned, and moved with a lightness and grace belying his years. He was quietly spoken, almost shy, but his face often creased into a friendly grin. He had fought in the War and could still speak a little Italian, delivered with a broad Kentish accent. Unlike most old soldiers, it was difficult to get him to talk about the War, but when he did it was fascinating to listen to his stories of Apennine battles like the ferocious assault of Monte Cassino.

We drew clear of the city and began to climb gently. It was slow, back-breaking progress but I consoled myself with the thought that at least we would be getting fit. The first few days are always the worst; one is unused to the weight, and the essential rhythm of walking has to be re-learned until the mind and feet are hardened to the task. We walked until evening and then dropped down into a quiet, wooded ravine with a stream splashing down its smooth rocky bed. If the first day is the worst, then in compensation the first night spent out is the most enchanting. It was delicious to rest my aching body, to lounge around a glowing wood fire, smell the wood smoke and allow the night to creep up before retiring to sleep.

The next day was hot and sultry and we walked on gaining height slowly. I began to feel the pricking sensation of developing blisters and was soon hobbling painfully, wishing the walk over and nursing feelings of resentment. Hell, I hadn't really wanted to walk in the first place; it was a compromise holiday. Why didn't Max and Ernie get bloody blisters? At this rate I'll never get to the Dolomites. Storm clouds gathered and soon it began to bucket with rain, drowning such dark thoughts. We struck off the road into a thick wood and rapidly strung up our shelter – my ancient US Army bivouac tent of heavy enduring canvas. The rain was cold and heavy, turning to snow a few hundred feet above us. Cowering under the tent, we sat it out all night and next day, becoming more damp and miserable as the hours dragged by. The only relief was an occasional drink brewed with tremendous difficulty from a smouldering and unwilling fire.

The following morning dawned bright and clear with the bite of frost in the air. Thankfully, we packed up and emerged from our dank, oppressive campsite, out on to the open road where we were confronted with a dazzling view of mountain ranges sparkling under new snow. We strode out with new vigour, reached the col and gazed with wonder into Italy, the beckoning Dolomites spread out before us. Impatiently, I longed to be there, to be climbing. A train waited at the railway station. Where was it going? Dobiacco, on our route. In a moment of weakness I suggested we take it, and was surprised when Max and Ernie agreed. A few minutes later we were rattling uncomfortably in the slowest train imaginable, downhill through South Tyrol, towards our goal. I felt a little guilty, as the instigator, but Max pointed out that we would have plenty of walking in the Dolomites. It looked a boring walk in any case. We reached Dobiacco and got a tantalising view of the Tre Cime di Lavaredo but we had to get to Cortina, so caught a bus and arrived by evening.

Cortina lies in a huge, bowl-shaped valley surrounded by Dolomite peaks and precipices coloured red, yellow and purple in the fiery sunset. The effect was theatrical, an awesome landscape of luminous vertical shapes leaping out of sunlit greens; too startlingly savage for beauty, but raw, primeval and exciting. My heart quickened at the sight of so much rock. I couldn't wait to get started, but first we had to buy some climbing equipment.

We visited Lino Lacedelli's climbing shop and Lacedelli himself was there – a huge bear of a man with a grizzled face and powerful hunched shoulders. As one of the first men to climb 'Kappa Due' – K2 – he was an Italian hero. We bought pitons, karabiners, hammers and etriers, loaded them into our already huge rucksacks and set off for the Tre Cime di Lavaredo.

With mountains in view and the anticipation of climbing to come, the walk was pure joy. By now I was feeling fit and strong after the early tedious struggle. Even my rucksack, loaded with tins of corned beef, rope, clothes and tent, felt light as we walked up through pleasant woods and alpine meadows humming with grasshoppers and bedecked with flowers. I walked along half in a world of fantasy, reliving the epic climbs of Riccardo Cassin, Emilio Comici and Hermann Buhl, turning the names of peaks over and over in my mind: Tofana, Monte Cristallo, Marmolada, Civetta.

We reached Misurina and rested by lovely green lakes before starting up the track towards the Tre Cime di Lavaredo and soon camped. Impatient, anxious to climb, I rushed off in the dying light to scamper up some decaying minor pinnacles of rock. The remainder of the walk was, in contrast, most unpleasant. It coincided with a national holiday, and it seemed that half Italy was driving up the track, now thronged with cars, motorbikes and buses, grinding ever upwards and fouling the air with a mixture of dust and carbon monoxide. It was a relief to get to the road head, a vast rifugio set beside a dismal scree slope under the backside of the Cima Ovest. We continued until the Cima Piccolo came into view and a great yellow prow of rock, the *Spigalo Giallo*, or *Yellow Edge*, towered over us. This must be our first climb, I thought. Hidden in the boulders, and away from tourists, we sought out a quiet campsite. It was hardly a lovely place, but at least it had a spring of fresh water and the litter of boxes from First World War military emplacements provided enough wood for our fire.

Max and I made no special effort to get off early next morning and soon discovered our mistake. The start of *Yellow Edge* was already crowded with parties; cries of 'Achtung' and 'Attenzione' warned of the dangers of being hit by stones dislodged from above. We waited for things to quieten down and the climbing, when we got on it, surprised me. The rock was steep and bristling with pitons of every type, battered and bent, in every possible crack; but the holds were ample and the main difficulty lay in avoiding the use of dubious pitons. We climbed quickly, paying little heed to where the route went; one merely looked for the next piton. Then we came to a steep section of loose red rock. A piton stuck out of it and so I climbed over two difficult overhangs to a tiny ledge. Something was wrong; the climbing was much harder and looser than anything so far. I belayed and brought Max up. His pitch, if anything, looked worse; a crack and groove up disintegrating yellow rock reared up. Max climbed nervously, aware that a false move could send tons of rock crashing on my head. Anxiously, I watched him inch upwards to a bent and very rusty piton. 'We're on the wrong route, you know,' he calmly observed. Someone had to say it.

'Yes, I think so – I'm sure so – but push on for God's sake, the thought of reversing … ' I replied, leaving the thought unfinished. He placed another piton and tapped it gingerly into place.

'Be careful, Martin,' he said as he brought me up. There was one more awful rope length and then the angle eased, the tension subsided and soon we were on the summit. Although a little shaken up by our dangerous diversion, after a long and thoughtful laze in the sun we shrugged off the memory and clambered back down, abseiled down our ropes and ran back to camp. Ernie received us with a relieved and friendly smile. 'Christ, you buggers scared me to death. I watched you – but didn't you go the wrong way?' We could only laugh.

Having decided to take it easy the next day, we climbed the *Preuss Crack* on Cima Piccolissima, a delightful cleft. Then it was time to think of tackling a serious route, the obvious choice being the North Face of the Cima Grande. This is a famous route, first climbed in 1933 by Comici and it takes a direct line up an awesome, overhanging wall. When first done, this was the most sensational and sought-after route in the Eastern Alps and heralded an era of Dolomite climbing during which many unclimbed walls fell to an onslaught from competing climbers prepared to use artificial techniques where they thought free climbing was impossible. Today it no longer has a reputation for great difficulty, but is still a fine climb, both intimidating to look at and, above all, steep.

We walked round to the north side of the massif to inspect our route that evening. At the col the three north faces loomed into view, three great fortresses of smooth, grey rock, all incredibly impressive: the sheer Piccola, the Cima Grande standing proud with its vast impending wall and beyond the monstrous overhanging bulk of the Cima Ovest. We sat and looked, tracing out the line. A wafer of ice fell from a gully high on the face, sailed into space and sunlight and disintegrated into a splintering cascade incredibly far out from the base of the wall.

Determined to avoid queuing this time, we breakfasted before first light. But although it was still quite dark as we neared the North Face we heard voices: Italian and German. Groaning with disappointment, we took a short rest and started climbing. Ahead of us were two teams, a pair of fast-moving Italians, all in black, and two thickset Bavarians with double boots and large rucksacks. They looked ominously slow. I gave them a friendly greeting in German, half hoping, I suppose, that they might allow us to slip through, but was answered with a surly grunt. As we waited, another team arrived, an Italian pair whom we had seen on the *Yellow Edge*. The lead climber looked good, but his second was less able and looked somewhat shaky.

We climbed slowly – so slowly. After each pitch we would wait up to an hour, whilst Fritz and Otto – as we now knew them – kicked and cursed their way up. It was bitterly cold as we sat in the shaded wall, idly swinging our feet as we cursed as well, though silently, watching their progress above and below where the Italians were having the same bother. The second had fallen off the rock and was swinging limply, with a defeated look on his face. A stream of abuse poured from the leader's mouth, the second whimpered. 'Bambino! Bambino!' the leader screamed. The second stirred and struggled up hand over hand, to reach his tormentor. I anticipated a punch-up but instead they embraced each other. A discussion ensued, which was terminated when the leader pointed forcefully upwards.

We reached the route's artificial section and climbed up and out across the overhang, clinging on to pitons. It was my first taste of artificial climbing and while I didn't enjoy it, it was soon over. The face leaned back to become merely vertical and above us I could see the ice-encrusted chimneys. We sat for a further two hours, waiting for parties to clear this section before we followed up the awkward, slippery cleft. Above a traverse broke leftwards, and once again we waited.

Suddenly there was an ear-splitting scream, and Otto plummeted, ripping Fritz from his stance. We watched helplessly as Otto swung about, suspended from a piton over a terrifying void. His gyrations lessened and he began instead to twirl one way and then the other, until at last he managed to prusik up the rope. Immediately, as if this were a regular occurrence, the two Bavarians went on.

It was getting late but fortunately the climbing was easing considerably. We reached a large terrace and the parties ahead scuttled off along it. We wondered what to do; the top was still a few hundred feet above, and I wanted to go for it. Setting off, we reached a minor point but then reconsidered our plan and decided to beat a rapid retreat to avoid a bivouac. A descent gully, which seemed easy, became too steep for safety after we had scrambled down several hundred feet and so we threaded our 300-foot rope through a ring piton and abseiled down to a tiny ledge, in reality not much more than a foothold. As we tugged one end of the rope, it ran stiffly and then stuck fast. We heaved and pulled to no avail. So without saying a word, I started to solo back up the rock and, in the dying light, re-fixed the abseil and set off down again. Unbelievably, the rope stuck again. Frustrated, I climbed up once more, and this time prised the rope out of a crack. At the third attempt the rope came down, but had been so stretched by our tugging that it wrapped itself into an incredible tangle. In those days the books recommended one 300-foot rope doubled for abseil rather than two shorter ones tied together. Now I know better. We were perched on our footholds, in darkness, with a 300-foot knot. I was almost weeping with rage and frustration, but Max was quite calm and began the formidable task of unthreading loops to sort it out. It took God knows how long; I had almost given up hope. Our last view of the foot of the cliff had made it seem tantalisingly near, perhaps a couple of abseils. Max set off into the darkness, a few falling stones signalling his descent, and I followed.

'Stay up on the ledge above me, Martin. This one's very tatty and I think you'll get a better piton in. I think we'll get down with the next one.'

'I hope so!' I replied and found a good horizontal crack, smashed a piton into it and began to wrestle with the rope again. It seemed alive, like a 300-foot anaconda. As I threw the ends down into darkness, I prayed that they would reach the bottom.

'Max, you go down first, the rock is really crappy below; I might kick something onto you.'

'OK!'

Next, I heard a large rock crashing down the gully, echoing off to the side. It was terrifying. Then the rope whipped onto the piton with a terrific crack and I heard a simultaneous, blood-curdling scream and then a thud.

'Christ, what's up Max?' I got the worst answer; a deathly silence. I listened again but heard only my racing pulse. Then – a faint groan. Trembling, I hurried down the rope and there, 50 feet below, was Max crumpled on a ledge and moaning gently. He came round slowly and I comforted him as best I could. He was in great pain. The night was long and black and I peered down into the gully, hoping for an end to the nightmare, uncertain what the morning would bring. The cause of the accident was obvious. Between Max and me, the rope had snarled over loose blocks. When Max had tugged the rope to test it the blocks held firm, but as soon as he committed all his weight to it they had pulled out and there was suddenly 40 feet of slack.

At last I could make out the bottom. The ropes did reach the ground. We were so nearly there! Max was stiff with cold, but had regained his senses, and now his remarkable strength and courage took over. His back had received the full force of the fall onto the stony ledge and was almost certainly damaged.

'I'd better alert a rescue team,' I suggested.

'No, I'll manage. Just help us down the last abseil.' Somehow he managed it. The pain must have been frightful. I joined him on the snow patch and we made our way carefully down the hard, frozen surface. He slipped and desperately I clawed on, slowing his downward slide, until I was plucked off too. Together, we slipped down, coming to rest among some boulders. Max's face was drained white with pain and he couldn't stifle a cry of agony as he bounced to a stop. Somehow we reached the campsite, where we slumped in the morning sun as Ernie rushed around and prepared hot drinks. We discussed our next move and Max decided he would 'rest a day or so and see how his back felt'. To hear him talk about his back one could have supposed nothing worse than a pulled muscle or two but Max is a master of understatement. After a day lying in the sun, he made the admission that his 'back was pretty bad – probably broken'. Obviously he needed medical care, but was loath to go to hospital. We were short of money, totally uninsured and aware that medical treatment would mean large bills. 'I think I better get back home,' Max announced, as he slowly straightened himself up and began to pack. 'Ernie's decided to come back with me, but there's no need for you to come; you're bound to find someone to climb with.'

Of course, I wanted to stay. I had enough money for a few more weeks. Yet I felt I ought to accompany Max back home. Max, of course, realised my dilemma and, with typical generosity, insisted that there was no need for me to return. And so I stayed – more callousness of youth!

Sadly, I watched them pack and start the walk back down to Misurina. I had tried to get a lift for them but Max assured me he would rather walk than endure a bumpy, cramped ride. Wishing them a speedy journey, I waved goodbye as I watched them disappear, Max walking slowly, painfully erect, his back having locked solid into ridged knots of muscle. I returned to the tent feeling uneasy and utterly alone.

Several weeks later, on my return to England, Max told me of his painful trip home. When, eventually, he reached Britain he walked into his nearest hospital and told them quietly that he had broken his back. The doctor ridiculed this obvious 'nonsense', explaining that pulled muscles and strains could be very painful. He got Max on the table and made him try an excruciating press-up. Max was then X-rayed, as a formality, and told to return in a few days for the results. Once again, patiently, he tried to explain his back was broken and then suddenly people were scurrying around, holding up X-rays, and a rather embarrassed doctor returned to inform him that indeed he had severely damaged several lumbar vertebrae. Immediately, Max was encased in plaster and persuaded to stay for a few days. They did their best to keep him, but Max admitted that he had stayed more for the doctor's peace of mind than his own. After a few days of boredom he decided to leave and there was little they could say, considering the unusual circumstances of his admission. For many weekends Max trudged around in his plaster, warming his back against a fire and adopting various yoga positions, until the healing process had done its work. His back is now sometimes stiff and painful but, thank God, he is as fit and strong as ever.

After Max and Ernie's departure my first action was to shift camp next to the Rifugio Lavaredo. I wanted a change of scene, new company and a fresh start so I could put aside the memories of our nightmare on the Cima Grande. In the evening I would go to the rifugio and have a plate of spaghetti and a carafe of wine. It was a cheerful little hut, run by the widow of a climbing guide. She was kind and ran things with the interests of climbers at heart. There were always lots of German and Austrians gathered there and I had little difficulty in meeting and talking with them, although my ability to speak German did not help much with the various Bavarian and Austrian dialects. My problem was to find a good climber who was unattached. This was not easy, since most of them already had their partners. Even so, unpartnered climbers drifted around, although in many cases it was easy to see why they were alone.

My remaining ambition was to climb the North Face of the Cima Ovest, a serious and hard route first climbed by the great Italian Riccardo Cassin. The whole of the lower half of the face is a sequence of incredible projecting overhangs, but Cassin's route skirts round these on the right and then traverses above them to the centre of the cliff. The crux of the climb is the traverse left, on the lip of the overhangs, across very shattered rock. It was not a route to tackle with a weak second man, since he would have to climb as well as the leader, and without a protective rope from above. I had read accounts of the difficulties – people had died of strangulation, swinging helplessly in space. Hermann Buhl, an outstanding post-war Austrian climber, had written a hair-raising account of the climb and there was no doubt that it needed careful thought and preparation.

I did not have long to wait for a partner. One morning a young German student, Helmut, sought me out in my tent. Having made enquiries at the hut, the guardian had directed him to me. He also wanted to climb the *Cassin Route* but explained that he was unfit and needed a training climb or two first. He suggested a short, hard route on the Cima Piccolissima; I was only too happy to agree and so, after swallowing a hurried breakfast, we set off.

It was a fun route, though technically quite hard if one avoided grabbing the excessive number of pitons already in place. My companion suggested I lead and gratefully I accepted, keeping a watchful eye on Helmut from each stance. He managed well enough, but I noticed uneasily how he grasped for pitons without testing them first. When I offered him a chance to lead, he declined. He was 'not feeling well' and I noticed that his exuberant cheerfulness had vanished and his face now wore a thoughtful frown. A short traverse proved the last difficulty, an ideal challenge in fact, since it presented a similar if shorter problem to the great traverse on the *Cassin Route*. Helmut dithered for a few moments and then came across, but he was uncertain in his movements and nearly fell off.

By now my mind was made up; he was not ready for the difficulties of the Cima Ovest and I would somehow have to explain my decision without causing hurt feelings. I need not have worried. Helmut, too intelligent to be unaware of his shortcomings, admitted he was not up to a serious route like the *Cassin*. He was very disappointed and so was I, for Helmut was extremely likeable and I would have been happy to climb with him. After thanking me warmly, he decided it was time to go back home and do some serious studying for his exams.

Once more I was seeking a partner, and that same night was introduced to a striking Italian who had a day to kill before his comrades arrived. He was an impressive figure, of medium height, well-built and with a wild mane of straight, black hair falling onto his shoulders. His face was that of a biblical prophet, dark and sun-beaten, with piercing black eyes that looked slightly mad. Having already climbed most of the routes I wanted to do, he suggested the *Demuth Route* on the Cima Ovest. This takes the arête on the left of the North Face and was easy for the most part, with only one short difficult section. I readily agreed to his suggestion and next morning the Italian set off at a tremendous pace that I had great difficulty matching. Communication was difficult and fragmentary, we spoke no common tongue but there was little enough time for conversation in any case. We scrambled to the start, uncoiled ropes and he rattled out a quick explanation, very little of which I understood. I was totally dumbfounded – and more than a little apprehensive – when he bowed his head, muttered a prayer, made the sign of the cross and then exploded up the rock face with the speed of a cat chased by a large dog. The rope ran out, he shouted something like 'Corda!' and I followed.

I just kept climbing, following the rope as fast as I could, desperate that it should not go tight, for he was at the other end, climbing furiously. We came to the difficult overhang; he paused for a few seconds until I arrived, and then swarmed over it. Within an hour and a half we were on the summit. He patted me on the back, pointed at his watch, said 'Record!' several times then promptly hurtled off down a scree gully. I followed. Doubtless he was going all out for another record, for in what seemed like minutes we were careering down scree slopes to the Rifugio Auronzo at the back of the Tre Cime. We ran back to the Lavaredo Hut where we were served a free lunch after which he gave me a bone-crunching handshake and disappeared.

Climbing companions were now coming fast and furious; another German climber introduced himself and expressed enthusiasm for the *Cassin*. Once again I climbed the practice route on the Piccolissima. By now I was climbing superbly; I knew the route backwards and hardly touched a peg. My companion, however, was totally incompetent and repeatedly tumbled and fell. By the third fall I had had enough, and had no qualms about informing him that I had no desire to climb with him again.

It was Friday night and I was hopeful for the weekend, when it was usual for crowds of climbers to arrive at the hut. I was not disappointed and found Gunther, a willing partner from Munich, who wanted to do the *Cassin Route*. His climbing companion had cried off at the last moment and his two friends were after the formidable *North Face Direct* on the Cima Grande. I chatted to him for a few hours, gleaned a certain amount of information about routes he'd done and made discreet enquiries about his ability from his friends. They assured me there was no cause for concern; he was a thoroughly competent climber with a good record of ascents. I stopped worrying. It didn't even seem necessary to carry out a training climb, something I had promised myself I would always do with each new partner.

We made our plans, sorted out some gear and prepared for an early start. Setting off soon after dawn, the day was cold and clear and the north faces loomed above, pale yellow in the morning light. We scrambled up easy rock and Gunther led the first difficult pitch. He was infuriatingly slow

– surely it wasn't difficult? It was cold, though. Perhaps he hadn't warmed up sufficiently? But the seed of doubt was sown.

'How are you feeling?' I asked, in a tone of voice that hinted strongly at my unease.

'Nicht schlimm,' he answered unhelpfully. 'Not bad.' He'll be alright, I told myself, he must be pretty good to have climbed the things he's done. Anyway, this had to be my last chance to do the route. It was surely worth a try, and, with my spirit buoyed by a surge of optimism, I launched myself onto the crucial traverse.

It was easy enough at first and there was no cause for concern until the ledge petered out into an overhanging yellow wall. The difficulties were obviously about to start, judging by the large number of bent pitons sticking out at a hundred crazy angles. I climbed carefully, testing pitons first and using them where necessary as hand holds. I distrusted them utterly. Reaching a tiny stance with a piton belay at knee level, I sat on the ledge, tied on and prepared to bring Gunther across. Then I watched in horror as Gunther swung from one piton to the next, treating each one as if it had a guarantee label attached.

'For God's sake, treat the pitons carefully.'

'They are fine,' he replied, rather gruffly. Then came the hard move, a gap of six feet between two pitons. I watched in amazement as he tried to swing his body across the gap in a desperate lurch for the next peg. He failed completely and I had to suppress a nervous laugh at such a ridiculous manoeuvre.

'You might have to climb that move.'

Pointedly, he ignored my sarcasm and once more threw himself across the gap. His body leaned almost horizontal; I shouted in alarm, but too late. His feet jerked upwards above his head and he toppled out of his etriers and bounced on the rope, swinging well clear of the rock. He fell 20 feet and began to spin as he thrashed around, trying to regain contact with the rock. The rope ran tight and bit into my waist. Desperately, I clutched at it, but Gunther seemed to settle lower and lower, inch by inch. A piton sprang out with a clatter; the taut rope 'pinged' as Gunther dropped another five feet with a terrified scream. I was jerked against my belay and the slack rope wound round my trailing etriers and hammer. By now I was bent double and could hardly move. Something had to be done.

'For Christ's sake, prusik up. I can't hold you forever!' I bellowed.

'I'm trying,' came the desperate reply.

'Well hurry.' I was pleading now. My grip on the rope was weakening.

I had one option – to tie it off onto the belay piton, and this I did but only with great difficulty for I couldn't afford to let any more rope out. This manoeuvre offered me little relief, since the rope still ran round my body and, like a noose, bit deeper and deeper as Gunther jerked up and down in his private struggle for survival. With a strangely detached horror I watched as if I were merely an observer that the belay piton was pulling down. I could see a bright gleam of metal where it had worked out of the crack, and thought vaguely of a prusik sling to relieve the unbearable strain on my body, but could not find one.

'Come up,' I cried.

'It's difficult,' he replied and then burst out into hysterical swearing which subsided into a whimpering prayer.

I was blacking out, breathing was difficult and the upper part of my body was doubled over, hanging into space like a grotesque gargoyle. Sweat ran down my brow and dripped off my nose to plunge a thousand feet into the void. Becoming unconscious of pain, oblivious to my situation, I drifted into a dream of kaleidoscopic images, vivid, fragmented, which flashed through my brain: green grass, cool wells, emerald sea caves, a soft embrace – oblivion. I awoke once or twice with a shock of reality; Gunther was still there. Should I cut the rope? A crazy thought – but was it? I struggled to think and relapsed into the comforting blackness inside my skull.

I dreamt I heard voices and slowly regained consciousness. The blackness dissolved into grey and I was aware once more of the sweat dripping inexorably off my nose. Suddenly, Gunther was shouting. I twisted my lolling head and saw two climbers moving rapidly towards us. As they came level with Gunther they dropped a doubled loop of rope, which he clutched and clipped it on to his waist. They heaved and Gunther swarmed up. The pressure suddenly eased and blood surged into my numbed legs. Miraculously, I was alive. Our saviours were two climbers from Stuttgart and they proceeded to set up a fixed line back down. Gunther was clipped on and he slid down like a sack of potatoes. I retreated back across the traverse.

'Danke, danke sehr,' I mumbled inadequately. 'How long have we been here?'

'At least two hours – we saw you a long way off.'

In fact, we had been there for three and a half hours, which seemed to stretch into eternity.

Gunther and I regained easier ground and I threw the ropes down. We began abseiling without a word being said. Walking back to the hut in brooding silence, I was angry and disgusted, both with myself and with Gunther. He had a forlorn and pathetic look of guilt and insisted on buying me a huge meal for which I had little stomach. Afterwards he said goodbye sheepishly, and walked off. I returned to my tent feeling crushed.

Lazing around for a few days, recovering from my aches and bruises, I was about to hitch back home when a group of English climbers arrived. The temptation to stay on proved too much and I enjoyed a couple of easy scrambles. Then another character called Tokyo Joe appeared. He was from Manchester, belonged to the infamous Gritstone Club and was a cheerful vagabond who had drifted around the world and regularly enthused about Japan. He was on his motorbike – a sturdy Sunbeam – and, as he was short of cash, he invited me to join him on the way home.

It was almost a relief to pack up and leave Tre Cime; I had spent too long there, had suffered too many disasters. Bumping down the stony track, stripped to the waist, we enjoyed a magnificent ride through the Dolomites, freewheeling down passes and rattling through huge gorges to the apple orchards of Merano. It was hugely enjoyable and a wonderful tonic to be on the move, riding free and easy through the Alps. We passed through a sleepy South Tyrol, drove into Switzerland in a blazing heatwave, viewed the Eiger and swam in every lake. Arriving in France we visited Chamonix; it was the end of the season and like a ghost town when compared to the crowds of summer. As far as we could make out we were the only English there, which meant there was no chance of borrowing equipment. We caught up with the news and heard the terrible disaster involving Bonatti on the Central Pillar of Frêney and also of its eventual ascent by Chris Bonington, Don Whillans, Ian Clough and Jan Długosz just a few days earlier.

The perfect weather continued and we were compelled to take advantage of it, scraping together enough money to hire crampons and ice-axes for a couple of days to do a pleasant scramble around the Requin. But my eyes were drawn to the tawny granite slabs of the Dru and the icy buttresses of the Grandes Jorasses. I felt my lack of experience painfully; my climbing ambitions seemed utterly unattainable, as yet, mere dreams.

Everything had seemed so marvellous; by midsummer my A-level exams were done, school was finished with, university was to come, and I had the prospect of a long leisurely holiday in the Alps. Now once again my Alpine plans had turned sour and I returned home in a state of panic, expecting the worst.

As soon as I got back I visited Max and found him at home encased in a white plaster carapace. I listened with horror as he retold the story of his journey back home. At least he was feeling better, quite cheerful in fact, now that he had left hospital. He was already back walking and camping out. He had taught himself a series of yoga exercises to relieve the pain. It was only later when I suffered similarly that I fully understood all that he went through.

My other great worry was exam results. If I passed sufficiently well, I had a place waiting for me at Manchester University; if not, I dreaded to think. Rushing home to learn my fate, to my relief I found I had a place at Manchester. I could relax; the next few years were taken care of.

Although I hardly had any money I was determined to enjoy the remaining weeks of autumn until university started. I set off to visit Wooly in Sheffield, within a few miles of gritstone. I knew Jack Soper was also around and that as the marvellous possessor of transport, he would almost certainly take us in his Dormobile to the Lake District.

Wooly shared a flat, known as 'The Doss', with a whole crowd of climbers and students. I staked a claim to some floor space and on the first available day we hitched the few miles to Froggatt and Curbar. It was a lovely mellow autumn day and I felt enthused with a delightful anticipation. As soon as I touched the warm, rough rock I knew I was in for a special day – one of the best days climbing of my life. I drifted up and down with incredible ease, caressing the holds. Nothing could stop me. I climbed practically every route above Very Severe, including the second ascent of *Cave Wall* and the first lead of *Chequers Arête, Great Slab* and innumerable others. My appetite for rock was insatiable. Although Wooly had by now done enough I was at fever pitch. I continued with *Elder Crack, Peapod, Left Eliminate, Insanity, Maupassant* and a dozen more. To finish the day we walked down to Stoney Middleton to meet Jack Soper and while we waited did *Sin* and *Glory Road*. At last I could feel my fingers tiring.

The next weekend, Jack was going to the Lakes. There was one route there I wanted to do more than any other; it was then called *Entity*, later renamed *Extol*, and had been climbed by Don Whillans and Colin Mortlock. Already a whole series of legends had sprung up around it; it was reputed to be fantastically hard, intricate and loose, threading a line through enormous overhangs. It was rumoured that after the climb one or both of the climbers had stayed for days in a darkened room to recover from the trauma.

Extol had thwarted me the previous Whitsun when Max and I had set out to hitch to the Lakes. Max succeeded in getting a ride but I had failed to move at all from a dismal roadside verge for a whole day and returned bitterly disappointed to sandstone. This time I intended to get to grips with it.

We drove up late on Friday night over Kirkstone Pass, descending into a heavy shower. The rain was infuriating but we didn't give up hope. Walking up to Dove Crag the next day, I surveyed its impressive dome. It was far too wet but we climbed *Hangover* and realised the fresh breeze was drying the crag out.

On Sunday we set out again, this time to climb *Extol*. Jack belayed me below the last long pitch and I started up its initial vegetated groove. The rock was still slightly greasy – the cracks were wet – but after delicately negotiating a tricky groove I reached the meat of the climb – a bulging wall impossible to see. I had a couple of feeble line runners draped over tiny creaking flakes, my nearest protection as I set out on a series of strenuous moves that brought me into a cramped recess below an overhang. There was only one way to go and I prayed I would soon find some good protection. Traversing left on sopping wet holds, to my intense relief I found a 'thank God' piton. Above me was a livid green groove and I escaped from it by moving blindly onto the right arête. Only a short wall remained before grass ledges which led to the top. There was just one good hold, which I needed to pull up and then stand on. I had a go, nearly made it – but not quite. Trying for a second time, my foot shot off. The hold was greasy. Badly frightened, I placed a sling round a spike, stepped up in it and reached the top. I felt very bad about cheating on that last move; on subsequent ascents I have been hard pressed to even notice that final step up.

At the end of the holiday I went home via Wales. There were several acquaintances camped in the Llanberis Pass and I was pleased to see Peter Crew. He had had a miserable summer, seemed depressed by Oxford, and had taken a couple of big falls. To make matters worse he was disastrously in love; it was not his year. I climbed with him one afternoon and made an ascent of *Erosion Groove Direct*. It was hard and fierce and I had the quiet satisfaction of watching Pete struggle and ask for a tight rope. We were still rivals. For my last significant climb that summer I joined up with Don Roscoe who was writing the Llanberis guidebook. There was only one route he had yet to climb – *The Cromlech Girdle*. I was keen to help him plug this gap but such was its reputation for difficulty that Don was hesitant.

As a member of the Rock and Ice he had always been one of the 'back-up men' – overshadowed by Don Whillans, Joe Brown and Morty Smith. Early on he had taken a tumble from the top of *Cenotaph Corner* and wasn't convinced of his own ability. As soon as we embarked on the climbing all went well. It was not particularly hard going and soon we were climbing across the superb sheer walls of *Cenotaph Corner* on surprisingly large holds. It was the last of the great Brown-Whillans routes and our second ascent was practically the end of an era. It was no longer possible to enumerate every ascent of their routes, as we had once been able to do. A new generation of hard climbers had arrived and the stage was set for a further surge in climbing standards. There were new routes to be done and I hoped I would have my share of them. I couldn't wait to arrive in Manchester where climbing opportunities were to open up for me.

SIX

MANCHESTER

My choice of Manchester University was baffling to almost everyone except me. I thought it was obvious, almost automatic in fact. Only I knew the extent of my climbing obsession; I was steeped in the myths of the Rock and Ice, which had strong links to Manchester and its environs. For me, Manchester represented the climbing heartland and, as such, had a romantic appeal that overshadowed its grim reality. I felt ready to break out of the south-east, to escape the loving clutches of family, to leave behind the shattered memories of first love and throw myself into a new life where I could indulge fully my passion for climbing.

As events turned out, I had little choice in the matter of universities. I applied to several, as a matter of course, but at London and Bristol failed dismally to impress the interviewing academics. Mercifully, Manchester accepted me without the formality of an interview for which I was profoundly thankful.

By late September I was ready to come up to Manchester to inspect the lodgings the university provided. I was also invited to the preliminary freshers' conference. I wasn't keen. I did not feel 'fresh' and, in any case, have always maintained a mild antipathy for conferences. Still, I had to go to Manchester some time, to settle in to my digs, and the weekend seemed as good a time as any. By a stroke of luck, a teaching colleague of my mother's was driving up to the Manchester area with her fiancé. I got the impression my mother had taken the initiative in suggesting the lift; I got a chilly reception climbing into the car.

My mother's friend was an oddly aggressive woman: an 'advanced motorist', whatever that means, a keen rally enthusiast and generally proud of her driving prowess. Her fiancé was meek and submissive, overwhelmed by the challenge of circumnavigating London via the difficult Northwest Passage. It was a hilarious ride and I had to summon all my powers to suppress my giggles. We got lost repeatedly. For no obvious reason we would suddenly turn off main roads and hurtle up dead-end cart tracks. At one point we were almost submerged in an unexpected ford. After many hours driving, much of it in reverse gear, we reached the A6 and from then on it was a straightforward run through Leicestershire, Derbyshire and on to Manchester.

My lift ended abruptly at the large iron gates of Lyme Park, on the edge of Disley, still some distance from Manchester. It was far too late to think of doing anything but sleep, so I dropped down over the park wall and stretched myself out in the deep litter of leaves at its foot. It began to drizzle but, past caring, I merely tucked my head inside my sleeping bag and slept on until my sleeping bag was sodden on the inside. By early morning I was damp and dishevelled, so I packed up my things and caught the next bus into Manchester. It was a depressing ride and a bad intro-duction to my new home. The overriding impression was one of greyness, of blackened stonework, grubby pavements and all framed by a leaden sky. The bus crawled through mile upon mile of depressing streets; Manchester was not looking its best.

The bus pulled into a dismal bus station and as I prepared to get off I heard a familiar voice. 'Bloody 'ell! It's Martin. Where did you spring from?' It was Richard McHardy and some of his pals. I explained I was on my way to my new digs to drop off my enormous trunk before going on to the freshers' conference. They were going to Buxton, back the way I'd come, and then hitching to the Roaches in Staffordshire, if the weather improved. I didn't need much persuasion to change my mind and join them. The bus conductor looked justifiably perplexed as I got back on board the bus I'd just arrived on to retrace my route. Once more we passed through suburbs; they looked no better the second time, but at least I was growing used to them. At last, we climbed up onto the moors through thick hill fog and finally descended into Buxton – that most bracing of British spas – swathed in a characteristic cold mist. Nevertheless, the mood on the bus was cheerful. Richard began a long and energetic monologue in the course of which he led me up many a Roaches classic. 'You swing out on these flakes, see, and tuck your legs up behind them like this, then you reach out for this superb hand jam and … ' As he spoke, his body contorted into various climbing shapes, frightening the other passengers.

The news at Buxton was not encouraging. Young Al had driven out to the Roaches on his new motorbike and reported that climbing prospects were nil. The rocks were weeping with water and green with algae and lichens. We returned to the spa lounge to ponder and, after several pints and games of darts, we agreed to head for Hathersage and the cleaner rocks of Stanage. Stumbling out at closing time, we began hitching, Young Al giving his brother Stan 'the Man' a lift on his bike. A home-made sports car stopped almost immediately for me, and I climbed into the cockpit, clutching on to my trunk as we roared off, albeit without much speed, towards Hathersage, through grim Dove Holes, dusty Sparrowpit and on over Mam Tor. As we cleared the crest and dropped down into the lovely Hope Valley, the mist lifted, the clouds dispersed, and the sun broke through; it was, suddenly, a marvellous day.

I dumped my cumbersome luggage, fished out some climbing tackle and waited for Richard, who soon arrived. We then set off at a keen pace, up the hill and onto Stanage Edge, which rolled away into the distance for mile upon mile of delectable gritstone, cresting the gentle wave of brown and purple moor. It was a day when the sensations are heightened; I was filled with a glorious sense of freedom, of tingling elation as we raced from one buttress to the next, glorying in the views of distant Kinder Scout, Bleaklow, shapely Lose Hill and the emerald patchwork of fields and woods below. We climbed as though possessed; soloing up and down routes with ease and all the time bubbling with enthusiasm as we savoured the rough, sound rock.

Towards evening, when our pace had slackened a bit, a youth in a flat hat and curly boots insinuated himself into our company and began alternately to pester us with his naive questions. We felt inclined to ignore him, but our interest perked up when he announced that he was a man of property. He owned – or more probably, his dad did – a tiny wooden shack called, to our huge delight, 'Heaven'. Heaven was crowded that night, for half the Alpha Club crammed in, shamelessly taking advantage of this fortuitous hospitality. The alternative accommodations were numerous, but less desirable, and included the rickety cricket pavilion and various draughty outhouses known and unknown to the local constabulary.

We had no food with us, so next morning we flocked into the local cafe – Ma Thomas's. This was in reality a corner of her downstairs room, crammed with a wide selection of disintegrating furniture liberally coated in diluted Daddies sauce. Richard was well in and got the prodigal son treatment, which involved long disappearances into the kitchen. Part of this special attention was the chance to interact with young Elaine, a precocious and well-developed young woman, much given to sidling coyly around in imitation of the era's celluloid sirens. Ma was a fine woman. From South Wales, and then in her sixties, she was well-preserved and vigorous, with a matronly manner and a head of white hair. She talked quickly, in rapid scolding bursts, like an excited hen, and she very definitely ruled the roost. Although she clucked and told us off and always had the last word, we all felt great fondness for her, which was returned. Her only weakness was her eccentric cooking. On my first and only previous visit, some years earlier,

I had caused a major scene when I had innocently returned a plateful of white chips and a woefully under-done egg back to the kitchen to be 'cooked a little more'. Mrs Green, who helped out, shook her head and pronounced, 'she won't like it, you know.' She didn't – and came storming out of the kitchen, puffed up with rage, and fixed me with a beady stare. 'Is it you?' she demanded. Then without waiting for a reply: 'No-one ever complains about my food.' I could easily see why. Chastened, I beat a hasty retreat in the face of a tongue-lashing from this little white-haired lady. Now I knew the pitfalls of ordering and stuck to safe options, so all was well.

After breakfast we caught the train the few miles to Grindleford, where we walked pleasantly up through the trees and on to Froggatt and Curbar Edges. I had already climbed a lot here so we sought out some quiet corners, eventually finding the ominous Deadbay Area where we climbed its *Crack* and *Groove*. Then we lazed in the warm sun until it was time to catch the train back to Manchester. The train was a sort of 'outdoor special', laid on with the roughest carriages available, inevitably packed with scratched and scruffy climbers, squelching potholers and red-faced ramblers. There was little give and take between the various sporting factions, though the potholers, with their huge pit boots and muddy ropes and ladders, were understandably unpopular with the rest. Fortunately, they were at an immediate disadvantage; they had to get on a few stops later, by which time a boot was firmly lodged against the compartment door. Their vengeance was predictable, and fortunately directed at the lighting system so that it was a matter of course to pull into the vast, cast-iron maw of Central Station in total darkness.

Before the train had stopped, doors sprang open and people were leaping out and rushing to the barriers in an effort to catch onward buses and trains. Amongst the jostling throng there were always a few without tickets, and these would leap the barriers to evade waiting officials. We said our hurried 'goodbyes', made plans for next time and dispersed, Richard and friends to their homes, and I to my unknown digs. Suddenly, I felt very lonely and hung around hesitantly before plucking up courage to ask the best way to Moss Side. 'Little Africa, you mean? Oh, that's easy; just get the bus on't corner. Where are you from, lad? I'll give you a lift with your bags to the bus stop.' I was learning already there was more to this city than grimy bricks and mortar.

My digs were located in a 'respectable' terraced house, in a glum little street parallel to Princess Road. The houses were of uniform glazed red brick, each with its scrubbed doorstep directly off the pavement. In each front room were little lace curtains, a bowl of plastic flowers, or occasionally a proud aspidistra. The house numbers ran into the hundreds. I knocked on the door and waited with heavy heart. Mrs Burtonshaw came to the door. 'Mr Bagstone is it? We've been waiting for you, you know.'

She was a woman of stunning ugliness, late middle-aged and overweight, with a sad, flaccid face crowned with a mop of frizzled grey hair. She was, poor woman, nearly blind and wore glasses of astonishing thickness. She moved slowly, shuffling round the house in worn slippers, her nylons collecting in folds around her swollen ankles. Mrs Burtonshaw shared the house with her daughter, a thin, weary woman, and her granddaughter. Her main hobby was grumbling, and she was, incredibly, a terrible snob. Daily, she would tell us that we lived in the 'respectable' end of Moss Side. There were no 'darkies' in her road – yet. The problem of explaining an absent son-in-law obviously troubled her, and she was compelled to put my mind at rest with the information that he worked 'out of the country'. Poor Mrs Burtonshaw; she needed the money, but she was kind enough.

Mercifully, a German student called Peter, who was on a two-term visit, joined me a week later. He was a cheerful character, a football fanatic who was quite happy to forgive the squalor and lousy cooking so long as he was near Maine Road, where he could witness the steady decline and relegation of Manchester City while his compatriot Bert Trautmann made the odd guest appearance in goal. Together we endured the most awful food, an unvarying menu of cheap, greasy meat and washed-out vegetables. Anything which had touched fat swam in it; anything boiled was utterly so. We faced it as bravely as possible, but often were too embarrassed to leave it uneaten, and would slide whatever remained into paper bags which could be smuggled out and dropped in the nearest litter bin. I lived in constant dread of discovery, my briefcase always bulged with uneaten cabbage, mutton fat and other disgusting scraps which rapidly went mouldy if not cleared rapidly.

The university was within walking distance but the walk was not a pleasant one. The whole of Moss Side and its neighbouring areas were then a squalid slum. The worst was Hulme, and I would look on with horror as I threaded my way through the awful houses. The slums were straight out of Dickens – low, mean and unbelievably decrepit – and housed a dispirited and impoverished community. Scattered among the dismal terraces was the odd, lovingly cared-for house, bravely resisting the tide of decay. The shock was profound. I had, of course, read of poor housing and I had looked down on slums from fast-moving trains, but never before had I been forced to look closely, to touch and smell the dreadful decay. Later I would see squalor in India and South America, but seldom has it seemed worse than those awful, grey slums which were ready to be swept away.

I craved greenery and fresh air and found some consolation in the local park, with its blackened trees and struggling grass. My chief delight was a huge, Victorian cast-iron greenhouse – alas, no more –filled with flourishing plants – lush banana and pandana, bougainvillea, hoya, orchids and vast cacti – forever threatening to grow through the roof. In this miniature jungle it was possible to forget the outside world, to lose oneself in the smell of growth and peaty compost.

The university itself was an odd mess of buildings of assorted styles and ages, bisected by one of Manchester's busiest roads. The main building was Owen's College, a Gothic Revival structure of character blackened to the colour of soot by a century of coal smoke. Surrounding it were lesser buildings: a chemistry block apparently built from lavatory bricks, a Doric Arts library and a great number of more nondescript buildings including a miniature and – to me – mystifying department of audiology. The area was being rapidly redeveloped as tall and seemingly ugly skyscrapers took the place of the surrounding slums being knocked down to make way for them.

The university did not provide the atmosphere of freedom and learning I had hoped for. In many ways it was a continuation of school, with compulsory lectures, essay writing and exam after exam. We were treated much like schoolchildren; registers were taken at each lecture and, except for this stratagem, many would have been poorly attended. The lectures, by and large, fell into two categories: those which resulted in pages of undigested notes, scribbled like fury, and those which resulted in a page largely filled with thumbnail portraits of surrounding students and arabesque doodles. The master of the second type was the botany professor, a silky-tongued Highland gentleman who bored us to unconsciousness with hours of banal twaddle largely devoted to the subject of bananas. His opposite number in the zoology department, Professor Graham Cannon, was anyhing but boring – extremely amusing in fact – and totally unorthodox in that he expounded his own famously cranky Lamarckian views on the theory of evolution. He was about as successful as King Canute in stemming the overwhelming tide of neo-Darwinism. He was a stout, pompous, blustering man, gout-ridden and fruity-faced. His lectures had their moments of drama; several times he was on the point of collapse and was forced to swallow a pill or two. We watched in horrified fascination, wondering but not daring to offer assistance since any interruption was taboo.

Once, early in the term, a bumptious student, recently transferred from a social studies degree, had the nerve to interrupt his even flow with a question. An awed and ominous silence followed, the professor spluttering with incredulous disbelief as he slowly coloured from pink to red and then purple. 'You insolent young pup, what's the meaning of this?' he bellowed.

'But the question seems important to me … '

'Answer your question? Get out. Never, in all my years of teaching, has anyone behaved like this,' he expostulated as the baffled and embarrassed student fled to leave the door swinging on its hinges.

As an honours botany student, I came under the wing of an eccentric and brilliant lecturer who was at his best when being scornfully dismissive of any authority but his own. His sarcastic phrases spattered you with saliva and a smile as withering and as friendly as a crocodile's. His reptilian leer terrified nervous first-year students, the girls especially, and as far as one could judge he seemed to gain satisfaction from doing so. One of the unpleasant tasks that he set us was writing essays on the collected hundred most obscure and boring subjects known to botany. I slaved worthily a couple of times, delving in dusty Victorian tomes for research. I was rewarded for my efforts with derisory marks of one and two out of 10, accompanied by hurtful and sarcastic comments. The overall effect was totally dispiriting, and I gave up writing essays in the hope that I would be dropped from the honours course.

The botany department was housed in the corner of Owen's College, a quaintly old-fashioned and vastly overcrowded building with students crammed together on the mahogany benches. We worked hard in the labs, endlessly classifying and drawing a profusion of specimens, which ranged from frantically wriggling unicells to potted palms. I was pleasantly surprised to find that the cryptogam lecturer, Alan Alsop, was a climber of past distinction. One would hardly have guessed it, for he was a comically rotund little man, with a rolling gait reminiscent of a 'knock-me-down' man. Before starting a lecture he would take a huge breath, inflate himself to a tremendous size, and then rattle off Latin names at breakneck speed until, pouring with sweat, the hour had passed. By this time he was deflated again; after panting for a bit, he would give us a cheery 'goodbye' and leave. In his youth he had obviously been a good climber and extremely athletic. He would often pause at my bench and have a friendly chat about past glories, the highlight being 'when I was considered for Everest'. Dr Alsop apart, the rest of the staff maintained a frosty remoteness. In many ways I had enjoyed more freedom to think, and more encouragement to learn, at school than at university.

One main memory of that first term was the thick fogs. They could linger for weeks, and slowly infiltrate the labs and lecture theatres. At times it was difficult to see the lecturers through the wraiths of fog, but it hardly mattered and did nothing to improve the dramatic impact. It had been a strange and disillusioning start to my studies. I was, in fact, unhappy, lonely in my own personal fog of mixed feelings and emotions. The only part of life that was clear and bright was my weekend existence as a climber. Climbing was, for me, a joyous release, a wholehearted commitment that allowed me to cast aside all these worries and disappointments. In my climbing world I was master of my own destiny. I was confident of my ability, aware of my limitations. If my academic ambitions were limited to survival and no more, my climbing dreams were boundless.

I did not form friendships early in my first year. This was partly because I was a year or so older than my fellow students, but it was mainly because my interests were outside university. The honours students were, to some extent, segregated from the others and I shared little in common with my colleagues. The male students struck me as immature and prissy, the females as earnest little swots. The friendships I did eventually form were with second-year students, who were a much more colourful lot.

It was only natural that an early preoccupation was to find a girlfriend. I did not have to look far, for there were numerous female biology students. I first noticed Maggie pulling faces over a half-dissected frog. She was good-looking and had an interesting, mobile face that I couldn't help looking at. We met later during chemistry and it wasn't long before we were engaged in exploratory chatter and 'accidentally' meeting in coffee bars and on lecture hall benches. The attraction was mutual; we had both recently broken off relationships and both had that consuming need for love which youth and emotional insecurity demands. We also had a lot in common; Maggie – Mags – loved the outdoor life, was sensitive to natural beauty, loved hill walking, and was keen to take up climbing. She had a strong character and a typically direct northern manner. Intelligent, lively and lovely, she was disarmingly scatter-brained at times.

It was too good to be true; we were in love, and yet there was no conflict between the often-contradictory demands of a relationship and climbing. But despite the happy discovery of mutual love, I was in many respects immature and unready for the demands of a steady relationship. I some-times felt trapped; it had come too soon. I had not had my sexual fling. Yet although there were bad patches, where I behaved with unfeeling selfish-ness, there was always a sufficiently strong bond of love to keep us together.

Our relationship has, in fact, survived and grown stronger, and enriched my life immeasurably. Maggie has been and continues to be my vital support and I would find it hard to live without her.

It was difficult sometimes to convey the extent of my climbing obsession, especially as at first I had played it down in the interests of courtship. For two weeks I made what seemed then the ultimate sacrifice, pursuing conventional rituals like the pictures, eating out and escorting home. Finally, I could stand it no longer and at the next opportunity took Mags climbing in Derbyshire. It was a glorious, golden October day, the first frosts had turned the leaves, and the bracken was warm and brown. We walked up to Stanage End from Bamford Station, through lovely woods and over heathery slopes, breathing in the cold tingling air. It was a delightful start to what was to be an eventful and idyllic day.

I was climbing especially well; I was, after all, in love, full of exuberant confidence and ready to show off. I climbed *Kelly's Overhang*, disposed of several other notable routes and pointed out the jutting neb of *Quietus*, which, I thought at the time, was awaiting a second ascent. Mags seemed totally unmoved.

'Why don't you do it, it's only little?'

I didn't know what to say. Maggie – like other strangers to climbing – was confusing size with difficulty. I determined to have a go, feeling like a latter-day Sir Lancelot, but first we retired to the heather.

A large crowd of noisy students wandered into the area, curtailing any amorous advances. They identified themselves immediately as being from either Oxford or Cambridge judging by their crisp, public school accents and jaunty indifference to 20-foot falls. Two of the party demonstrated considerable ability; they turned out to be the Honourable Wrottesley, wearing a remarkably silly trilby hat, and a grinning, gap-toothed character whose face seemed familiar. It was Nick Estcourt from Eastbourne who had, like me, wandered around Harrison's Rocks as a schoolboy, looking for someone to climb with.

They slung a top rope over *Quietus* and everyone had a go. Top-roping gritstone routes is generally frowned upon by the cognoscenti. According to the strict, unwritten ethics, climbs should be led or followed if necessary. I watched with interest, and with disapproval, as several characters lurched off into space, unable to manage the last hard moves. It was obvious they had paid too much attention to a guidebook photograph of Peter Biven dangling from the lip of the overhang – a position from which upward movement is difficult.

'Would you care for a go?' I considered it briefly and gave in to the idea – and it seemed so easy, feet tucked under the roof on a flake, two hand jams and up. 'Could you do it again, please? Only this time swing out on your arms, as it makes a better picture.'

'Get stuffed, what do you think I am? A performing ape?'

I was genuinely annoyed, but more with myself; in a moment of weakness I had deprived myself of a 'sight lead'. I knew the problems of the climb and to lead it now would be less rewarding. Nevertheless, almost as a penance, I decided to lead it and tied on to the largely symbolic rope, trailing it behind me. There was a large, rounded flake at the start of the roof and I placed a sling over that to act as a running belay. The protection before the advent of nuts was largely psychological, a fact tragically driven home when Dave Sales was killed falling from the overhang. I swung out and made the now familiar moves, but was just that bit more tired. There was a moment of horror when I failed to reach up to the good hand jam and rapidly my hand probed and explored the crack for any favourable contours. A sensation of fear swept through me and I began to feel my strength fail. A poor finger jam turned up for one hand and with my other I found a barely adequate hand jam. This allowed me to haul myself thankfully over the top.

It was time Maggie learned something about climbing from personal experience, before she precipitated my premature death.

'What am I supposed to do with this crack?' she asked, a note of surprise in her voice.

'You put your hands in it like this, press your thumb against the palm and there, you have a hand jam,' I said, demonstrating with my hand.

'But it hurts!'

'Yes.'

'And you expect me to tear the skin off my hands?' Maggie was astonished.

'Well, eventually you build up a thick layer of callous tissue, and then … '

'You must be crazy.' And so, Maggie won her first hand jam scars and was put off gritstone climbing for some time.

We wandered pleasantly along the edge, in the warm afternoon sun, pausing here and there to climb some choice route, until we bumped into a crowd of friends. It must have been a gathering of the Alpine Climbing Group; Chris Bonington, Ian Clough and many others were present. Chris was in an exuberant mood, bubbling with enthusiasm. He had just left the army and had only recently returned from an Alpine season in which he had bagged the outstanding first ascent, with Don Whillans, Ian Clough and Jan Długosz, of the Central Pillar of Frêney. Having said goodbye to the regular army, he was now about to pledge himself to an army of a different sort – that of Unilever's – in a management training group with Van den Bergh's, with a view to joining their sales force as a margarine rep. Chris has an amazing ability to sell ideas to himself; he was utterly convinced he was doing the right thing.

'God, you know Martin, it really is terrific to be settled into a challenging and worthwhile career,' he explained, before going on to extol the capitalistic system in general, and Blue Band margarine, in particular, to the rather sceptical audience.

After that day on Stanage, Maggie and I enjoyed many more weekends together, camping under Frodsham, or in deep snow below Froggatt Edge. When a lift was available we tramped and climbed in Wales and the Lake District. During the Christmas holidays I made my way up to Maggie's home in Calder Vale, beneath the Bowland Fells near Lancaster, where I was introduced to her not unnaturally suspicious father. We left to spend the New Year in the Lake District and a freezing week in Keswick, sleeping in a barn along with a group of lads who were the nucleus of the Alpha Club.

Back in Manchester, I was drawn increasingly into the Alpha Club's fold and was soon spending Wednesday evenings at Richard's house, where we arranged weekends and talked climbing as Richard slowly demolished a basin of 'cow pie' closely followed by a vast pudding and custard, served up by his diminutive and doting mum. Winter passed and spring arrived before I met Chris again, this time in Wales. He was now a slightly disillusioned margarine salesman, whose task was to visit the grocers of Hampstead in a natty little trilby, delivering the latest sales promotion speech as naturally as possible. His dreams of becoming an overnight tycoon had taken a bad knock as longstanding customers closed their accounts, sales plummeted and area managers became restless. On the positive side, he now had the use of a small Ford Popular, though he had to disconnect the odometer to take advantage of it. He had brought with him his girlfriend, and future wife, Wendy. Mags and I had hitched there, and we all met up, along with Ian McNaught-Davis and the poet and critic Al Alvarez, in the field of Ynys Ettws in the Llanberis Pass. Mac and Al were showing a group of Parisian friends around the sodden hills and we were gratefully drawn into the party as 'guides'. We all joined forces, and struggled up a cold and wet Cyrn Las.

There were still huge snow patches around, and Chris scrambled up to tackle the icy *Fallen Block Crack* on Clogwyn y Ddysgl. The others began the traverse of Crib Goch and it was now that Wendy made the alarming discovery that she had absolutely no head for heights and was a total and terrified non-climber. She was accompanied down by Mags, and carefully attached to the belt of the French veteran, Serge – to his immense amusement.

Despite the appalling weather, the meet was a huge success, with Mac making the most of a rare opportunity to joke and bullshit in two languages simultaneously. Even the weather improved on their last day, and before they left I took Simon, the oldest of the French climbers, up *Cemetery Gates* in the first light of morning.

The Easter weekend crowds departed and a high-pressure system built. I was now climbing fit and the crags were fast drying out. I joined forces with Chris and we moved up to Cwm Glas, and occupied a bedroom each. First we visited Tremadog and repeated many newly climbed routes, including *The Fang*, where I mistakenly climbed an amusing direct variant. We also made plans to visit the latest crag from the 'secret' list – Castell Cidwm – where Joe Brown had made several excellent routes. By chance we heard that Pete Crew and Baz Ingle intended to make the second ascent of the most impressive of the routes – *Dwm*. We decided, as a joke, to beat them to it and so left early next morning.

Unfortunately, the Ford 'Pop' was slow, and Chris was not exactly Stirling Moss. In our ignorance we also chose the longest approach to the crag. We walked along Llyn Cwellyn, by now expecting to be already beaten, but not caring if we were; there were many other equally excellent routes to do. Climbing over a little knoll, we spotted our rivals. They had come the short way. We were now equidistant from the crag, but we had the advantage of height already gained and scrambled up, panting, to gain a position at the foot of the climb.

'You bastards,' yelled Pete, not totally amused, until Chris, unable to restrain his natural urges any longer, whipped down his breeches and presented a large, white arse to the appreciative audience.

Towards the end of the holiday we returned to Cwm Glas to find it occupied by a formidably respectable family, and after retrieving our wildly scattered odds and ends which included the all too evident debris of love-making, we made an embarrassed exit. Mags had to go home and it was time I went to see my parents; and so the holiday ended. Chris drove me to London after a hard day's climbing. He seemed incredibly tired so after a few hours we turned into a lay-by, where he slumped over the wheel in a deep sleep. I sat, bored, until a huge lorry pulled into the lay-by, lights full on, from the opposite direction. Chris sprang upright with a terrific scream and almost wrenched the wheel clean off to avoid the imagined collision before he awoke fully to the real situation.

I stayed the night at Chris and Wendy's flat in Highgate and left next morning as Chris donned his suit and trilby. Before he left we arranged an evening's climbing on sandstone. When we arrived at High Rocks we barely had an hour's climbing before the gates were shut. Chris and I have probably never ever climbed as well as we did that evening. It was an orgy of activity in which we managed a dozen of the hardest routes before going on to Bowles Rocks, where we continued until the gloom of evening was replaced by silvery moonlight. Although our efforts that night were trivial, measured in mountaineering terms, it was a day I vividly remember, a day of beauty, when nothing seemed impossible. I was feeling fit and climbing better than I had ever done before. And I could not wait to get back to Wales.

Nexus   **450 feet**   Extremely Severe

Takes the slabby arête of the Plexus buttress. The groove on the upper pitch appears to be impossible, thus spoiling the line a little, but the second pitch is one of the finest in Wales, on perfect rock and in superb position.

Start   As for Plexus, directly below the arête.

1   **30 feet.** Heather scrambling up to the tree belay.

2   **150 feet.** The object is to get up to the square-cut overhang on the arête on the left. Start on the wall on the right and make a semi-hand traverse at a low level to reach the slab under the overhang. There is a fine natural thread on the arête itself. Layback up the arête and round the overhang to gain a standing position in the crack above, and climb this to a resting place. Continue up the narrowing slab above until it is necessary to make a difficult move round the arête on the right to the foot of an overhanging crack. Up this on good holds, and up the grooves to a good stance at the bottom right-hand corner of the overhangs.

3   **40 feet.** Up the slab on the right, and back left past a large block to a stance below the final groove. Peg belays.

4   **100 feet.** Make a difficult hand traverse round the corner, using a peg, to join the upper reaches of Plexus.

5   **120 feet.** As for Plexus, pleasant slabs and grooves to the top.

SEVEN
THE ALPHA CLUB

My first task after settling down in Manchester was to find climbing companions, and as a consequence of meeting Richard McHardy and his friends these were to be outside university. Richard, along with Al 'Festy' Parker, Paul Nunn and several other lads I had met in Wales, were part of the embryonic Alpha Club.

The Alpha started among a group of youths who walked and climbed in the Peak District and for a short time they had a barn in Edale as their base. In the course of weekends, acquaintances were made, friendships formed and the group enlarged to include Paul and a whole contingent of his friends attending the same Catholic grammar school in Manchester. For a period it remained in this casual state but after an early flirtation and rejection by the Rock and Ice Club, Festy Parker conceived the grandiose vision of starting a club to rival and supersede the Rock and Ice. To this end, new recruits were sought, and when Paul went to Sheffield University a whole bunch of Yorkshire lads including Clive Rowlands, Oliver Woolcock, Tanky Stokes and Ted Howard were signed up. In time, many more joined and I was soon one of them.

The Alpha Club was not a club in the usual sense. There were no elected officers or any of the normal trappings of organisation. Once my one-off club fee had been extracted, the impromptu treasurer wisely spent it on a Lake District high tea. Qualifications for entry were mysteriously unspecific: one had to be 'one of the lads' and a character; it helped to be a good climber but it was more important to be a humorous companion. After a probationary period, a straw poll established whether you were 'in' and no amount of hanging around or brilliant climbing would help if you were 'out'.

On Wednesday evenings the Manchester contingent gathered at Richard's place, a comfortable, if slightly rundown house in Droylsden. We would talk climbing, decide where we would go at the weekend and drink endless cups of tea whilst Richard sat in state and slowly demolished his usual basin of pie and vast pudding and custard.

I was pleased to discover after several such gatherings that I had passed muster and was now a member along with two other recent arrivals in Manchester, Pete Crew and Baz Ingle. Pete I already knew, having climbed with him in less happy times. Since then he had made the first of several drastic changes in direction by leaving Oxford. He had been unhappy there from the start, unable to stomach the rituals, the dressing for dinner, the vintage port and upper-class mores. It was so different from his down-to-earth Barnsley mining background. To compound the misery, his climbing had suffered. His burning ambition to be the best climber was as fierce as ever, but Oxford was too far from the crags. He was nothing if not single-minded, so abandoned Oxford to throw all his energy into climbing. He had teamed up with Oxford graduate Peter Hutchinson to open a climbing shop, selling cheap equipment from modest upstairs premises in an old office block in a back alley off Deansgate in central Manchester otherwise occupied by Armenian cotton merchants. I would often pop in for a cup of coffee and a chat and sit undisturbed; customers were rare. The shop was under-stocked, poorly financed and difficult to find but it made a good meeting place for a select band of climbers.

Abandoning the shop, the two Petes turned their hand to manufacturing down equipment. Once again it proved difficult to establish the business, especially as Pete Crew was off climbing at every opportunity using the shop's most vital asset, a grey Morris van. The early prototype duvet jackets leaked down; worse, because of inadequate sterilisation, the feathers retained a lingering smell of decomposing oriental waterfowl. But if the cut and quality were poor, the price was right. Half the Alpha club could be recognised by their ill-shaped jackets moulting feathers.

Peter Hutchinson was an amiable, reclusive figure. While Pete commandeered the van as often as possible, Hutch spent most of his time in his bungalow at Broadbottom near Hyde. I spent several days with him in Derbyshire and he pointed me at some local new routes. Peter didn't fit the mould of a manufacturing entrepreneur. He seemed more interested in obscure mystical philosophy; perhaps not surprisingly it was many years before his business was transformed into the successful Mountain Equipment.

It was at the shop that I met Baz Ingle, who was to partner Pete Crew for several crucial years. He presented a sharp contrast to Pete, both in character and appearance. He was small, even frail-looking, with dark hair and a mournful face. He was reserved, almost withdrawn in unfamiliar company, to the extent that he was sometimes accused of being 'miserable'. This was untrue. He had a wry sense of humour and could be a lively and amusing companion. He had moved to Manchester to study electrical engineering from his hometown of Nottingham.

Baz was one of the best climbers I ever met. He moved over rock with a neatness and lack of effort I envied. He was always cool and unruffled, quite unlike Pete who attacked the rock and often struggled mightily. Pete never looked calm. He was forceful and daring; his great strength lay in his utter determination. He overwhelmed a climb. Although Baz was technically far superior it was Pete who drove the most effective climbing combination since Brown and Whillans. There were tensions and rivalries, just as there were with Brown and Whillans, and these split them up from time to time; but as a climbing partnership they were ideal. I have often reflected regretfully that my own inability to form such a relationship held my climbing ambitions back.

Although Derbyshire was on a bus route from Manchester, Wales was the magnet for our attention – especially Cloggy. Pete with his van could come and go with ease compared with my tedious hitchhiking. That summer Pete had still been climbing with Jack Soper. They had already achieved a notable coup by climbing *The Pinnacle Girdle* and *Scorpio*. Just before Baz became his regular partner I had gone down with Pete on a foggy October weekend and led up *Shrike* through damp swirling mist. It felt like the end of the climbing season on the high crags, but it wasn't quite so; the following weekend Pete and Baz teamed up for the first time and climbed a fine new route on the East Buttress, called *Serth*.

As winter encroached and climbing became more limited we spent the weekends in Derbyshire climbing and drinking in the evenings in large and relaxing groups. It was the 'social season', a time when the club jesters rather than the outstanding climbers held the stage. Tanky was our senior buffoon, always outrageous but ready to disarm bemused outsiders with his devastating charm. Clive Rowlands, with his heavy tortoise eyelids, was the club clown. John Smith had a manic sense of humour; Arthur Williams had a deadpan face and a corpse-like pallor, which only added to a stream of jokes that kept us laughing.

Highlight of the winter was the annual club dinner, the Alpha's only organised event. Our favourite venue was the Wasdale Head. Each year, under an assumed name, the Alpha would arrive driving a motley collection of vans and motorbikes. The landlord, Wilson Pharaoh, was a magnificent ruin of a man, an ex-wrestling champion and athlete now in alcoholic decline. When he saw who had booked, his face would drop. He would threaten to throw us all out – something he looked well capable of doing – but would always soften. The supper was cooking and inevitably he would still be there, semi-comatose, propped on the bar, a cigarette burning into his great hands until the cock crowed.

After Christmas the club met for a few days in the Lake District, and after spending the holiday at home I decided to join them with Maggie. I travelled up to Lancaster by bus to take the opportunity of visiting Maggie's parents at their home in the Bowland Fells. At the bus station I rang up and then waited for a few hours, wondering what had happened to my lift. Maggie finally appeared in her father's car, distraught. It seemed I had precipitated a family quarrel. Her father refused to give her the car keys and it was only after Maggie's mother had reminded him that the car was half hers that Maggie had managed to get hold of them. I was given the frosty welcome of the prospective son-in-law, although Maggie's mother's concern for her daughter was mixed with kindness towards me.

Maggie lived in the midst of lovely upland country in the Forest of Bowland. The house sat above a wooded ravine on the edge of moorland. We walked over the wild heathery tops next day under a cold glowering sky and next morning the landscape was transformed by a deep layer of light powdery snow. We packed our bags in haste and set out to tramp downhill to Garstang to catch the bus to the Lakes. In Keswick we met up with the Alpha and enjoyed several days wading through deep snow. I also made my first winter climb up the impressive cleft of Piers Gill on Scafell Pike. Derwentwater froze over and we skated and slid all over it. The nights were not so enjoyable as we slept in the back of Jack Soper's van and Maggie revealed her sleeping bag to be merely a blanket sewn together.

In March the snow melted out of the high crags and our thoughts turned to rock. I begged a lift off Pete and Baz and we went down to Wales with the intention of climbing on the low sheltered crags around Tremadog. On our way there we met Joe Brown and learnt he had developed another nearby crag called Carreg Hylldrem. He mentioned a fine little route called *Hardd* and suggested we give it a direct finish. It was only a tiny morsel of unclimbed rock but it wasn't every day that the inscrutable Joe Brown gave away a new possibility. The crag was impressively overhanging but bathed in spring sunshine and we felt eager to touch the warm rock. Without discussion Baz and Pete took the lead. I was, after all, the weekend passenger, not unwelcome but equally uninvited. I was already aware of a conspiratorial air between Pete and Baz. I felt I was intruding.

An overhang guarded the first pitch. Pete tried to get round it and failed, then Baz tried and did likewise. Then it was my turn, and I felt a modest satisfaction in getting past it and completing the pitch. The final section of the climb, where Joe had roped down a short way to gain an escape left, was a series of jutting roofs. Pete tried it and quickly retreated. Baz whittled away and after placing a very poor piton managed to hook a sling round a spike. By this time he was too tired to continue so I was given the lead, and with all the protection in place it was not too hard, with the aid of the final sling, to swing over the overhang and reach the top. It was a pretty worthless addition to the climb but it was not quite as silly as the later description made it sound.

Towards the end of April an unseasonal heatwave dried out the high crags and the race to climb the hardest routes, and more importantly to climb new ones, really started. I was desperately in search of partners and relieved when Oliver Woolcock arrived as the vanguard of teams from Sheffield. I climbed with him one day and on the next did *White Slab* and *The Mostest* with Paul Nunn. The day after, I was reduced to climbing with one of the least talented members of the Sheffield University Climbing Club, a great gangling youth much given to falling off. Even so, we did *Woubits* and *Slanting Slab*, both routes which had reputations and had still only been done a handful of times.

It was during this period of frenzied activity that Baz, Pete and Jack Soper arrived. Pete and Jack had come to complete their girdle traverse of The Pinnacle, so Baz and I joined forces for the day. As we walked up once more to Cloggy, we examined the great expanse of rock known as Great Wall and determined to look at a tenuous line of grooves at its left edge. As we passed over the last dried streambed before entering the crag's gloomy shadow we picked up some rounded tapering pebbles to serve as chock stones.

Baz took the first pitch, which led, after a tricky first move, round a detached flake to a good ledge. My pitch was obviously going to be the crux and I felt a delicious, nervous excitement, which only eased when I got to grips with the shallow groove above the ledge. As I gained height, small rough holds appeared on either side, allowing me to bridge; most gratifyingly, at the back of the groove was a thin crack filled with wet earth. When I dug this out, I was able to slip in pebbles threaded with line slings. Utterly engrossed, I continued until my groove ran out into blank rock. The only way to continue was up another hanging groove to the left. The traverse on small holds leading to the as yet unseen groove gave me great trouble. I felt anxious but with great effort placed a piton into the base of the second groove and swung round into it. Above me was a bulge swathed in wet sods of grass. I placed another piton above it and using the peg as a hand-hold moved on to easy rock, which led to the top. It was an excellent climb, one of the best lines on Cloggy yet to fall. That I had rested on a sling and used two pegs did not seem unreasonable at the time. It would never have occurred to us to clean out the crack and vegetation first and without modern nuts, placing protection was extremely difficult. I felt inordinately proud of our new route, which we called *Daurigol*, the Welsh for diglyph, a feature with two grooves, and the name of Joe Brown's neighbouring route. *Daurigol* pointed to the possibility of the even more impressive wall just to our right, attempted several times by Joe. This was the 'great problem', one which Pete Crew had set his heart on – and one I intended to examine closely as soon as possible.

As the summer term advanced first year exams began to loom. I had spent too much time climbing, and to make matters worse my grant had run out. In desperation I moved to the two Petes' bungalow, known as 'the shack', which lay on the edge of a wooded ravine in Broadbottom on the edge of the Peak. It was deserted for the most part by its residents and I bedded down in the tiny wooden hut among the discarded clothes, dirty dishes and ubiquitous duck down to live as cheaply as possible.

Almost immediately I began to feel unwell. I fell into a state of torpor, felt all energy drain away, and found it more and more difficult to drag myself to lectures. The weather in May 1962 was hot and humid, the woods and hedgerows were bursting with life and the heavy scent of hawthorn blossom hung in the air. I could take no joy in it and lay sweating and feverish in the middle of the squalor, listening again and again to the sumptuous tones of one record – a Brahms symphony. Days passed unnoticed. I stopped getting up, abandoned revision and could not bear to think of climbing.

After several days of not appearing, Mags arrived, like a redeeming angel, to rescue me from my plight. She took me home to her parents' house where Janet, Maggie's younger sister, kindly vacated her bedroom for me. A doctor was called and glandular fever diagnosed. It was a long time before I recovered sufficient strength to get out and about. One day I would feel slightly better and then a relapse would follow. The exam results came out and inevitably I had done badly, failing chemistry. I now faced a special test to determine whether I continued on the honours course.

It was a bitter blow but worse news soon followed. The weather had been glorious in Wales and Pete and Baz had not been slow to take advantage. On Cloggy, *Great Wall* was finally climbed. *Haemoglobin* followed and, in the Lake District, *Hiraeth* on Dove Crag. These were all routes I had wanted to climb. They followed up this fine tally with an Alpine holiday during which they climbed the *Bonatti Pillar* and other hard routes. Meanwhile I was tottering around on short country walks revising once more for exams.

By the end of June I had recovered a little and Maggie and I set off on a short walking and camping trip in the Bowland Fells. I was still far from well, and extremely weak, but I could not bear to languish any more. At last I felt strong enough to climb, and Maggie and I set off for Wales. I was determined to get something from the summer. The hitchhiking went badly, but even though I was impatient to get there I couldn't resist the pleasures of loitering on the roadside verges thick with primroses and campion, ears and eyes pricked for passing cars. At last we arrived at Pen-y-Pass, the hills green and inviting, and as we bowled along down the valley I felt the joy of returning vitality. Colin Mortlock and his wife Annette were at the campsite and to my relief he was looking for a climbing partner.

I chose as my objective an obvious unclimbed line on The Pinnacle, a clean bold prow known as the *Pinnacle Arête*. By the time we had scrambled up to its base it was obvious to me that I was still weak but I resolved to try it. Every move proved a trial. I was shaking with fatigue and extremely nervous, and as if to underline my weakness Colin sauntered up with an ease that emphasised the fact he should have been leading, not me.

Pinnacle Arête was to be my only crumb of satisfaction that summer; again and again I discovered how weak my illness had left me. In late summer when everyone returned from the Alps I climbed with Paul in the Lake District and failed repeatedly on a variety of routes, hauled ignominiously up *Hiraeth* and *The Niche* in Borrowdale. It was a season I wanted to forget.

As autumn came and university started up again I was determined to fight my way to physical fitness and erase the memory of a miserable summer. Some good had come out of it. I passed my re-sit exams and more importantly realised the extent of Maggie's love and support and how much I needed it. Partly as a consequence of our deepening relationship, Maggie decided to spend her small savings on a vehicle.

A friend of a friend was in the motor trade and he found us a 'good little runner' in the form of a Ford Thames van. It might have been painted an appalling maroon and blue but it was love at first sight. We adopted it as our baby and like doting parents could see no wrong in it. Not that it was trouble free; on our inaugural journey it exhaled clouds of noxious black smoke and guzzled oil at an alarming rate. We stormed back to the garage and remonstrated till a new engine was fitted, after which we had no more serious problems, merely the irritation of windscreen wipers that slowed down as one picked up speed, and an engine that overheated in summer. We kept the van for several years and Maggie never regretted it.

It is not now fashionable to sing the praises of the internal combustion engine but to us the van was the equivalent of a magic carpet. Buying it did more to raise the quality of our lives than any other single object. Immediately, we were free to go where and when we wanted, to escape from Manchester to the hills of Derbyshire, Wales and the Lakes, and during the holidays plan trips to Scotland and the Alps.

This was the beginning of the 'van era'. Previously motorbikes had been all the rage – huge black Vincents, gleaming Nortons, Triumphs, Velocettes and BSAs. They certainly had glamour but this wore thin in midwinter and the accident rate was high – far exceeding that of climbing. By comparison, a van had many advantages; it was a mobile tin tent into which all the gear could be thrown and a comfortable bed made. Drives to Wales and the Lakes became fun and often developed into burn-ups between battered and underpowered vans. As a driver, Mags was fast but safe, and many a male hackle was raised at the sight of her long fair hair as she swept past.

In the late autumn we spent most weekends in Derbyshire. On Saturday morning we would pick up Al Parker and Richard and drive in high spirits over the Snake Pass, returning on Sunday evenings with sinking hearts as we looked down on Manchester's spangled ribbons of light stretching towards the horizon. To solve the weekend accommodation problem the Alpha Club toyed with the idea of a club hut. We acquired the use of an old explosives bunker below Millstone Edge and set about converting the grim concrete block into something more comfortable. We secured the door and windows with metal shutters, fixed up bunks from discarded doors, and gave pride of place to a pot bellied stove. Unfortunately our elaborate security must have suggested goods worth stealing. At the very least, it presented a challenge to local vandals and on successive weekends the doors were smashed open, the stove stolen and the woodwork fired. We gave up the unequal struggle and returned to sleeping in our vans.

The winter of 1963 turned out to be one of the most severe – and memorable – of the era. A deep frost gripped the country from New Year until March. As usual the Alpha Club spent the holiday in the Lake District and Baz Ingle and I climbed together. We were both keen to learn as much as possible about snow and ice climbing and as the watercourses turned to ice we gleefully attacked as many classic routes as we could.

I was puzzled at first that Baz should climb with me rather than his usual partner Pete Crew. I knew Pete was not particularly keen on winter climbing but Baz hinted that this was not the main reason. Baz and Pete, although forming the most effective climbing team then operating, were not always the best of friends. There were strains and stresses in their relationship, which caused periodic estrangements. It was not an equal partnership. Pete by his sheer force of character dominated; it was Pete who stuck his neck out and grabbed the limelight. For Baz, quiet and brooding, the small resentments would periodically build up to breaking point. For a while they would go their separate ways but would always draw together again. This situation continued for several years and became even more fraught when they jointly bought a Welsh cottage and vied for the same girlfriend.

Baz and I climbed on Great End, Raven Crag Gully and several frozen waterfalls. It was a different and dazzlingly beautiful world. Familiar crags and hills were transformed by frost, great icicles festooned the rocks and snow was piled and sculpted by the winds. The gentle hills became real mountains, simple hill walks became adventures and there was a whole new craft to learn. Our equipment was primitive – especially mine. I had an old long ex-WD axe and 10-point crampons. Baz was better equipped with 12-point Grivels and a shortened axe and at first he was far better than me at cutting steps and handholds and tiptoeing up icy slabs. Even so, I was learning all the time and relished the physical exertion and race against time that the short days demanded.

After New Year it was back to university, permanently frozen water pipes and lots more snow. It was miserably cold in my dingy flat and without water and heat I spent as much time as possible inside the students' union. The winter was declared a national emergency, roads were blocked, farms cut off, blizzards raged but I was happy at the thought of winter climbing – as long as we could get to Wales.

As soon as some of the roads were cleared, we ventured out to Derbyshire, astonished at the banks of snow that had obliterated the rocks of Stanage. On Millstone we climbed several desperate snow walls and made plans for Wales. As soon as lectures finished on Friday we packed the van, picked up Baz in Chorlton and began the epic drive. The tarmac was packed with snow, new drifts were constantly forming and the roads were almost deserted. Wales was white and empty of people; we could pick and choose our routes. Little winter climbing had been done as yet apart from the obvious gullies on Snowdon and in the Carneddau. We had heard that Joe Brown had climbed hard routes on Lliwedd and the Black Ladders so we decided to follow these leads up and see for ourselves.

On our first day we broke trail to Lliwedd through thigh-deep snow. The crag was covered by a chilling mist. We had no idea of our bearings and as we ploughed blindly up a steep snow slope we heard the whoosh of a powder avalanche and were suddenly immersed in a billowing cloud of snow. Retreating quickly, we confined our efforts to some icy buttresses around Dinas Mot and admired the tremendous frozen pillars of ice plunging down Craig y Rhaeadr.

We resolved to make an early start for Western Gully on the Black Ladders and were rewarded by a brilliant sunny day. Reaching the crag exhausted us; we floundered and swam our way up the bottom section of powder to the upper rocks, which were mercifully clear of snow although still coated in thin verglas. It was almost dark by the time we emerged, crusted in ice with frost-nipped fingers, and we stumbled down thankfully to the van, where an anxious Maggie was waiting with hot tea. On the long drive back to Manchester, we discussed our next objectives. It was obvious that the big gullies were out of condition; there was plenty of snow but without a thaw it would remain as unconsolidated powder. We decided to turn our attention to the icefalls and Craig y Rhaeadr in particular.

The following weekend, with Craig y Rhaeadr in mind, we installed ourselves comfortably in Ynys Ettws, the Climbers' Club hut in Llanberis, with a group of Alpha lads that included Pete Crew and Paul Nunn. Then we set off to inspect our route, daunted by the verticality of the ice pillars, which were far too continuous to climb by traditional step-cutting in the days before ice screws and curved axes. There was however a series of ice ramps which zigzagged between the pillars with one short vertical section, the line of a summer route called *Waterfall Climb*. This we followed to produce a highly entertaining route without special difficulty.

It was time for a sterner test and next day we all set off to Cloggy to investigate the obvious line of *The Black Cleft*. It was a glorious day, freezing cold with a wind whipping plumes of snow into the clear blue skies. We waded slowly up the steep slopes from the hut, crested the sunlit ridge and then plunged into the deep gloom of Cloggy. It was an impressive sight, heavily iced and dusted white. *The Black Cleft* corner was choked with a huge tapering pillar of ice; we knew immediately we would a have to try it. A race developed to reach the base of the Cleft, for although we had not discussed the climb it was obvious we would all want a go at it. It was equally obvious that there was only room for two. Pete, with typical impulsiveness, started to solo up the initial icy approach. Paul hung back uncertainly, but Baz and I, using our newly acquired expertise, easily climbed past as Pete came to a halt on an awkward step. Having staked our claim, Pete and Paul retreated crestfallen and left us to struggle on alone.

I tackled the first pitch, a mixture of ice, frozen vegetation and rock and reached a little cave at the side of the ice pillar. Baz joined me and began to fashion delicate hand and footholds in the initial vertical section. He had one ice piton – a coach bolt with a brazed ring on the end – and after great effort managed to place it. The ice was so steep he had to hang on with one hand and cut with the other, an extremely slow and strenuous business. As he gradually disappeared from sight, I shuffled from one foot to another, dodging lumps of ice and whistling to keep my spirits up. Eventually I heard the unmistakeable ringing of a rock piton being driven in. Baz was safe and shortly after lowered himself off utterly exhausted. It was late so we abseiled down and retreated to the cosy warmth of the hut.

Next day we resumed our attack but were woefully late when we regained our high point. I took the lead, climbing quickly up the line of steps and handholds to Baz's peg. Beyond, the ice tapered up for 80 feet to where the spring normally gushed out below a small roof of rock. It was now my turn to chop holds and experience the precarious excitement of one-handed cutting. I was fortunate to dig out a crack between ice and rock and managed to hand jam a short section until I was forced out once more onto the thin ice. With my last strength I cut a series of nicks and tiptoed into a minute stance where I could just about sit, crouched uncomfortably. I was beginning to realise how inadequate my 10-point crampons were compared to Baz's front-points. I couldn't believe it when Baz told me it was far too late to follow me. I had spent all afternoon completing the pitch. Once more we roped down, leaving the rope to speed our progress next day. We could not afford to fail again.

The weekend was over but we had no intention of leaving until we had completed our climb. That night was an anxious one, cloud drifted in and snow began to fall lightly but by morning the weather was as bright as ever. We left very early and as an extra precaution we carried a bivouac sack. Having quickly retraced our steps, I belayed at the high point and Baz climbed over the roof and onto the thinly iced slabs. The rope stopped moving out; there was a scratching of crampons and I cowered in antici-pation of a fall. It never came and after a while Baz advanced and reached the safety of a good ledge. With relief I heard him call weakly: 'Cracked it!'

I scuttled up on a tight rope to join him and scenting victory threw myself at the final overhang. This beat me back temporarily until I hammered in a piton and swung round onto the final easy snow-fluted slopes leading to the top. It was midday, the sun was shining brilliantly and at last we had escaped from the Cleft and could saunter down content.

We climbed together on several more weekends, picking off various good climbs but nothing matched *The Black Cleft*. As spring slowly arrived I climbed with Paul Nunn and picked off, between hail showers, a fine little route on Dinas Mot called *Nexus*. In doing so I incurred the wrath of Baz who had also spied it as a possibility. Baz returned once more to climb with Pete. Meanwhile I had arranged to spend the summer in the Alps with Paul.

The mainstream climbers in Snowdonia were, during the early Sixties, starting to run out of possibilities, and the pursuit of 'Crag X' had become a favourite game. One of the most active groups around that time was the Alpha Club, and it was two of their members, Bas Ingle and Martin Boysen, who 'discovered' Gogarth, and climbed the first two lines: *Gogarth* and *Shag Rock*. They returned with Pete Crew, and beavered away to produce nine routes, after which, astoundingly in retrospect, they felt that the cliff was worked out.

EIGHT

HARD CLIMBS, MODERN TIMES

I couldn't wait for the summer holiday of 1963. It just had to be a good season. This time we had saved enough money; we had a van and I was climbing with Paul Nunn. Our plans were ambitious; we would start in the Dolomites and continue in the Western Alps. Final arrangements were made; we bought the obligatory rations of tinned meat and tea, proofed the tent and booked our ticket. All that remained was to visit my parents for a few days in Tonbridge, where Paul would join us for the journey south.

Our day of departure arrived with no news of Paul. We waited as long as possible and then set off that evening to catch the boat, hoping he would be waiting for us in Dover. He wasn't and we were faced with the awkward decision of where we should wait. It was the holiday weekend, the boats were fully booked and so we crossed over to Ostend where we resumed our anxious vigil. All night and the next day we scrutinised disembarking passengers from every ship; in between we catnapped in the van parked up alongside a chip stall, next to the stinking dock. I was beginning to give up hope when at last we spotted Paul's red head bobbing above those of the jostling crowd. He acknowledged us with a sheepish grin, but I was too relieved to be angry. When we at last got underway he told his story. A few days earlier he had suffered a typically bizarre accident, crashing into a head-high scaffolding pole in a Sheffield street. He suffered a mild concussion, temporarily lost his memory and forgot both the time and place of our rendezvous. He vaguely remembered Tunbridge Wells, arrived there, and with the help of the police was directed to Tonbridge. He arrived at my parents' house after midnight, knocked them up, consumed a vast supper, and next morning my mother put him on the Dover train. I still don't know if this is the whole story. Nothing was ever simple in Paul's life; he had a genius for complexity and confusion.

Our journey started through Belgium and towards my birthplace of Aachen, over the same cobbled and potholed roads that I had travelled out on in 1945. The German border police showed a keen interest in my passport and took it away for examination for an uncomfortably long time. Was I about to be arrested? Or would I be pressganged into the new Wehrmacht? My passport was returned, and I breathed a sigh of relief.

As we pressed on south down the autobahn, the van began to suffer chronically from overheating. Our progress during the day was punctuated by obligatory stops to cool the engine. We tried every remedy we could think of, including swathing the petrol pipe with wet rags, but to little avail. So, instead, we adjusted our pace to suit the vehicle, pre-empting stops by frequent halts at beer cellars and sausage stalls, and so made halting but not unpleasant progress to Innsbruck and the Brenner Pass. Our entry to Italy on the crest of the pass was dramatic; as we swept downhill into the warmth of Italy's valleys a violent thunderstorm swept in, lightning flashed around us and rain hammered on the windscreen. The van seemed to appreciate it and raced through the night towards Cortina, where we found the old military road to the Dibona Hut and drove up this through dark dripping pines to fragrant Alpine pastures, where we stopped, tired and thankful.

I awoke from a deep sleep with the sun streaming in. Flinging open the van doors, I gasped. Surrounding us were towering cliffs wreathed with mist, seeming unearthly and insubstantial. It was as if an enchanted landscape had been conjured up around us in the night – the Dolomites.

Our objective soared above us: the Pilastro on the Tofana di Rozes – a great pink pillar of rock. It was a classic Dolomites route, climbed in 1944, and had once enjoyed a reputation for great difficulty. Indeed, in his book, my early climbing hero Hermann Buhl devoted an entire chapter to it with the title 'We had to bivouac after all'.

There was no danger we would follow suit; next day we romped up the introductory slabs and walls to the crucial overhanging section and were comforted to see all the pitons were in place. Paul and I swarmed up and over the roofs, reached a difficult chimney pitch and were soon scrambling over easy summit rocks to the descent which led through a labyrinth of gun emplacements and catwalks strewn with wire and shell cases, relics of the grim mountain warfare that took place here during the First World War.

We set off in high spirits to drive to Alleghe, delightfully situated by a lake below the Civetta, the 'queen of the Dolomites.' The mountain was famous among climbers and we could understand why, with the whole vast north face displayed above us. The golden evening light picked out its architecture, its pillars, walls and isolated towers, a vision of unparalleled grandeur. There were lots of routes we wanted to do, but one in particular compelled us: the *Philip-Flamm*, renowned as the hardest and finest free-climbing route in the Dolomites if not the Alps. First climbed in 1957, by 1963 it had seen fewer than 10 ascents and one of these, the first by British climbers, was by Pete Crew and Al Wright.

First we needed a training climb. We camped for the night and next day slogged up to the Vazzoler Hut and pitched our tent. Rising early, we drank strong black coffee and set off to walk the few miles through wet alpine meadows to the foot of the Cima Su Alto. We had chosen the *Livanos Diedre*, a hard free and artificial route, which had been climbed by several British parties and was highly recommended. Unfortunately, after a few miles of fast walking Paul started to feel sick; the coffee had upset his stomach, but not sufficiently for us to turn back. We soloed up a long introductory apron of grey slabs until the rock changed colour and a huge yellow groove reared steeply above. Paul was feeling distinctly poorly so it was my task to lead until he improved. I climbed pitch after pitch in the vertical corner, mainly up strenuous cracks, until blocked by a repulsive yellow overhang. This was the artificial section and I wished Paul had been feeling better, for I hated trusting myself to the twisted ironware, bleached slings and broken ring pegs which were the only means of progress. Paul was experienced at pegging on Derbyshire limestone but I had done none; it must have been obvious to him as I made hard work of it and mismanaged the double ropes till the drag was almost unbearable.

It was late afternoon by the time we reached the summit wall of pink and white rock with the texture and appearance of sugar candy. We reached the top, tired and with little light left. The descent looked obvious, but the description talked of abseils. We dithered for vital minutes and then sadly but wisely elected to bivouac. It was a bitterly cold night, but the following morning, after gingerly tiptoeing in our smooth-soled rock shoes down a huge gully full of frozen snow, we arrived weary at the camp just as the morning sun struck it, and Maggie stirred from sleep.

With a training climb done, it was time to focus for the main challenge of the *Philip-Flamm*. This was more easily reached from the other end of the mountain, so we descended to Alleghe, stocked up with more food, and drove round to the rough track leading up to the Coldai Hut, parking at the last ramshackle farm which seemed to be largely occupied by a family of half-wits. When we later returned, the van and others cars had been crudely broken into and chewed at by goats, yet nothing was missing.

We pitched our tent on some rough grass between some huge boulders a short distance from the hut. Our tent was a joke, my primitive US Army bivouac shelter made of thick green canvas, supported by two wooden poles. The three of us could just about crawl under it, but the awnings sagged and flapped on our faces and by morning Paul's feet inevitably stuck out of the end. The sight of us caused much hilarity and some fairly ribald speculation amongst the good-natured Italian climbers.

The proximity of the hut alleviated much of the discomfort. It was run by a couple of motherly ladies who obviously felt sorry for us, for they occasionally insisted we spend a night in the hut and enjoy a good bowl of soup. Evenings in the hut were warm and convivial. It was generally full of Italians and Germans, and after a jug of wine we would joke and chat and glean information about routes.

The weather seemed to be set fair, so there was time for one more route before we got to grips with the *Philip-Flamm*. The *Andrich-Fae* was our choice, a fine route with a short, hard crux on perfect grey rock leading to a comfortingly secure summit chimney system. A sudden change to cold wet weather upset our plans for the *Philip-Flamm*, and we settled down glumly to await an improvement. Our mood cheered up when several British teams arrived, including Scots Johnny Cunningham and Wee Davie, Sheffield climbers Dave Gregory and Gerry Rogan, Oliver Woolcock, Clive Rowlands and Dave 'Pod' Potts with Richard 'Lou' Lewis. Despite the miserable weather, we enjoyed ourselves making social tent-calls exchanging news, while crowded around a roaring Primus stove cooking pans of chips and mouth-searing curries. Pod and Lou had come from the Tre Cime where they climbed almost everything and were particularly cock-a-hoop at having done the *Brandler-Hasse* in record time. Johnny Cunningham had just returned from Antarctica, and told us tales of blizzards and penguins. Amazingly for one so well-travelled it was his first Alpine season; he had come 'to climb the Eiger'.

For days there was little to do except sleep, eat and read. Supplies ran low, and our hunger increased. A rescue call-out one night offered a break in the monotony and also the chance to be well-fed as a reward. I also remember the guilty pleasure of finding a package of succulent ham sandwiches left by a tourist, which Maggie and I devoured in secret.

An improvement in the weather was heralded by the mass arrival of German climbers. They included the team that had done the first winter ascent of the 'super-direttissima', a bolting extravaganza on the Cima Grande. I suspected they were heading for the *Philip-Flamm* and went to investigate. I discovered they had already set off that afternoon and gained a march on us. Obviously the forecast was good, and sure enough towards evening the cloud parted, it grew cold and before dark we feverishly made ready and packed intending for an early start.

We left camp in darkness, clad in light clothes and climbing shoes with a bag of rolls and a big bottle of orange. The stars shone brightly as we crunched over the stony path, locked in our private thoughts, until we made for the vague looming darkness of the North Face, slipping on the moving scree up to a frozen snow patch, which marked the start of the climbing. Dawn was almost breaking and I could just make out the brooding shape of the Marmolada on the horizon when we reached the first rocks. Here we settled for a while to wait for better light.

The climbing was immediately hard. We moved urgently, establishing a rhythm, and as the route unravelled we felt a reassuring confidence that all would turn out well. By 7 a.m. we had caught up with the rival German team standing miserably and shivering mightily on a tiny ledge below a pitch of grade VI. We were now in full flight, warmed to the task and eager for hard climbing. I climbed past, wished the Germans a cheery 'Guten morgen!' and continued without stopping. Paul drifted up behind me and carried on in his most majestic style, but after a few more pitches we came to a halt. A series of wet overhangs loomed above us, blocking the way. This had to be the famous unprotected traverse pitch. A line of tiny footholds led left, and for the first time I felt nervous and uncertain of the way ahead. I wasn't sure I'd chosen the correct level and was uncomfortably aware of the huge drop and the consequences of a fall. At last, I reached a ledge and a belay peg, brought Paul across and we took a well-deserved rest.

Above, the difficulties appeared to ease, but we began to wonder at one point when progress became impossible. Then we realised we had taken the wrong route. Retreating from this impasse, we picked up the correct route via a devious traverse, and reached the last major difficulty, a steep and friable wall that Paul led with apparent ease. It seemed nothing could stop us now. We were going to be on top by early afternoon, having done the route in less than nine hours. This was a fine effort considering the *Philip-Flamm* had never been done in less than a day and a half.

My mind was musing joyfully on these thoughts as I started up an awkward little crack. I grasped a large chockstone but was shocked to feel it rotate inside the crack. Gently pushing it back into place, I moved gingerly past it. Suddenly I heard a grinding of rock, glanced down and to my horror saw the chockstone cartwheel out of the crack. Time slowed as I caught sight of Paul's fearful expression and heard a sickening soft crunch. Paul gasped in pain and I saw blood spurting from a severed artery. I leapt down, tore off my shirt and staunched the flow. Paul was white, suffering from shock, pain and loss of blood. His leg seemed to be broken. We sat for some time until he recovered his composure and then contemplated the unpleasant alternatives. We were still hundreds of feet below the summit ridge. The situation seemed bleak. But then, to my surprise, Paul made the decision to carry on.

The last haul was slow and agonisingly painful. I heaved on the rope and Paul hopped and crawled up the rock. A final overhang with a traverse on pitons was particularly harrowing; I could offer no help and winced in sympathy every time Paul bashed his leg. It was almost dark when he finally hopped on to the ridge and slumped there exhausted. He was in no state to move any further. It had been a remarkable feat of endurance and courage to get where we were. I knew there was a hut somewhere, but in the dark I was not sure of finding it. I didn't want to leave Paul who was now overwhelmed by the delayed shock and pain. He was shaking violently so I dressed him in my sweater, placed him in the bivouac sack, huddled up and massaged him intermittently through the long night.

A wet mist followed by light rain increased our misery, but in the watery light of dawn we could see the way off was straightforward. I took Paul's arm and we slowly staggered on three legs to the tiny summit hut. It looked boarded up but I hammered on the shutters anyway and then waited with a growing sense of despondency. Then I heard someone stirring, the latch clicked and a sleepy hut guardian appeared. No explanation was needed and after gently manoeuvring Paul onto a bunk, he rushed around, prepared bowls of milky coffee and pressed us to drink a good slug of brandy. As these warming liquids eased our cold stiff bodies, I felt the weight of responsibility lift. I told the guardian to marshal all the British climbers he could find; we had no insurance, so couldn't afford an official rescue. He seemed to understand and as he sprinted off down the mountain I drifted into sleep.

It seemed a matter of minutes rather than hours before the guardian was back, seemingly untroubled by his strenuous efforts, and a few minutes later, Pod, then Lou followed by Clive and the others arrived. It was immensely reassuring to see how everyone, including some German climbers, had turned out for the rescue. With amazing dispatch, Paul was hustled down the mountain, shuffling and sliding down snow slopes and screes, whilst anchored to various ropes. We had almost reached the path when we encountered the official rescue team, which had somehow got wind of us. For a moment it looked as if they intended to snatch him away from us, but we pretended ignorance and fended them off. A bearded giant emerged from the mist carrying a rescue chair on his back. He examined Paul, mentally weighed him, and came to the obvious conclusion, shaking his head gravely. We continued as before.

While the main party carried on down to the valley, I traversed back to our camp to reassure Maggie and arrange our departure. The tent was empty so I entered the hut to find her being consoled by the guardians. She turned, gasped in surprise and said: 'It's you!' I was puzzled until I realised the source of her confusion; everyone thought I had been injured because the guardian had described the pullovers we were wearing, and Paul was wearing mine on top of his.

We packed up camp, hurried to the van and drove off to Bolzano to visit Paul. We found him in cheerful mood, laid out on his back attended by silent nuns dressed in white in a splendidly modern hospital. His leg was broken, not badly, but it was severely lacerated and bruised. The doctor appeared, suave and handsome. He sniffed at our rude appearance, lit an American cigarette, and explained that he was unhappy about the risk of infection. Paul then said he was going home. The doctor was horrified and angrily began to shout for us to get out. The nuns cocked their heads and we stood still, considering the next step in our planned abduction. Suddenly the doctor realised we were serious. 'OK, OK – you go. I wash my hands. It is very dangerous.' He produced a letter absolving him of responsibility, the X-rays were bundled into Paul's hands, and we wheeled him down to Dave Gregory's van. We drove in convoy to Venice, booked a seat on a plane for Paul and then sat about uncomfortably for a day and night in the hot, humid marshes, anxiously examining Paul's swelling leg, and fighting off swarms of vicious mosquitoes. At last his flight departed.

Maggie and I were now alone, privacy we had missed to that point, yet I felt Paul's loss keenly and felt torn by a mixture of emotions. Were all my Alpine holidays to be jinxed? Was it my fault? What should I do now? Maggie now took over; we visited Venice, relaxed and I regained my composure as we made our leisurely way through Switzerland to Chamonix. I was sure to find someone to climb with and maybe snatch a good route before we ran out of money and were forced home.

We arrived in foul weather and were gratified to learn that nothing much had been done. The town was full of dissatisfied climbers and long-faced tourists mooching disconsolately around the wet streets staring wistfully at menus and drifting inevitably into the Bar National for *grandes bières*. We splashed our way to the scruffy and sodden Biolay campsite, hunting for friends in the polythene shanty town, and were pleased to find Richard, Festy Parker and John Peck in residence. It was Maggie's 21st birthday, so with the last of our money we had a meal out and ended up in a small club much frequented by French alpinists, called The Bivouac. It was an unpretentious place; the main attraction was a jukebox with all the current Beatles numbers, including *Give Me Money*, much beloved by Festy Parker. At the time there was a certain amount of animosity between the French and English; Charles de Gaulle was in power, we were trying to join the EEC, and there were too many scruffy English about. I was vaguely aware that we were not welcome in The Bivouac, but was greatly enjoying myself dancing in a back room when Richard burst in and announced: 'There's trouble with the lads next door.' We pushed into the bar and saw a climber, obviously English, staggering around with blood streaming from his head and a shattered bottle on the floor around him. For a few seconds no one made a move. Then Richard, boiling into a fury, shook his fist and grabbed the climber's swarthy, thickset assailant, who was holding the neck of the shattered bottle. A chair sailed through the air, shattered a mirror behind the bar and sent more bottles crashing to the floor. Suddenly it was pandemonium. Tables overturned, chairs crashed onto heads, bottles flew and bodies wrestled and kicked. I felt very frightened, especially when the French armed themselves with broken bottles, which they looked like using. We grabbed chairs, fended them off, edged out to the street and made our escape.

Next morning the riot police – de Gaulle's hated private army –swooped on our campsite with sirens wailing and pistols drawn. Our passports were seized and we were warned not to move. We felt very vulnerable, discussed our plight and wondered what the outcome would be. We were told that police had no right to take our passports, so we marched to the station and demanded them back. We received short shrift and were unceremoniously kicked out. Then we tried ringing the British legation in Lyons and were told very politely not to bother them; it was the holiday.

At this point, Don Whillans arrived and through him we contacted the *Daily Express*. The paper was engaged in a longstanding crusade against EEC membership, so it was delighted to report the 'vicious attack' and we made the front page. Other support arrived in the form of a renowned American climber, Gary Hemming, and his French girlfriend. Once more we confronted the police, this time with our interpreter, and to our surprise our passports were handed back with the warning that civil proceedings would follow. We had no inclination to stay longer and packed up immediately to leave. At the last moment, the injured youth, Brian Shirley, whose attack had precipitated the fracas, asked us to take him home. He was a steelworker from Sheffield and so we learnt the full story. He had entered the bar on his own, dressed in boots and breeches and gone to the bar to order a drink. To his utter surprise, the barman took a swing at him and hit him hard on the face. He crashed against a table and was just about to pick himself up and trade blows when he received the *coup de grâce* from behind, in the form of a bottle smashed on his head. His attacker turned out to be a famous French climber, Lucien Bérardini, well-known for his mean temper. The rest we had witnessed. Fortunately there were no repercussions; a court case followed and was dismissed. Thus finished an eventful but not entirely unsuccessful Alpine season.

I returned for my third year at university. Finals were approaching and with them the unwelcome realisation that I was going to have to work harder. My aspirations were not high; I had been far too lackadaisical as a student to achieve anything but an adequate pass. University had not met my expectations. It had felt very much like an extension of school. I was a bad student, barely scraping through my preliminary exams, attending too few lectures and forever putting off assignments until the last minute. I was not popular with several members of the teaching staff and I did little to hide my contempt for some of them. Part of the trouble stemmed from my own inconsistency and lack of conformity. For certain lecturers I worked hard and showed great enthusiasm and this held me in good stead. I was also diligent and good at most of the practical work. Indeed, it was one aspect of work that I thoroughly enjoyed and I could sit happily absorbed at my own piece of gnarled mahogany bench slicing plant sections, preparing slides and looking in wonder at the jewel-like micro-structures of cells and plant tissue.

In the winter term I moved into a new flat with Maggie. It was very small but cosy with a glowing coal fire and a fold-down bed, which creaked and clanked alarmingly. We dragged out all our collated bundles of notes – a dreary pile – and began to read and memorise them. It was a task I dreaded but while the weather was cold and wet I dutifully continued to study. Maggie was a great encouragement. She worked with a fierce and thorough determination while I picked at it less wholeheartedly.

Spring came and through the windows I watched the miraculous transformation of buds growing into delicate greenery. I conceived a sudden yearning for Wales and became ever more fretful at the thought of what I might be missing. Baz visited and offered a lift to Wales in his newly acquired van. Maggie was happy to pack me off and I comforted myself that a bit of spiritual and physical refreshment would do me no harm.

Baz, Arthur Williams and I travelled down on Friday night but our expectations were dashed when it rained all Saturday and we chased from one wet crag to another becoming disconsolate. On Sunday prospects seemed little better and on the spur of the moment we decided to drive to Anglesey, which generally enjoyed better weather, having heard there was some climbing on Holyhead Mountain.

We drove first to South Stack, ran down the steps to the lighthouse and were appalled by the contorted bands of rock twisting 500 feet out of the sea. Already the ledges were occupied by thousands of guillemots and razorbills prospecting for nest sites. Climbing there seemed a dismal prospect. It was raining gently as we made our way inland over desolate heath to the mountain – a rocky bluff laced with pale quartzite. We were pleasantly surprised that the rock was firm and there seemed to be a number of worthwhile little routes. When the sun suddenly burst through the sea-ward clouds, we cursed ourselves for leaving our climbing gear in the van. We ran back to fetch it, determined to salvage at least something from our journey. As evening approached we completed a few pleasant climbs and were on the point of leaving when our curiosity got the better of us; surely, we reasoned, the band of rock we'd been climbing must outcrop on the sea cliffs below. And if so, it should provide worthwhile climbing.

I ran down the slopes to the sea, leaping through the dwarf furze. A sea cliff in the bay began to reveal itself and my excitement grew. We reached a rocky shoulder and peered incredulously at a vast crag of grey and yellow rock, seamed with vertical cracks and corners.

'Looks like a seaside Cloggy,' Arthur remarked, after we had stood for a while staring in silence.

'Better go and have a closer look before we get too excited,' Baz said.

A convenient dirt gully led to a slippery slope of earth, which we crossed cautiously under a fine steep white wall.

'Plenty to go at there for starters,' I said, 'although it needs a lot of cleaning.'

The tide was at the lowest spring ebb and taking advantage of this we scrambled over mats of seaweed to a rock island where we gained a wider perspective. We were impressed; the encroaching gloom served to exaggerate the scale and its menacing effect. We clambered to the foot of the crag and began to traverse along its base, fingering the rock, peering round corners and gazing up cracks. We would have to return; one line in particular was an obvious classic of rock pillars and cracks and accessible at any state of the tide.

For years climbers had boasted, often half jokingly, of finding secret crags, a quest not unlike that for the Holy Grail. Now at last we had found one and were filled with an appropriate sense of awe. We swore an oath of secrecy and returned to Manchester.

I could hardly wait for the following weekend. Sadly Arthur was doing exams and couldn't join us. Baz had not been idle in the week. He had refined his collection of slings and added to them a collection of nuts of various sizes with threads carefully filed off. Pebbles were becoming redundant although the range of sizes and shape of ordinary nuts was limited; it was still necessary to carry pitons and hammers. We arrived at the Padarn Lake Hotel bar, the latest climbers' haunt, feeling the smug superiority of people who know a secret. We deflected enquiries as to our weekend plans. On Saturday morning we drove away from the overcast mountains and into the sunshine of Anglesey. The cliffs were now ablaze with colourful flowers: bluebells, primroses, pink campions and thrift. Seabirds clamoured and sailed in the mild sea breezes. The tide was in but that didn't worry us.

We traversed to the first pillar, which Baz climbed, and then I took his bundle of slings and surveyed the way ahead. A short vertical wall guarded a slab leading easily to a second pillar split by an obvious wide crack. All this was a bit premature since I found great difficulty in stepping off the ledge. I placed Baz's favourite brass nut in a crack and clawed my way up on tiny holds until my hands were brushing the slab. My foot shot off and suddenly I was surveying the sea upside down with Baz chuckling above me. We swapped places and he tried with a similar lack of success. I then moved rightwards, following a line of holds to an overhang that proved easy enough except that the holds creaked and I had no runners.

Easy climbing led to the crack, which provided a pleasant romp at Severe. The way ahead did not look so inviting as the rock was covered with hairy sea lichen and the top cracks were filled with earth and a luxuriant growth of pennywort. The obvious final groove was difficult to enter and involved an airy traverse. I could tell Baz was nervous and he climbed hesitantly until he had bashed in a piton and swung up into a bridging position across the groove. His problems had only just begun for the groove was blocked with long thin slithers of rock hanging like rotten teeth waiting to be plucked.

Baz rarely lost his composure, but on such large loose blocks he was understandably scared. With the utmost caution he tapped the flakes, glanced anxiously down and continued like a cat walking across a cluttered mantelpiece. He dared not pull anything off in case the falling rocks guillotined the ropes. I re-examined my belay and fed the rope out tenderly, inch by inch, as he manoeuvred round the worst parts and reached the last earth-filled cracks. As he clawed at the greenery, fat leaves of pennywort floated down. Baz dug away with his piton hammer, gingerly moved up and then disappeared from view. A tug on the rope was my signal to climb. As I gained height, I kicked the loose blocks off as I passed them and watched with horrid fascination as they hit the sea in a watery crump. Despite my best efforts, there were still plenty of loose blocks left in place by the time I reached the top where Baz still looked shaky.

We called the route *Gogarth* after the name of the bay and subsequently the whole crag was referred to as Craig Gogarth. We were puzzled how to grade the route; we agreed it was not very hard but it was certainly extremely dangerous, a fact borne out when a few years later someone suffered a bad accident on it. It was in many ways an unfortunate first choice of routes. It had been a marvellous adventure but was far too gripping to be enjoyable. We assumed wrongly that the rest of the crag would be similarly loose and would require an enormous amount of cleaning from abseils, something I was always loath to do.

The joy and elation I had experienced discovering the crag was now somewhat tarnished. Perhaps this feeling of disappointment was self-inflicted; whatever happened I was now out of action, committed to full-time exam revision. In the circumstances I could hardly blame Baz for introducing other climbers to the crag, but I could hardly bear it when I heard he had teamed up with Pete Crew again and on successive weekends climbed several of the lines I had jealously cherished. Later, after exams, I visited the crag again with Clive Rowlands and after failing on our route found ourselves deflected onto another loose and rather undistinguished route.

Strangely this first phase of exploration fizzled out shortly after and nothing more happened for two years until Joe Brown and Dave Alcock took a fresh view. This began a frantic spate of activity, and Anglesey became the most fashionable climbing venue. Magazines began to publicise it and new routes and unexplored areas were discovered and developed. I picked off one or two pleasant lines myself but my enthusiasm had faded; I didn't enjoy the carnival atmosphere, preferring the seclusion which climbing in Snowdonia still offered.

I went back to weeks of intensive work, of midnight cramming and last minute revision and then the examination hall doors opened and we filed in apprehensively. The exams came almost as a relief; a catharsis in which jumbled knowledge could be committed to paper and forgotten. It was suddenly all over, the culmination of three years of effort. For days afterwards we felt dazed by it. All that remained was to meekly await the results.

When the summons came, all the faculty students assembled to hear the best or worst. A terrible hush descended as the names were read slowly off in alphabetical order, so I didn't have long to wait.

'Boysen, Martin – Two, Two, but withheld until he satisfies the statistics requirement.'

I was happy with the result. I knew I'd fail the statistics and although I doubted if I would ever pass, I didn't feel too concerned as it represented such a tiny part of the course. I was mistaken in this; my failure was used as a stick against me for some time to come. Maggie passed without any complications and she went on to do a year's post-graduate teaching course. This was barred to me without my degree. I retook and failed my statistics once more and then set about the equally depressing business of finding a job at the local labour exchange. The building looked as defeated as the shabby customers, who dragged on cheap cigarettes, then still available as packets of five, and grumbled about missing 'cushy numbers'. I reached the front of the queue, was called into a cubicle and asked what qualifications I had to offer – very few seemingly. After several fruitless visits I was offered a job at a small chemical works called FEB.

'You must be fucking desperate mate – up to your neck in shit all day for a handful of washers,' was the succinct comment from my neighbour in the queue. It seemed FEB was well known as a last resort for the workless, useful merely for gaining enough insurance stamps to go back on the dole. From what I gathered the pay was less than the dole, but as I had no stamps that was denied me. I duly walked up to the factory, a miserable scattering of sheds and tumbledown outhouses at the edge of a railway shunting-yard. I sought out the foreman, a bald-headed sour-faced man called Albert who looked me over, sniffed scornfully and finally announced: 'You'll do.'

I arrived next morning to be issued with overalls and facemask, which I could 'wear if I wished.' A half-witted lad, without overalls and stained from head to toe in garish dyes, showed me into a poky black room and demonstrated my task, the trowelling of coloured powders into bags. The factory made cement additives, to help it set in cold weather, to colour it or somehow improve its performance. As far as I could judge the raw materials for our products were based on a noxious white powder of anhydrous calcium chloride, a pinch of resin and in my case potent aniline dyes. The mixture was ground up and delivered to me by a cheerful bowlegged bantam of a man indelibly coloured. He scoffed at my mask. 'Never done me no harm,' he boasted while coughing deeply and treading a multi-coloured gob of phlegm into the dirt floor. After a few days a huge and mysterious Nigerian joined me. He muttered to himself and when I asked revealed he was putting a curse on Albert learnt from his Yoruba auntie.

At the end of the day we were allowed five minutes to wash but as there was only one squalid shower and the hot water lasted a minute at most I complained to Albert.

'Are you some kind of troublemaker? Because if you are you can bugger off now,' was his curt response. I innocently mentioned the Factories Act, at which he spluttered with incoherent rage. I was taken aside by a workmate who explained 'he probably thought you were in a union. The last lot to join up were sacked on the spot.'

Despite the awfulness of the work conditions, the workforce shared a grim subversive humour. It was almost a point of honour to perform as little work as was humanly possible and a secret code of pipe taps alerted us to Albert who specialised in creeping round and then peering furiously through the door. After a week I was removed from the solitary confinement of my black hole and put to work with a gang grinding and packing another product. My companions were made up of a confidence trickster just released from gaol, two West Indians recently arrived, and an Australian research student. I was quickly initiated into the art of skiving, with a warning to look out for the handful of Albert's spies, old retainers who had shares in the company and received separate wage packets. My own wage was barely £10, a sum that did not inspire me to any great exertion, or any guilt for lack of it. To rub salt in the wound, wages were delivered by the factory owner who arrived in a gleaming white Rolls-Royce.

To get our own back we resorted to sabotage. Whenever Albert announced there was a 'big rush on', the grinding machine would develop inexplicable faults and much to Albert's disgust he would have to ask us to do overtime. Following this request we would work flat out for a few hours, achieve the required quota and hide it until the end of the day. As soon as Albert departed we would find the product and go home having arranged for the night-watchman to stamp our cards for a couple of hours extra.

Easy as the work was, it was impossible to save any money, which became a problem as the summer holidays and Alpine season drew near. I heard that Kellogg's were recruiting night shift workers and that pay was much better so I applied for a job and was taken on.

For the first week new recruits were given training, shown films about the marvels of cornflake manufacture and the hallowed beginnings of the Kellogg's cereal empire on the windy plains of Nebraska. We were shown round the clamorous factory to lewd whistles and gestures from factory girls who introduced us to the repetitive and mind-numbing work.

When I started on the night shift, I was put on one of the packing lines in front of a giant dispenser which gushed cornflakes into packages which I checked now and then for weight. The machine was noisy, it was impossible to talk and there was no shared laughter. The machines were our masters and how I enjoyed it when my dispenser went berserk and cornflakes came gushing out like an avalanche, swamping me before I found the stop button. My life reminded me of the film *Modern Times* by Charlie Chaplin; like him I was demoted for my failure to cope with the machinery. For a week I popped plastic novelties into a never-ending row of boxes until my rehabilitation began on the All-Bran line. The irony was this proved to be one of the most troublesome products, continually blocking the machinery with miniature logjams.

The work was unbearably tedious, the hours crept by and I continually examined the skylights for the first sign of dawn. At six in the morning the night shift ended and I would stumble into the deserted streets and walk several miles home to collapse into a warm bed as Maggie got up and left for teaching practice. I slept until four when she would wake me and five hours later I reluctantly dragged myself back to work. I began to loathe it. The malty smell of toasting cereals, discernible at a distance, became ever-more nauseating. I had nightmares – or rather day-mares – of working the rest of my life on nights. There was one consolation that kept me going; I was saving money and this was going to buy me freedom. It would allow me to climb in the Alps, and forget all about cornflakes.

NINE

THE WALKER

The day of double departure arrived. I collected my last pay packet, waved goodbye to the handful of workmates I had grown to like and then fled gleefully through the factory gates. Maggie was waiting for me in the van, already packed and ready to go. All that remained was to drive across the Pennines to Sheffield and collect Clive Rowlands.

Clive and I had joined the Alpha Club at roughly the same time. We climbed together occasionally, enjoyed each other's company and so it made perfect sense to join forces for an Alpine season. Clive was a few years younger than me but you couldn't tell; he displayed a remarkable maturity for his age and even looked old, with a prematurely weathered face, hooked nose and heavy-lidded eyes, all of which contrasted strangely with his boyish figure. He was tough, crafty, and had a sharp sense of humour, mercilessly so in the face of pretentiousness. Somehow he had wangled six weeks holiday from his job in a steel mill where he held down a responsible and well-paid job. He disliked the work; it involved shifts, which upset his stomach and messed with weekends, but as he had left school entirely without qualifications it was the best job available. He was already determined to set himself up in business and was saving up to do so.

Clive was an extremely good climber, and, most importantly for the Alps, utterly steady. We had talked little of our plans; we had suffered enough Alpine misfortunes to cure us of over-optimism. The routes we wanted to do were obvious: the *grandes courses* of the Vallot guide, the six north faces of Gaston Rébuffat's *Starlight and Storm*, and most of all the *Walker Spur* on the Grandes Jorasses.

We arrived in Chamonix in the early hours of morning, weary and dazed after driving all day and most of the night across the pitted hog's back roads of France. Chamonix came all too abruptly without the gradual transition from plain to mountains. Once more the jagged skyline of the granite Aiguilles shocked us – made us appreciate we had arrived. In the Bar National – the British bar – Maurice gazed short-sightedly at us from behind the counter and then his face broke into a smile of recognition. He gave us each a small beer on the house and we followed them with large coffees served in thick green cups.

Afterwards we bumped up the dirt track to the Biolay campsite, past the washing trough, the old wooden hut and into the patchwork of meadow and woods scattered with tents. The campers were largely British, recognisable by the scruffiness of the tents and their white torsos lounging in the sun. There were lesser numbers of Germans and Austrians, spruce and brown, while the French, being better off, stayed in apartments and chalets. The Italians stayed in Italy.

The camp was stirring as we arrived, climbers recently down from the hill were placing steaming boots in the sun and airing damp clothes and sleeping bags. Others were trooping through the trees, back from the shops with baguettes under their arms. The thrumming sound of Primus stoves filled the air. We wandered around the tents, seeking out friends, eager to pick up news of climbing conditions and find out who had done what. I was greatly cheered to come across Little Mick – Mick Burke – taking his ease in the morning sun while waiting for the kettle to boil. He grinned from ear to ear, welcomed us to join him and filled us in on the gossip.

Mick was from Wigan, climbed mainly in the Lakes where I had met him often, but had recently been living in Manchester. He had a mischievous and mobile face, framed with dark curly hair, and he peered owlishly through thick and battered black-rimmed glasses. His hand trembled slightly as he puffed on a Gauloises, an impression of nervousness accentuated by his slight stutter. His appearance belied his nature, for he was a pugnacious and argumentative character, much tougher than he looked and well able to look after himself. He was to be a dear and generous friend to me. I first met him on a trip to the Lake District when we were both passengers in a van. He introduced me to the exquisite agony of a dossing site under an Ambleside bridge and next day we set off for a Wasdale dinner of the Langdale Lads. We stopped on the way and climbed a classic route on Heron Crag in Eskdale. At first I was alarmed to see him shaking violently as he stood on small holds; he seemed to have more courage than ability. He must have seen my reaction because he assured me he always climbed the same way and had had surprisingly few accidents. What he lacked in style he made up for in determination.

Mick was teamed up with Bill Bowker, a laconic, soft-spoken individual from Blackburn, nicknamed with characteristic cruelty 'Bivouac Bill'. He had earned his name in the previous Alpine season when he had climbed with stoic indifference to the appalling weather and consequently suffered a record number of forced nights out on stormy mountains.

We discussed plans, swapped news and learnt that the weather had been fine and that the high routes were coming into condition. Mick and Bill were also recently arrived, and since we all had to do a training route or two and wished to do the same routes, we naturally joined forces. The arrangement increased the safety margin and companionship on the mountain as well as boosting our collective morale; although we were ambitious we were still in many ways Alpine novices.

After a gruelling but mercifully short training climb on the appropriately named Aiguille du Peigne, we set off to climb our first 'proper route' – the East Ridge of the Crocodile – involving a hut walk, glaciers and mixed climbing. I had a score to settle with the Crocodile, having failed on it during my first unhappy season. Then bad weather had forced us to stay at the Envers des Aiguilles Hut. This time we intended to camp, determined to eke out our limited supply of money.

We settled down comfortably enough by some boulders, cooked supper and drifted off into a restless sleep. The pre-dawn silence was shattered by the sound of crunching boots and torches flashing against the tent as parties left the hut. We realised we were late once more. This was a disadvantage of not using huts, but at least the sky was clear, the stars shining with startling brightness, and we could use the other party to guide our path up the glacier.

After a rapid breakfast we stowed away our sleeping bags and stove and hurried after the bobbing torches ahead. Dawn broke as we reached the start of the climb where a French party waited. We were impressed to recognise the burly, bald-headed figure of Lionel Terray with a lady – his client. He gazed at us with disapproval, recognising us immediately as English. He announced rather imperiously: 'Please do not interfere with me on this climb.' We stood back respectfully, watched with rapt attention as the great man thwacked at the ice and followed on only after they had got some distance ahead.

It was a dangerous place to hang around; the large accumulations of winter snow were being sloughed off in the morning sun. We had just reached the safety of a rock rib when an avalanche thundered down, narrowly missing our last man Mick who disappeared briefly in a cloud of pulverised ice before emerging covered in white frosting. 'Nearly got me that time,' he shouted shaking his fist in the direction of heaven. Crossing another hazardous couloir, Mick was again nearly wiped out and once more he tempted fate by admonishing the almighty. 'For Christ's sake, leave off Mick, his aim is getting better all the time,' Clive said.

Above us was a rock tower, which constituted the route's main difficulty. Terray was dragging himself up a steep wall at its base. I was sure he was off route and after adopting a suitably humble tone dared to point this out to him. He responded rather forcibly that he knew where he was going; he was a Guide and had done the route before, whereupon he set to with renewed vigour, hauled himself up on his arms, teetered a little and then scuttled back down. He was obviously a stubborn man but I saw a little doubt showing on his client's face.

I was not prepared to wait so after signalling Clive we climbed easily up broken rocks to a dark chimney I recognised from my previous attempt. The others followed and then Terray began to rope down to join us. We were determined to acquit ourselves well and not cause any hold-ups and consequently charged up the chimney. An additional reason for speed was also making itself obvious. Angry grey clouds were boiling up for a storm. We were just about to leave the chimney when Terray shouted up and requested our help to haul up his sack. We were happy to oblige but shortly after our ice-axes started to hum with electricity and we realised the danger we were all in. We left several karabiners and all our etriers to help Terray's escape and as we reached the summit, lightning struck nearby. It was a horrifying experience; a loud hiss, a simultaneous flash followed by a rock-shaking crash. We hurled an abseil rope down, descended helter-skelter and raced for our lives along a snow-ridge, with the rope left behind, until we were out of danger, sliding down snow slopes to the Requin Hut.

Having collected our sleeping bags, we left a message for Lionel Terray and set off in teeming rain down the grey polished ice of the Mer de Glace. We slithered helplessly, lost our way briefly and arrived below Montenvers in pitch darkness, very tired, very wet and utterly fed up. To compound the misery we missed the ladders leading off the glacier so for an hour searched and felt our way like blind men through the crevasses and boulders. I had just about given up but Clive persisted and at last a clang of metal announced his discovery. We plodded up them mechanically and then trudged down the rack railway to Chamonix, reaching the Biolay in the early hours of the morning.

After two hard and exciting days in the mountains it was bliss to rest for a while without a gnawing conscience as we lay in the sun contentedly looking up at the snowy summits. We could rationalise our idleness as 'waiting for conditions to improve'. A message arrived a day later from Lionel Terray, telling us to collect our equipment from the Guides' Office. With it was a note expressing thanks for the help we had given – especially our abseil rope and etriers. Later we met by chance in Chamonix and he explained: 'At first when I saw you I thought you were a typical

English party – slow, always getting lost and poorly equipped. Later I could see you were good climbers.' He also explained his own bad form; he had only recently recovered from an avalanche, which had killed his client and badly injured him. He also pronounced our storm to be the worst he had ever experienced. He was lucky to survive. It was clearly some storm.

I must admit to feeling some pride in such distinguished praise, even if the compliment was slightly backhanded. There was certainly some substance in his poor opinion of British alpinists. They had long been a byword for incompetence, particularly when it came to snow and ice climbing. So used were the French to seeing bivouacking English on the Requin that it acquired the local nickname 'Dortoir des Anglais'. British climbers also looked scruffy – an unpardonable offence to the French. With the notable exception of Joe Brown and Don Whillans, very few British climbers had done much. Most Europeans knew nothing of British climbing, in fact, they were surprised to learn there was any. We were part of a new generation despairingly called the 'blue jeans' by Toni Hiebeler, then editor of the influential German magazine *Alpinismus*. Maybe Hiebeler had seen lightly-clad British climbers in the Dolomites, myself included, dressed in jeans and PAs. One thing was certain; unencumbered with heavy boots and great racks of pitons we could climb fast and enjoyably unlike many of the heavily equipped Germans we overtook. We were the start of a new generation reacting against the over-mechanisation of climbing. We had no time for pointless bolting exploits and the devaluation of fine free climbing routes by over-pegging.

The *Bonatti Pillar* on the West Face of the Dru was our next objective, a challenge I had long desired. Early in my climbing life I had read accounts of the amazing solo first ascent by Walter Bonatti. I had studied photos and struggled through articles in *La Montagne* and at last I had seen it for myself; a tawny, radiant sweep of rock lit by the evening sun. I had often longed to be on it, sat high on a ledge in the evening, observing the Chamonix valley as it darkened. Now my dreams would become reality. I was ready for it and felt an inner calm that transcended my outward show of nervous excitement.

In the early afternoon we loaded up our sacks and set off through the trees to trudge back up to Montenvers where we allowed ourselves to gaze briefly at our route before crossing the Mer de Glace to the foot of the huge lateral moraine which cuts off the slopes leading to the Rognon du Dru. This rocky spur is where we intended to bivouac. Bill, Clive and I rashly thought we could climb the moraine direct and were led on by the initial easy slopes, but as we climbed higher the angle became insidiously steeper, retreat became less and less desirable but progress became more and more difficult. Finally, we were stuck, each of us clinging precariously to a boulder insufficiently cemented in what looked like mud. We shouted for Mick, at first trying to hide our desperation but later losing all inhibition. His head popped over the crest of the moraine, a wide grin pasted across his face and then a rope trickled down till it was almost within reach. Mick couldn't miss the chance.

'What will you offer us for an end?'

'Anything – you name it.' We pleaded for our lives until he relented. The remaining slog was less eventful but totally without humour.

When we arrived, we found the best bivouac cave was already occupied but as we searched for another the occupant came bounding down the boulder field, blond hair streaming. The figure was bronzed and magnificently muscled, far too well-maintained to be British. Sure enough, he was an American who introduced himself as John Harlin. We had heard of him. He lived in Switzerland, and with Tom Frost, Gary Hemming and others had done several hard rock routes including the South Face of the Fou. Harlin hadn't bothered to speak with us for long but a little later another figure, this one obviously English, staggered down. Harlin's partner, sent as an emissary, turned out to be Nick Estcourt. Nick was embarrassed to recognise me and went on to explain, stuttering slightly, that John was attempting a new direct route on the Dru's West Face. He was jumaring up behind carrying the hardware.

'Like a white Sherpa,' Mick cruelly interjected.

Nick was uneasy in the face of blunt Northern humour and he was even more embarrassed when he finally delivered his message from Harlin: we were not to leave before them next morning as he did not want to be slowed up in the Dru couloir.

'Who the hell does he think he is? God?' I replied.

'He can get stuffed,' was Clive's curt response. Bill chuckled. Poor Nick, he had not enjoyed being errand boy, but he made as graceful an exit as possible, shrugging his shoulders and smiling sheepishly.

Mick was still fuming hours after the meeting and perhaps this first meeting set the tone for future confrontations. It was a case of instant dislike. For Mick, Nick was a representative of class privilege – public school, Cambridge and a profession. He talked too loudly, was garrulous and argued with the enthusiasm of a young terrier tackling a bone. He was a vivid character, engagingly open and consequently vulnerable to the cutting humour of Mick.

We settled down for the night, watched the mist creep up until it engulfed us and then saw it dissolve to leave the Dru glowing like a dying flame. A cold breeze stirred, scented with the hard smell of rock. I shivered, nestling into my duvet, but was glad that a frost would bind the loose rocks and make the couloir as safe as possible.

At first light we set off up the snow cone disgorging from the Dru couloir. Above us danced the lights of Harlin and Nick. We reached them a few minutes later, stood in the grey dawn light below the entry pitch to the couloir. We nodded to each other but said nothing. Harlin began to climb, clumsily and without intuition. He placed a piton, disappeared from view and Nick followed, apologising again before removing the piton. I was gratified to find the pitch easy and we kept at their heels until they left the couloir across grey dusty ledges and we continued directly into the icy neck of the gully. We were heading for a dark and ominous prison of rock, a crucial passage that focused any falling rocks. With our ears and eyes alert and our hearts racing we scuttled through to a sizable snow basin, which we traversed to reach the sanctuary of the pillar's base.

The pillar was perfect red granite, soaring up in one wild surge. A crack split its base, like a flaw in a diamond. I set off up this crack, hand-jamming around a succession of rotten wooden wedges far too dangerous to be of use. We climbed slowly up a succession of strenuous cracks into the sun and it became unbearably hot. Eventually we reached a fine ledge where we could sit and admire the staggering exposure. This must have been the ledge where Hamish MacInnes had suffered a skull fracture after being hit by a falling stone. Chris Bonington had told me of their epic ascent, and bearing this in mind I crouched close to the back wall, smoking a cigarette until Mick and Bill joined us.

'Is that it? Can we bivvy now?' Mick chirped as he arrived gasping on the ledge. It wasn't a particularly amusing remark but we laughed anyway and it was for this quality – the ability to defuse tension, to make us laugh at ourselves – that I loved to climb with Mick.

I swallowed a salt tablet to alleviate muscle cramp, wished we had carried more water, and set off up a difficult chimney followed by a great split wall. Cracks, grooves and wall continued – an infinity of climbing. I no longer consulted the description. The route was obvious enough and my horizon was limited to the next piton. It was late and we had had enough by the time we gratefully stumbled on the tiny ledge nestling below a formidable dripping roof. This was where Bonatti had performed his hair-raising solo acrobatics. I shuddered at the thought of it as I climbed into my *pied d'éléphant* and prepared to cook up some soup.

In the morning we were cold and stiff with discomfort. We wolfed the remaining bread with chocolate and cheese and washed it down with a mouthful of disgusting tea heavily contaminated with our fish soup supper. The roof above us was now iced up and we had the alternative option of a steep wall split by a thin crack that bristled with pitons. It was straightforward enough, simply a matter of clipping in etriers and standing up, a process I repeated until the rope was finished and Clive was forced to follow. Above the angle eased slightly and we were able to climb more quickly but then a piton suddenly shot out with Clive standing on it and he clattered down a few feet. Then we emerged onto the North Face where conditions turned icy.

Weary from the previous day, dehydrated and short on energy, each pitch was a strenuous effort, and time slipped by unnoticed. Clouds, small and insubstantial at first, but then thick and grey, began to boil up and stream past the Dru. A reverberating thunderclap heralded the storm just as we reached quartz ledges, which allowed us to traverse into the ordinary route a hundred feet or so below the summit. It was not the time to go there, or linger, as rain began to bucket down and lightning crashed around us. We hurried to lose height but with sodden ropes, electrified after each lightning flash, and waterfalls gushing down every crack, it wasn't easy. Eventually the misery became too much and we elected to spend a wet night in safety rather than blundering on in a state of exhaustion.

The storm rumbled on, coming and going throughout the night, but by morning its force was spent; a watery sun broke through to cheer us as we stumbled down. By the time we reached level ground on the glacier, we were dry and happy. We wobbled along on tired legs, but could now safely contemplate luxuriating in the delights of the valley.

A spell of unsettled weather suited us; we rested our weary bodies and allowed our rock-torn hands to heal. Bill Bowker had to return home to his job, so Mick cast around the campsite for a partner until he found Alex Fulton, the brother of Stuart Fulton who had played a major part on the first ascent of the Fou's South Face. Unlike his brother, Alex was quiet and thoughtful but he was equally keen and fit.

There was no question about our next objective: the *Walker Spur* of the Grandes Jorasses, in the words of the guide 'one of the most formidable among the great Alpine routes'. It certainly looked it; four thousand feet of ice-glazed rock towering above the remote Leschaux glacier – the culmination of the Mer de Glace. It was the irresistible challenge to every ambitious alpinist. Although the *Walker* had been repeated many times, with ascents from British climbers like Robin Smith, Don Whillans and Hamish MacInnes, it still held a tremendous reputation.

As soon as the weather improved we packed up; I kissed Maggie goodbye, she hugged me desperately and I weakly told her 'not to worry'. Then we set off, by train this time, to Montenvers. Pausing on the terrace, we saluted our mountain and set off on the long walk to the site of the old Leschaux Hut, a sad ruin of splintered wood and crazy-angled beams but, despite the drafts, a welcome shelter.

We were not alone. Two Germans were in residence and we didn't have to guess what they were waiting for. One of the Germans was a dour young Bavarian, the other a Saxon refugee who had a dry wit not unlike our own Northern brand of humour. He was surprised and delighted when he found I could share his jokes, largely at the expense of his humourless companion. He informed us there were two British climbers ahead. He had seen their lights approach the face. He had not gone on to the route as the weather looked slightly unsettled and sure enough, later that afternoon, cloud swelled around the Jorasses and it snowed high up on the route. As darkness fell we could just make out tiny lights flickering high on the spur. We guessed they belonged to Nick Estcourt and prayed fervently we too would be up there as soon as possible.

Another day of uncertain weather passed, leaving us fretful and concerned about our food rations. After gathering it all together we decided one of us would have to go down for more and Clive drew the short straw. He set off immediately. By evening all the cloud had gone and the sky was cobalt blue. The Germans left at midnight and we waited with growing frustration for Clive's return. He arrived early next morning, feet blistered from his frantic pace. His news was good; the weather forecast was excellent and we decided to start that evening and bivouac below the first difficulties a few hundred feet up.

The time had come to distribute the food, pots, stove and pack our sacks ready for departure. We waited in silence until late afternoon and then descended onto the glacier, threading our way through a maze of crevasses to the bergschrund and then scrambling easily up shattered rock to a ledge below the Rébuffat Crack. While Mick and Alex started brewing up, Clive and I climbed this first hard pitch and left the rope hanging ready for an early start next morning. We were in rare good humour. Mick was cracking jokes, Alex was singing heartily and by the time we arrived back at our ledge, there was a fine stew ready to eat. We settled down for the night, chatting intermittently, observing the sparkling constellations and in the periods of silence brooding on what the morning would bring.

I dozed fitfully, jerking awake each time the clatter of falling rock broke the unearthly silence. A trail of lights began to zigzag below us; others were coming and we would have to get a move on if we were not to be overtaken. We bolted down our breakfast, crammed our feet into cold boots and prepared to climb. I set off hand over hand up the rope thankful I did not have to touch the freezing rock. Easy climbing followed across broken ledges to ice bands that led to the right edge of the spur and a second step cut by a clean groove of perfect red granite. The morning sun touched the spur, warming the rock and our stiff bodies.

I began climbing, feeling full of energy and light-footed despite my heavy sack. The dark forebodings I harboured in the night were dispelled. I now delighted in the surroundings and joyfully absorbed the mountain's immensity and its exquisite detail, the cushions of lichen and a cluster of smoky quartz crystals tucked in a pocket in the rock. We climbed with an easy rhythm; it was never particularly hard, but always enjoyable. Only once did our composure falter when Clive led a desperately thin slab. We were off route but quickly regained the proper line and moved right to a tension traverse beyond which, the guidebook warned, 'retreat might be impossible.' A rotting fixed line precluded this awful fate but it led to a repulsive overhang, icy and black.

Having overcome this barrier we romped up a glorious stretch of slabs at the top of which was a voluble band of Italians. As soon as we reached them Clive wrenched off his boots and examined his heels. He had complained mildly about his hurting ankles but I was horrified to see huge infected blisters. One of the Italians produced a first aid kit and administered iodine and lint. We sat and had a breather, waiting for Mick and Alex to reach us and the Italians to move ahead. It was annoying to be held up on the route but we were not worried by it. We had made excellent progress, the weather was still perfect, and we would be above all difficulties by evening.

We climbed sedately now and reached the Red Tower where the rock was suddenly coated in snow and verglas, a reminder of the last storm. Overtaking the Italians, we pushed on up an icy chimney, balancing precariously on tiny rock spikes protruding through the ice. It was the last

1   Mum and Dad on holiday in Germany.   *Photo: Boysen Collection.*
2   Me, about to set off for the Cairngorms.   *Photo: Boysen Collection.*
3   Max Smart and me at Harrison's Rocks.   *Photo: Boysen Collection.*

4 The first ascent of *The Thing* at Bowles Rocks, possibly the first 6b on sandstone. Behind it, the birch tree which made the now-defunct route *Sloth* possible.   *Photo: Boysen Collection*.

5   Richard McHardy (climbing) and me on *Medusa Wall*, Esk Buttress.   *Photo: Chris Bonington Picture Library.*
6   Me at Gogarth.   *Photo: Ken Wilson.*

7

7   The diagonal crack on the South Face of the Fou.   *Photo: Nick Estcourt.*
8   The chaos of the Biolay campsite in Chamonix.   *Photo: Joe Brown.*
9   L–R: Mick Burke, Mike Kosterlitz and me on the Dru rognon.   *Photo: Nick Estcourt.*

8

9

10 Maggie and me shortly after meeting in Manchester.   *Photo: Boysen Collection*
11 Maggie.   *Photo: Ken Wilson.*
12 Tom Patey and me on the Plan.   *Photo: John Cleare/Mountain Camera.*

13 Mucking around in the Embassy Club pool in Islamabad. L–R (on shoulders): Dave 'Pod' Potts, Bill Barker, Joe Brown. L–R (in the pool): Unknown, me, Ian McNaught-Davis, Mo Anthoine. *Photo: Doug Scott.*

14 The Cerro Torre team (L–R): Peter Gillman, me, Dougal Haston, Pete Crew and Mick Burke (crouching). *Photo: Boysen Collection.*

15 Cerro Torre.   *Photo: Leo Dickinson.*
16 High on Torre Egger with Tut Braithwaite.   *Photo: Leo Dickinson.*
17 Trango Tower.   *Photo: Leo Dickinson.*

18 Mo and Joe on the Trango Tower expedition. *Photo: Boysen Collection.*
19 Mick Burke after receiving a head wound on the last attempt on Cerro Torre. *Photo: Pete Crew.*
20 Malcolm Howells and me at the final bivouac on Trango Tower. *Photo: Tony Riley.*
21 Clint Eastwood and me filming for *The Eiger Sanction*. *Photo: John Cleare/Mountain Camera.*

22 The knee-jam crack on Trango.   *Photo: Mo Anthoine.*
23 Tom Frost (back) and Mick Burke on Annapurna   *Photo: Chris Bonington Picture Library.*

24 Ian Clough on the South Face of Annapurna. *Photo: Chris Bonington Picture Library.*
25 Making the first ascent of *The Garotte* with Dave Alcock, on Ogwen's Suicide Wall. *Photo: Ken Wilson.*

26 Heading to the final ridge of Changabang.   *Photo: Chris Bonington Picture Library.*
27 Looking down the South-West Face of Everest.   *Photo: Chris Bonington Picture Library.*

29

28 Leading P1 of *U-Ei*, Grey Wall Recess, Pabbay in May 2010. *Photo: Neil Foster.*
29 Following Rab Carrington across the crucial traverse on P2 of *Nexus* in July 2013, one of the best E1s in the Llanberis Pass. This was the second time I had done the route, the last time being when I did the first ascent, 50 years previously. *Photo: Neil Foster.*

30 Katie, Maggie and me.   *Photo: Boysen Collection.*
31 Hanging out at Indian Creek.   *Photo: Boysen Collection.*
32 With Maggie, Katie and family in Corsica at the end of a five-day hike.   *Photo: Boysen Collection.*

difficulty, and the Italians called for a rope, which we gladly lowered them before finding a ledge for the night. We cooked and melted snow, smoked our last cigarettes happy in the knowledge that the top was only a few hundred feet above.

It was a bitterly cold night. In the morning we were only too happy to get moving. After a few pitches a cornice of snow blocked all progress. I searched around, found a hole and crawled through it to the sunlit summit and gazed longingly at the green valleys of Italy. We sat and soaked up the sun's warmth until the jubilant Italians appeared. Then we started the long descent. We were too short of money to buy any refreshments at the Jorasses Hut and continued wearily down steep grass and slopes of rock to the valley. Here we suffered our only accident when I tripped, twisted my ankle and nearly fell down a cliff. Moments later a huge boulder dislodged itself and rapidly gaining speed hurtled towards Mick. He dodged from side to side like a startled rabbit but it seemed to follow his every manoeuvre until he flung himself flat and it skimmed over his head. Mick picked himself up and observed philosophically that 'you've only done the route when you're safely sat on a bar stool.'

Reaching the valley, we walked several miles to Courmayeur as Clive suffered in agony from his inflamed heels. Our next problem was how to get back to Chamonix. We had just enough money to take a cable car back up to the Torino Hut next morning but not enough for a meal. We were reflecting on our plight as we reached a group of tents where we were delighted to see the girlfriends of Oliver Woolcock and Rod Brown. We collapsed thankfully and they fed us an enormous stew before we crashed out. The following day we rode up to the Torino Hut and tramped down through the Géant icefall, down the Mer de Glace and back to Chamonix, reflecting happily on our great adventure and marvelling at our luck. We had done the routes we wanted to do; anything else would seem an anti-climax.

In Chamonix everyone was down from the hill. Chris Bonington was scuttling about from one team to another having just returned from an unsuccessful attempt on a new route on the Civetta with American climbers, Jim McCarthy and John Williams. Joe Brown and Tom Patey were in the Bar National. John Harlin had just returned with Royal Robbins from a successful assault on his Dru Direct. Nick Estcourt confirmed that it was his lights we had seen on the *Walker Spur* and everyone settled down to enjoy themselves, happy in the knowledge of routes safely done. The festivities were becoming distinctly lively when two comically obvious detectives in trench coats and slouch hats entered the bar. An uneasy quiet descended except for Nick, who, grinning from ear to ear, pointed at them and burst out laughing. They were not amused and unceremoniously frog-marched him out and flung him in gaol for the night.

The weather finally broke, relieving us of any guilt about idling away the last week of our holiday. It provided a marvellous excuse for a trip to the white limestone cliffs of Les Calanques on the Mediterranean. We formed a mass exodus, joined by Arthur Williams, Tony Riley and a large party of Americans. John Harlin was already there – a brooding Adonis posing magnificently on clifftops, flexing his muscles and fixing his majestic gaze at any unattended female. He pointed out a few routes and directed our attention to a delightful low-level girdle traverse a few feet above the deep clear water.

'I only know one person who has ever done that first time without getting wet,' he said. 'I'll buy anyone a bottle of beer who does it.'

Here was a challenge. I set about it immediately, passed the first crux and was just about to negotiate the second when he dived in and attempted to wrench me off. I held tight, kicked him clear and continued to the end. Arthur Williams, who was thin and sickly white, however long he sat in the sun, followed me. Traverses were his speciality and he made it look easy.

'Who the hell is he?' the blond god demanded.

We remained for a week camping out under the pines, sunbathing, swimming and occasionally climbing. It was a perfect end to a marvellous holiday.

But I never did get my bottle of beer.

1964 Sep 1 **The Medlar**   M Boysen, CJS Bonington (var), M Thompson
Three points of aid were used.

*'As I remember, it was Martin who had spotted the line and then suggested
to Chris and me that we go and take a look. There was a tree, somewhere near
the start, that Martin, as a professional botanist, proclaimed to be a medlar
(though I rather think he was wrong about that). There was a double meaning
to the name, however, since Chris hand-placed a piton in a little hole as
protection below the crux on the first pitch, at the same time jumping
at my idea that, since no hammer was involved, it could be regarded as
a rather odd-shaped nut!'*

Mike Thompson recalls halcyon new routeing days. An outstanding
climb and probably the fiercest undertaking in the Lakes at that time.
Pete Whillance, '*A Short History of Lakeland Climbing (Part III)*',
FRCC Journal 1986. First free ascent, C Jones, 1976.

TEN

MIXED FORTUNES

Back home, my first priority was to earn some money and see if I could obtain my degree, which would allow me to teach. I visited the university, something that now filled me with dread, and arranged an interview with the head of the science faculty. He was a sympathetic man who took an interest in my case and seemed genuinely disturbed by my situation. He promised to do all he could and let me know the outcome as soon as possible, most probably by the New Year.

In the meantime I needed employment. While climbing with Richard, we heard of a job felling trees in Beddgelert Forest in North Wales. Two friends of Arthur Williams were already working there. We could live in a caravan in the woods and work when and how we liked. It seemed an attractive prospect, living and working with Snowdon as a backdrop in fresh air scented with resin. As usual the reality was a grim disappointment. It was the wettest autumn for many years; for weeks the mountain was hidden in a cold mist, the ground was so sodden that logs sank in as we dragged them, the trees were small and far from the roads, the caravan leaked and our subcontractor, a shifty-eyed Welsh gypsy called Will, always gave us the worst sections to clear. After a couple of weeks Richard left but I soldiered on growing gradually more and more disillusioned.

It was during this time that the idea of marriage was first mentioned. Typically, I had hardly thought about it but the situation was becoming increasingly difficult, in a practical sense, for Maggie. 'Living in sin' sounds a ridiculous phrase now, but in those days it had force and meaning. We had already lived together for several years. I was committed to Maggie and loved her dearly. There was no reason not to tie the knot.

So Maggie visited me one weekend, we bought a ring at Caernarfon, the banns were read at Beddgelert, and at the end of November I left the woods, travelled to Calder Vale and we were married on a bright sunny day amidst snow showers which fell like confetti. We bundled up all the presents in the van, unloaded them in our tiny Manchester flat and then I left once more for Wales for the last few weeks of work. For a short time conditions improved, a frost cleared the air, Snowdon appeared snow-capped like some Himalayan peak, and with the seasonal bonus of Christmas treetops I earned a decent wage. By Christmas the work came to an end, and having had more than enough I returned to Manchester.

Then I got some good news. My degree was being granted, and several days later the parchment scroll was unceremoniously handed over in the porch of our tumbledown block of flats. I immediately set about applying for jobs as a biology teacher, and after several failures got a post at Stand Grammar School for Girls in Whitefield, north Manchester. Teaching a large class of girls was at first a daunting task but I tackled it with enthusiasm and after a while even began to enjoy it.

From Manchester I continued my climbing with a variety of partners, particularly Arthur Williams, Jud Jordan and Dave Little. I was also a frequent visitor to the Lake District when we stayed with Chris Bonington at his cottage at Woodlands, close to the Duddon Valley. They were happy times. Chris and Wendy were a close and loving couple; they had their first child and Chris was busy writing his autobiography and dashing about the country in his little Minivan delivering lectures. Despite overrun deadlines it was easy to drag Chris away from work. We enjoyed several memorable days, often with Mike Thompson, an ex-army comrade of Chris. Unlike Chris, the army had shown no eagerness to let Mike resign his commission but he was always resourceful and hit on the escape route of standing for parliament in a by-election. After Mike discovered this loophole, there was a rash of soldiers standing as candidates until the loophole was closed. Mike was stocky but with fine hair and a sensitive face, usually smiling with gentle amusement. He was the spotter of routes, had a fine eye for a climbing line, whereas Chris did not but was better equipped as a climber to do them.

On one occasion I was the instigator of the route; we piled into Chris's van and I told him to drive to Thirlmere without telling him exactly where we heading. A guessing game followed as to where the new route might be and eventually I told them – on Raven Crag, left of the prominent cave. It was a route I had looked at briefly on a cold spring day with Paul Nunn. I claimed first try but was in poor shape and hindered somewhat by climbing in large, worn 'RD' climbing shoes. I came back down to reconsider my strategy and Chris eagerly insisted on having a go. The climbing was steep and on small holds, but the most serious problem was a lack of runners. Chris attacked it with vigour, but soon the lack of protection began to slow him down and he began to toy with the idea of placing a peg. As belayers, standing safely on a ledge, we howled in protest as his resolve weakened. Finally, he slipped a piton straight into a slot by hand and that gave him enough courage to advance, get a thread runner and move over an overhang to a microscopic stance. He wanted to go on but I was furious with myself for allowing him to carpet bag his way up 'my route' and I forced him to belay to give me a pitch. I shouldn't have bothered. I made a mess of it. The groove was too green with lichen to move directly up, so I attempted to traverse left. I stood in a sling and was attempting to excavate a hold when the thin spike snapped. I grabbed my hold, hung for a second then struggled up and eventually reached round the final groove to the top. I named the route *Medlar*, after a stunted tree marking the start, despite the fact the tree was a sorbus – a whitebeam.

At Christmas Maggie and I went to Scotland with Chris and Wendy. First we visited Mary Stuart who lived with her children and animals outside Glasgow. Mary was a lovely warm-hearted lady who threw her house open to a large collection of climbers. Chris had arranged to meet up there with John Cleare and Eric Beard and then go north to join Tom Patey. We drank too much over New Year – inevitably – and drove north to Glencoe feeling worse for wear. There had been a heavy snowfall and after arriving Tom Patey announced in his mercurial way that we should go immediately to Craig Meagaidh. His choice had more to do with the hospitality found in the nearby hotel than his stated reason of better conditions. But Tom was a leader and, on his native heath, the bandmaster. I had heard much about Tom and read of his dashing exploits in the mountains of Scotland, Norway and Himalaya. He loved a good crowd, delighted in conversation, singing and playing on a squeezebox, and was generally the life and soul of the party. His face was appealingly rugged, his clothes dishevelled and he drove around in a battered Skoda, littered with Players cigarette packets, and mysterious pill bottles. Dr Tom liked to indulge.

When the pub shut we set off well-oiled, following Tom towards Craig Meagaidh, round Loch Leven, through silent Fort William, past the moonlit bulk of Ben Nevis to Spean Bridge and then over snow-packed roads to the Loch Laggan Hotel. Thankfully it was too late to rouse John Small the friendly hotelier so we slipped silently into the neighbouring ice-cold bothy where we huddled together deep in our pits. Next morning we breakfasted in style and in no particular hurry set off for the walk to Craig Meagaidh.

The broad glen was deeply covered in snow and our group was breaking trail, Tom to the fore, forging ahead with a bouncing stride, odd socks, no gaiters and a cigarette hanging from the corner of his mouth. 'Grand conditions,' he announced, chuckling to himself. There were six of us:

Tom, Mary, John Cleare, Beardie, Chris and me. Only Tom knew our destination, a huge cliff, a vast corrie of mica schist, cleaved by three gullies – the Posts. As we approached the base of the crag the snow became deeper and deeper until eventually progress became a fight through a bottomless, unstable white mass.

Tom loved uncertainty and ambiguity so in the face of hopeless conditions and too few hours of daylight he playfully directed us on to *South Post*. I was sceptical but Chris has a naive optimism and started struggling up the easy ground to reach the start of the climbing. After half an hour we had still not arrived. I was growing impatient and eventually suggested, quite forcibly, that we cut our losses and followed the others up the easier *Staghorn Gully*. Easy it was, but no less arduous, but after flogging upwards for several hundred feet we finally caught the others. Tom was hacking fiercely up the hard snow; Mary followed with difficulty. It was growing dark as bleak clouds crept up from the west bringing a gale. Chris and I overtook John and Beardie but he didn't rush up the last pitch. Tom had cut few steps and as the conditions worsened his footholds became covered and Chris had to cut more. Mary shouted and disappeared over the top as Chris made painfully slow progress. We all joined on one rope but by the time we were all assembled it was dark; blinding spindrift hissed and curled in mesmerising twists across the gently undulating summit plateau.

Tom and Mary had disappeared. We couldn't see their steps and none of us had ever been on the mountain before. We realised straightaway that descent would be a problem. Chris summoned us together for a council of war.

'Has anyone got a map?'

'No.'

'Has anyone got a compass?'

'I've got one,' murmured Beardie who burrowed in his sack and produced it. It was not much good without a map and for the next few minutes we guessed the configuration of the mountain.

Tom had told me the quickest descent was down an easy gully to the left but had also warned that it was easy to miss it and go down one of the Posts by mistake. We had also seen an easy col called The Window far to the right of the crag; we decided this would be the safest descent. The problem was locating the col in the poor visibility, especially as the entire edge of the corrie was heavily corniced.

We set off roped up, Chris in the lead; periodically we moved to the edge and Chris would cautiously peer over. On one occasion he crept over and thought he could see an easy slope below.

'Hold the torch Martin and come towards me and let me have a better look.'

I approached him while directing a shaft of light down until suddenly he shouted. 'Get back! We're standing on the edge of a bloody enormous cornice.' After this we weren't so keen to wander near the edge and probably as a result missed The Window and floundered on with only the vaguest idea where we were going. I was weary and beginning to feel the weakening effects of a recent bout of flu. I became a passenger, stumbling along tied between Chris and John. Eventually Chris located a less fearsome slope and we began to slide and scramble down huge unstable snow slopes fearful we would set off an avalanche. Finally, we reached the glen and were out of the wind at last but there remained many miles of trailbreaking in the pitch dark to reach the road. We stumbled on, seemingly without end, falling through holes in blocky scree or into streambeds. Suddenly I felt an overpowering tiredness. I slumped into the snow feeling strangely warm, almost in a state of euphoria, and I welcomed an enveloping unconsciousness. I dimly realised I was passing out and shook myself and stood up unsteadily. The others were standing around me and Beardie began to rummage through his sack again, bringing out a handful of raisins and a crushed Mars bar. I realised at once I was ravenously hungry and gulped down my share. Immediately I felt energy flow back into my limbs.

The rest of the way down followed more easily and eventually we dropped below the mist and spotted torches waving at the farm. A few minutes later we were in Tom's car, drinking coffee and then went back to the comfort of the hotel bar.

'Why didn't you follow our tracks?' he asked.

'They were covered in snow by the time we got to the top.'

'Just as well you didn't – I started down *South Post* by mistake.'

Tom and Mary had had their own desperate struggle. Mary had fallen into a stream and was completely soaked in icy water and Tom had started blacking out as I had done. It was caused he said by a sudden depletion of blood sugar and could have led to death by exposure.

My next trips to Scotland were less eventful but far more successful. I had started climbing with Jud Jordan, Arthur Williams and Dave Little. Jud was a member of the Black and Tans Club of Hyde. He was young, powerfully built with a broken nose and short dark hair. He had started climbing when very young, had found it easy then drifted away. But he was a tremendous natural athlete; he had taken up lacrosse and quickly mastered it, and later became an expert caver. For a short while he was sufficiently good at rally-car driving to be considered for a works team place. He had been working for his father as a window cleaner when he started climbing again and was very quickly doing the hardest routes.

At half term we drove up to Ben Nevis and walked in to the CIC Hut. As luck would have it, the place was empty except for a couple of English friends. We bedded down and awoke late next day to a perfect sparkling day. It was too late for anything big but we wandered up at midday towards *Zero Gully* to have a look. To our annoyance it was in perfect condition, but we had only brought our ice-axes – prehistoric in comparison to modern tools – and a rope. Without saying a word I started up the first pitch, nudging up a groove of crusted ice. I ran the rope out and without a belay Jud followed and effortlessly continued up perfect snow ice without even cutting holds. A couple more pitches and we were tramping up easy snow to the top.

The view was ominous with dark grey bands of clouds spread across a livid green sunset. A blizzard was blowing by the time we reached the hut and we decided to risk the wrath of the SMC rather than walk down. It was Friday night and sure enough a band of SMC hardies came crashing in later on after being blasted by gale force winds.

'Who are you? Have you booked?' was their opening conversational gambit. I explained our situation, climbed off my bunk and laid my sleeping bag on the floor. I told them politely they would have to throw me out but in the meantime I was going back to sleep.

'Wait till Sandy comes,' was the enigmatic response. I imagined a vast monster of a man tossing us into the snow like balsa wood cabers but when Sandy did arrive not much happened except that he asked what we had done; our answer obviously impressed them.

Our next adventure stands out as the finest ice climb I ever enjoyed. We were at Lochnagar in perfect conditions, and having climbed an easy route the day before, we'd got a late start to walk back up to have a go at *Parallel B*, a chimney and gully line first climbed by Jimmy Marshall. As far as we knew it hadn't yet had a second ascent. It was an extraordinary route, marvellous and varied, starting up frozen slabs with delicate climbing from one frozen grass tuft to another. The chimney was filled with ice but there were excellent runners in the rock. An icefall and then easy snow slopes led to the final steep section – two hard pitches, one up a verglassed groove and the other a vertical wall leading to the summit arête. It was dark by the time we reached the top but the air was still and in the starlight we had no difficulty finding our way down.

Throughout the spring and early summer I continued climbing with Jud, Arthur and Dave, partly because they were such fun. Arthur would drive us down in his huge Ford Zodiac and keep us laughing with an inexhaustible fund of jokes. We also managed to climb a number of excellent new routes on a wide variety of crags: *Aardvark* on Aran Benllyn, a girdle of Dinas Mot and the routes *Black Spring* and *Sexus*, and *Black Maria* on Gallt yr Ogof.

By the time summer arrived our van had just about died. I had made a loose arrangement to climb with Clive Rowlands again, but all hopes of repeating the previous year's success were dashed when Maggie and I arrived in Chamonix after hitching through France. Clive was with his girlfriend Steph in Tony Riley's car, who was clearly expecting to climb with him. Clive met us with obvious embarrassment. The weather was poor so Tony wanted to go to the Eastern Alps. There was no way we could follow, so it seemed best to cut ourselves off and find climbing companions on the campsite. I had no difficulty at first; Tom Patey was in Chamonix with a party of followers that included John Cleare and the Rhodesian climber Rusty Baillie.

Tom had been climbing with Chris Bonington as the British represent-atives of a *rassemblement* – an international gathering of mountaineers housed and fed at the expense of the French Guides' school ENSA. Tom and Chris had not seen entirely eye to eye. Chris wanted to go for the obviously prestigious routes while Tom was happy to pick off smaller but no less interesting new routes he had assembled in a large black scrapbook of photographs. When the course finished, Chris went off to the Vercors for a short spell. Now that the weather was improving Chris would be on his way back; he was nursing an ambition to climb the *Right-Hand Pillar* of Brouillard. The fact Pete Crew and Baz Ingle were after it added extra spice.

In the meantime Tom invited me to join him with Rusty and John on a new route to the left of one he had done with Joe Brown on the West Face of the Plan. He didn't know that Chris had already set off to do the same route with Lito Tejada-Flores, one of the American ENSA representatives.

We caught the first cable car to the Plan des Aiguilles and Tom galloped off up the frozen snow to the face with the rest of us in hot pursuit. He then soloed up the first buttress at tremendous speed. I followed while John and Rusty wisely roped up. Tom was renowned for his soloing; his soloing standard was just about as hard as he could lead on a rope – a comfortable HVS standard. Halfway up the initial pillar we came across a brand new piton, looked up, listened for a bit and sure enough heard voices: the loud babble of Lito and the stentorian tones of Chris.

'The bastard, he's stolen my route,' Tom muttered before springing up the next pitch.

Lito greeted us effusively, congratulating us on joining them. Chris was embarked on an icy groove system and after a chilly exchange informed us that the 600-foot corner would have to be pegged all the way.

'Good luck to you then,' Tom said. 'You deserve it. We'll bugger off right and join the other route.' So saying we traversed across mixed ground and reached the fine finish of Tom's previous route. No sooner had I got to the top of the rock and brought Tom up than he was sprinting up the final snow slopes solo. As soon as I had brought up John and Rusty, I set out to follow him and immediately wished I had put on my crampons; the snow was rock hard. Once started, however, it was impossible to stop. I was beginning to realise it was not always safe to follow the good doctor.

By the time I dropped thankfully onto the summit I was in a state of nervous exhaustion. 'Why didn't you put your crampons on?' I asked him.

'Because I forgot to bring them.'

We all set off down towards the Mer de Glace and then back to Chamonix. By the time we reached Montenvers it was dark and we were out of cigarettes. John and Rusty had had enough and elected to sleep out but we were both determined to carry on to Chamonix. As good fortune would have it I kicked against a cigarette packet; it felt heavy and turned out to be full. Tom was happy once more and we set off down the railway and through the tunnels to reach our tents by early morning.

A few days later we set out on an abortive attempt on the Chamonix face of the Fou, but the approach up a steep hanging glacier was too dangerous so we all decamped and went round to Courmayeur where we went up to the back of the Aiguille de Rochefort to have a look at a pillar only Tom had ever spied. Bad weather prevented us from starting the route and a few days later we had set off grossly overladen in his Skoda to visit the Dauphiné. I was ill with a sore throat by the time we reached La Bérarde so Tom and the others climbed La Meije while I took Maggie up the little Pic Nord des Cavales.

A few days later we were back in Courmayeur but the weather was still bad so we had a couple of day trips to the Gran Paradiso. The first time we set off to climb La Grivola, a fine pyramid dominating the Val d'Aosta, but mysteriously we missed it and went on to climb the Herbetet by mistake, resulting in yet another midnight marathon of a descent.

At the end of the holiday we found our way back through the tunnel to Chamonix to try and find a lift back to England. We were fortunate to bump into Nick Estcourt who was beaming with pleasure at having just done the first British ascent of the *North East Spur* of Les Droites. He had come out to the Alps with John Peck, an old friend who had unfortunately broken his leg. Now Nick had to drive John's clapped-out Morris back to Britain. Nick said he had another passenger for the trip home – Mo Anthoine. I knew Mo slightly from Wales but hadn't understood just how hilarious and quick-witted he was. Mo was from Kidderminster in the Midlands, fresh faced with a mop of black hair, his muscular upper body supported on surprisingly thin bandy legs. He had recently returned from a round-the-world tour and kept us laughing from Chamonix to East-bourne with his stories and ready jokes. It was a memorable journey home, first to Nick's parents in Eastbourne, where we luxuriated in piping-hot baths and had a splendid English breakfast. We visited Beachy Head, had a day at Harrison's Rocks and then Nick left us to return the car to its injured owner.

I was to see a lot more of Nick and grew to like him enormously. He was argumentative and a tremendous enthusiast. A weekend climbing with him was never dull. Although he was not a naturally gifted rock climber he made up for it with determination. His greatest strength lay as an alpinist. He had been climbing in the Alps since he was a boy and had deep know-ledge and experience, not things easily gained.

The following summer of 1966 I arranged to climb with Jud. We bought another van a few weeks before leaving for the Alps, but a crash nearly dashed our hopes for the holiday. On the way back from Wales with Jud and a black cat we had recently acquired, Maggie was driving with her usual verve but a rare error of judgment on wet roads sent us spinning into a very solid Volvo. There was a tremendous crash; the door sprang open and the cat shot out with a howl. Jud held his head while Maggie examined her severely dented van. I was leaping across the heather calling vainly for the cat. Fortunately the damage looked worse than it was. It was quickly repaired and we even found the cat, albeit the next weekend.

From a climbing point of view the trip wasn't hugely successful. Once again the weather was uncertain and since Jud was an Alpine novice all the decisions fell on me. As I expected it didn't take Jud long to get used to the scale of the Alps; for our first climb Maggie, Jud and I climbed the *Forbes Arête* on the Aiguille du Chardonnet. It was a delightful outing and Maggie's first real Alpine climb too, and we were doubly fortunate to have the route to ourselves as early morning cloud had put off all the other parties.

I was still interested in having a go at the Chamonix face of the Fou, an obvious and appealing unclimbed face easily accessible from Chamonix. Yet, once more, poor ice conditions prevented us approaching the face directly, so instead we traversed to it from the North Ridge of the Blatière. It proved to be an excellent little climb with several hard crack pitches, my first new route in the Alps. We both felt moderately pleased with ourselves but weren't quite so happy when several hours later we failed to find our way off the Rognon des Nantillons in the dark and were forced to sit out the night in a cold drizzle.

A week or so later we were back on the Blaitière but this time to rescue an acquaintance known as 'Nogs'. He had been hit on the head by a falling stone climbing the West Face. Fortunately his partner Billy Birch had been able to traverse off on one of the large ledges bisecting the face and descended the Nantillons glacier to summon help from the British climbing contingent. It was the usual tale; they were not insured and were unable to pay the expense of a rescue.

Some dozen of us left next morning and retraced Billy's steps until we found Nogs pale and spattered with blood, sitting forlornly on the ledge. He appeared to be fully conscious and made a tremendous effort to climb back down with our assistance. Once again we were blighted with foul conditions on the Nantillons rognon. Next morning Nogs was too weak to move by himself but we were able to piggy back him down to the cable car. Later that evening, when we visited him in hospital, we were horrified to discover he had a severely fractured skull and spent many weeks in hospital.

Jud's time was up but as Maggie and I still had a couple of weeks we decided to stay on in hope of a route or two more. I felt frustrated that after my successful season of 1964 two summers had gone by with so little to show for them. In this rather depressed state I came across Gary Hemming, a tall, loping American who had done the first ascent of the *American Direct* on the Dru and the South Face of the Fou. These routes had been done with methods and hardware developed in Yosemite, the first time that such techniques had been used in the Alps. Gary was a well-known character in Chamonix, a loner and hippy who lived mysteriously in a deserted barn.

I said I would love to do the Fou's South Face and to my surprise Gary said he too would like to do it again. He revealed that on the first ascent they had left fixed ropes to siege the face. He had fallen out with John Harlin on the tactics of the climb and over time the truth of how it was done was obscured. Gary had all the necessary hardware, the chrome moly pegs and so forth; the only thing he was not sure about was his own fitness.

He also wanted to see me climb, so we decided on the North Ridge of the Peigne. It was a suitably strenuous route following a fine corner crack, but Gary proved to be in very poor shape; his guts were bad, the route was littered with excrement and all in all it was a noxious experience. Gary had to postpone any attempts on the Fou and I then became ill with tonsillitis. Maggie packed up and whisked me off to the Adriatic, pleased to have me to herself for a while. After a few days' lounging and visiting the Basilica of San Vitale, Ravenna's exquisite Byzantine church, I began to feel better.

I dragged her once more back to Chamonix where the whole town was abuzz with drama; two Germans had been stuck high on the West Face of the Dru for several days in bad weather and showed no signs of being able to get down or up. The rescue services were slow to get moving so Gary Hemming was rushing around organising one of his own. He asked me to join him but I was still feeling weak and a cut on my foot had turned septic and so had to decline. Mick Burke, René Desmaison and several young French climbers formed his party and successfully rescued the Germans by climbing the West Face of the Dru and abseiling directly down the *American Direct*, the route Gary had first climbed with Royal Robbins. The rescue made him famous for a short while in France; his gauntly handsome face was splashed across *Paris Match*. He was sought out for interviews and hailed in the streets as a hero. It proved to be temporary halt to his decline. Already there were signs of psychological collapse, and several years later I was shocked but not surprised to hear he had blown his brains out in the wilds of Wyoming.

The summer of 1967 was more fortunate. I had been a member of the Alpine Climbing Group for several years, and when an invitation came for two British climbers to join that year's *rassemblement* at ENSA, I was delighted to be asked to go, along with the ACG's president Nick Estcourt. It was the perfect opportunity. For two weeks we'd have board and lodging, free cable cars and access to the most succulent bivouac rations imaginable. I made my way to Chamonix by train, met Nick and we made our way to the ENSA building where we were formally introduced to stern-faced alpinists from all over the world. The sombre atmosphere evaporated as we sat down to the first of many superb meals with unlimited bottles of red wine. We were soon chatting away in a mixture of English, French and German, establishing ties, swapping information. I immediately made friends with two Germans, Günter Sturm and Fritz Zintl, and the Austrians Peter Habeler and Martin Meier. The Poles could also speak English. Only the Russians, a watchful Muscovite Communist Party member, minder to the noted

Georgian climber Misha Khergiani, who had once climbed in Britain, were isolated by language. Every morning, before we had breakfasted, they were to be seen doing their regulation pull-ups and press-ups outside.

Making full use of the free facilities we shot up the cable car to the top of the Aiguille du Midi and climbed an enjoyable little route on its South Face called the *Contamine* to get acclimatised. We didn't start until late morning and our French minder insisted we give him a time next morning when we'd be back. We were back by mid afternoon that same day. Our next venture was on Mont Blanc du Tacul, once more using the cable car. We descended from the Midi in the afternoon and ambled up to the foot of the *Gervasutti Pillar*.

It is a fine looking route taking a steep narrow pillar of rock. For none too obvious reasons, apart from the fact it was not in the English guide-book, it had never been climbed by an English party. We climbed to a ledge, bivouacked and feasted on steak and fruit before settling down for the night. The climb next day was enjoyable and went without incident. The only unusual thing was finding an old rucksack that had half rotted away with ancient crampons inside. Our discovery reminded us that Giusto Gervasutti suffered his fatal accident abseiling off this route in 1946. Could this have been his rucksack?

Our next objective was the South Face of the Fou. This had been gathering a reputation for difficulty ever since its first ascent and hadn't yet had a second ascent despite some of the best French climbers having a go. I knew the route would suit my rock climbing ability but I wasn't sure about the extremely difficult artificial climbing on it – although I was certain it could be done with a lot less aid than on the first ascent. One section in particular intrigued me: the long diagonal crack which cuts across the face had a rating of A4, the most difficult grade for artificial routes involving huge 'bongs' and tiny 'RURPs', pitons the size of postage stamps. From the photos I was certain we could do this free. I'd have to; I lacked the specialised pitons to do it any other way.

We set out for the Envers Hut groaning under the weight of luxury foods, and by chance ran into Gary Hemming who was walking down the Mer de Glace. He felt the weight of our packs, and smiled. 'Ah, the Fou monster,' he said, and continued on his way, while we continued to the hut. As soon as we revealed our status to the guardian we were feted, our food was cooked for us and for the first time we experienced the luxury of using huts in the civilised French way, instead of being relegated to the cellar to fend for ourselves.

The weather looked superb so next morning we set out up the steep couloir to the Fou worried that the warm weather might cause avalanches down the gully. Our fears were justified; just as we cleared the gully onto a projecting rib, a huge block of snow the size of a car came hurtling down.

We had arrived at the start of the route, an intimidating place with a huge overhang cut by a diagonal crack, our first crux of A3 artificial climbing. It was the first time I had ever done any aid and I was slow and suspicious of my pitons. Fortunately we had a good selection of nuts with us and I was able to use them to great effect. The pitch consumed several hours and it was only when I had reached the top with my legs dangling on the edge that I could relish the situation. Nick let go of the sacks, which sailed out forever and then swung to and fro as I hauled them arduously to my stance.

The next pitch followed a steep crack. I was sure I could climb it free and I did so until suddenly I ran out of strength and was reduced to aid climbing the last section. We had now reached the great diagonal fault and faced a dilemma. Should we go on? We had all afternoon in front of us. Yet the crux lay ahead and there were no ledges where we could bivouac in comfort. We couldn't stay where we were, but there was a good ledge a pitch below where there was even running water. We stayed for a brew and inevitably stayed put for the night.

Next day I brought out my secret weapons, a pair of battered PAs, which I wore for the rest of the climb. It was joyful taking my boots off. Nick, although a good climber, insisted that I should lead. He would climb in boots, carrying the sack where I could not sack-haul. The arrangement suited me perfectly and although I ritually asked if he wanted to lead, he politely declined.

A hard free pitch brought us up to the famous A4 crack where an over-lapping roof broke the continuity of the slanting crack. I was certain I could free-climb round it by laybacking and set off full of trepidation over a vast drop to move boldly round the overhang. A couple of thin moves horizontally and I was moving round the crack, and above the angle relented into a perfect layback.

'It's a piece of cake,' I shouted gleefully.

'No, really?' Nick could scarcely believe me. He'd intended to get some photographs, but I was across the roof so quickly he didn't have time.

On the next pitch I once again avoided artificial climbing by choosing a slightly different line. A final mixed free and artificial pitch landed us on this section's only good ledge – big enough for us to lie down. This we promptly did, falling asleep in the blazing heat of the day. It was such a delightful spot and the weather was so perfect that there was no need to rush at all. We were enjoying the route so much we had no wish to end it and so made ourselves comfortable, cooking up the last of our food.

The remaining climbing was as fine as anything, up a system of thin cracks, the only flaw in a perfect sweep of the most glorious granite. We reached the top by late morning, sat and, plagued with thirst, brewed up on the first snow patch before making our way down. We caused a small sensation on our return to ENSA, such was the route's reputation.

For several days we rested, swimming and allowing our chewed up hands to heal. Maggie and Carolyn, Nick's wife, had now joined us and although they had to camp out while we lived in luxury, we did our best for them by smuggling out slices of meat. The *rassemblement* ended with a vast champagne buffet presided over by the illustrious Maurice Herzog, who had climbed Annapurna in 1950 and had become the French Minister of Sport. Everyone came, the girls wearing miniskirts, the latest fashion, much to the excitement of the Guides, and we ate and drank as much as we could. The weather was bad for a few days and Nick took Carolyn to the seaside to escape the rain, but when things improved we set out on our last route, the West Face of the Pic Sans Nom, another route in Tom Patey's book of climbing possibilities. He had tried it half-heartedly with Joe Brown and mentioned it as a worthwhile possibility. The route lay on the peak adjacent to the Dru, overshadowed by its North Face and not as clean or obvious, but nevertheless a good-looking climb.

We dossed at the Rognon du Dru, busy with climbers heading for the West Face, and then approached up a dangerous couloir right under the Dru's North Face peering with great interest at the Dru Couloir, a superb ribbon of steep ice running down between the Grand and Petit Dru. We were almost tempted to change our objective and have a go at it but were prepared for rock climbing, not ice. Avoiding an unpleasant loose chimney system, we followed a line up the face broken by ledges. A huge flake provided the only way past a steep wall and this proved to be the pitch of the climb, requiring a strenuous and bold layback with scant protection. Nick said it would even be 'Extreme' on Curbar.

Some mixed climbing followed and Nick excelled on this, moving with great sureness. Then we performed a tension traverse and as evening fell reached a ledge below the final dome where the rock rose up, smooth and steep, for the final 500 feet to the summit pinnacle. We bivouacked, pushing some rocks off to make the ledge bigger, and after taking a wary look at clouds gathering high above us, I tucked my head down and slept fitfully. In the middle of the night I got a dig in the ribs.

'It's snowing,' Nick said.

'So?' I answered shortly. 'Why wake me?'

'I thought you might like to know.'

I did not want to know; my peaceful sleep had been interrupted. But Nick was a worrier who always had to voice his feelings, and he needed to share his concern. I preferred to be an ostrich and bury my head away from the outside world.

Later a cold wind woke me; the sky was grey and an early storm was approaching. After a hurried brew I set out to reach the final pitches on the summit block. A shallow groove provided the only weakness. It was much harder than I hoped it would be, and I was very short of pitons to protect myself. The wind was getting up and I was buffeted around, causing me to hurry. Two more difficult pitches followed and then the angle eased and we crept to the summit, cowering from the wind and peering down over the Dru.

It was imperative to descend at once but we were soon disagreeing about which way to go down. A horrible couloir of grey ice was the obvious descent but it was steep and unpleasant and after some argument we took to the broken rocks at the side. For a while it was easy but then we ran into a band of smooth, water-worn slabs down which we had to abseil. We arrived in the middle of the slabs with just a couple of pitons left. I placed one, wrapped a new sling through it and set off. Nick joined me and we pulled at the rope, which instantly became stuck. I heaved at it, leant out and tugged again and suddenly the whole rope came free and I was toppling backwards. The sling had snapped. I shot an arm out blindly, my palm hit a solution pocket and I froze in a position straddling the slabs, teetering on the point of over-balancing. Manoeuvring precariously, I regained my feet and padded back up to Nick who had stood there horrified and helpless.

Without stopping and allowing myself to consider my narrow escape, I set up the next abseil and we gained easier ground. The storm was now upon us and we descended with furious speed to reach the Charpoua Hut just before night. We gained the hut as snow blotted out the visibility and the first bolts of lightning flashed around us. For the first time in two days we allowed ourselves to relax, safe in our bunks with the knowledge we had done our route and escaped the storm.

Next morning the sky was clear but the mountains were dusted white with snow. The season might have been over, but I could now look forward to something new – my first expedition, to the granite spire of Cerro Torre, in Patagonia.

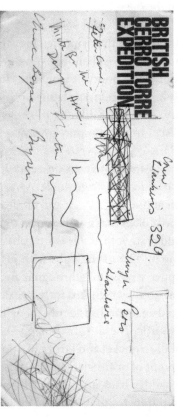

ELEVEN
CERRO TORRE

It started in a pub in Derbyshire, during an Alpha Club dinner. As usual the pub was packed with climbers, for the most part gatecrashers assembled from far and wide in anticipation of a riotous late night's drinking. They were not to be disappointed. The pub was decorated, perhaps unwisely, with an antique suit of armour, the perfect prop for an evening's jousting. It only stopped when the distraught manager threatened to cut proceedngs short, and the armour was returned. Martial arts gave way to trials of strength but these also came to an end when the bottle walking resulted in a badly lacerated wrist. Next was tug of war, which removed a lavatory cistern at one end and the leg of a grand piano at the other. The club secretary began to look nervous, but at last the glass was swept away and the record player brought out. As the thump of rock music blasted out and the dancing began, the drinkers converged on the bar.

Battling through the throng, I caught a pungent whiff of Gauloises smoke and homed in unsteadily on its source: Mick Burke and Pete Crew.

'I suppose you want one?'

'Well if you're offering ... '

'We were just talking about expeditions.'

'Moaning you mean.'

'It's time we went on one,' said Mick.

'Yes, we noticed. Getting a bit grey to be the Wigan wonder-boy for much longer.' But Mick was very serious.

'It's no good waiting for an invitation to pop through the letterbox. If you want to go on an expedition then organise one', Pete said with characteristic bluntness.

'That's exactly what I've been thinking, but idle buggers like me and Martin need a human dynamo, a whizz-kid like yourself to whip us into action.'

'OK. Think of a fourth and decide where to go.' Everything Pete did was done quickly. He climbed fast, drove fast, talked fast and made decisions with impetuous speed.

'It's no good thinking about the Himalaya,' I said. 'They're closed from end to end. What about the Andes? The place that fascinates me is Patagonia. Have you seen the pictures of Fitz Roy and Cerro Torre? Then there's the Paine.'

'Clough's mob is going down there to climb The Fortress. Do you know of any good unclimbed peaks then?' asked Mick.

'Not really, but the peak which grabs me is Cerro Torre.'

'Been climbed', said Pete.

'I know, but we could do a new route on it. Anyway I've heard a few interesting titbits about it recently.'

The history of climbing Cerro Torre was already being questioned. Walter Bonatti and Carlo Mauri had tried it from the Patagonian ice cap in 1958 while a rival Italian team including Cesare Maestri had looked at it from the other side. The following year Maestri pipped Bonatti to the prize when he returned with the Austrian ice climber Toni Egger. They succeeded, Maestri claimed, after an incredible epic, which involved nego-tiating hundreds of feet of near vertical ice. On the descent everything started collapsing. Ice sloughed off and they were forced to abseil from bolts drilled into the granite. Halfway down, Egger was swept away by an avalanche and Maestri, practically demented, only just escaped death when he fell the last hundred feet to the glacier. Unfortunately Maestri had no photos, no one saw them during the last few days and Egger's body was never found. After I explained all this, Mick and Pete looked uncertain.

'So where does that leave us?' Pete said.

'Nowhere really, but the lack of evidence has caused some doubt to creep in. I heard Lionel Terray refer to it as the greatest feat of mountain-eering ever. But he added a telling comment: 'if it has been climbed'. I even spoke to an Italian who was frankly doubtful about the ascent. Anyway we'll never know. But if we climb it, it will be a fantastic achievement – first ascent or not.'

'Sounds interesting,' replied Mick, after a moment's thought, and Pete also nodded his agreement. 'I know who would be the ideal fourth man – Dougal Haston. Don't expect him to do any organising work though; he's worse than Martin.'

Mick and Dougal had just completed a successful winter season during which they had climbed the Matterhorn's North Face. They were both based at Leysin in Switzerland. I had met Dougal a few times but hardly knew him well. He had seemed easy enough to get on with and he would certainly add strength to the team. He was, in almost every way, the opposite of short, cheerful and outgoing Mick. Like a lone wolf he had retreated from the pack. He was tall, lean, quiet and introspective. His climbing record was impressive and proved his toughness and ruthless determination. Pete knew him by reputation only but events conspired to bring them together for the outside broadcast from the Old Man of Hoy a few months later. A phone call to Dougal confirmed his interest in the expedition so we now had a team, an objective and a year in which to raise money and organise supplies.

The year passed quickly. Having enjoyed one of my best Alpine seasons, I set about organising the food. Pete meanwhile took on the main burden of expedition work; for him it was a frantic year during which he charged headlong into a disastrous marriage, had a child, wrote several guidebooks, bought a house and just about kept down his regular job as a computer programmer. Fortunately, his appetite for work was prodigious. He worked feverishly at his various tasks all day and much of the night sustained by black coffee and innumerable Woodbines. Even by Pete's standards he was overdoing it, burning a candelabra of candles at both ends. But as a result of his efforts the expedition became a certainty; money had been raised from the Everest Foundation, the *Sunday Times* and the sale of postcards. Food and equipment came flooding in along with the Welsh rains of autumn, which nearly inundated the expedition stores packed away in Pete's outhouse. The job of packing now began, and only when the boxes were finally sealed and their destination stencilled did the reality of what we were about to do sink in.

Before the task of expedition planning was complete two additions were made to our party: Peter Gillman, a correspondent for the *Sunday Times*, and a leading Argentinean climber – José Luis Fonrouge. We had no choice about taking on a reporter; the *Sunday Times* was sponsoring us. But to take on an unknown climber could be risky. Another snag was that food and tentage had been planned for four climbers, not six. Even so Fonrouge was obviously an able climber and his local knowledge would be invaluable. Also, he hinted that we could use his father's private aircraft to ferry goods and personnel, although in fact this never happened. Peter Gillman had already worked with Dougal and Mick on the Eiger Direct saga. Although at first this seemed a fortuitous choice it did in fact cause difficulties. Ever since Peter and Dougal had collaborated in writing a book on the Eiger Direct, relationships had been strained and this underlying tension was never resolved, making it difficult for Peter to be accepted fully as an expedition member.

By November Dougal and Mick were ready to leave England by boat along with all the equipment. Before they departed we were invited to make a television appearance on *Blue Peter* along with Pete's brainchild, a large gaudy red plastic igloo. We stood around it rather sheepishly being blasted with artificial snow, fog banks of dry ice, and wind machines recreating the Roaring Forties while a hyperactive John Noakes scurried in, out and around the igloo asking all the familar questions.

A dock strike nearly caused a last-minute disaster but we managed to load the equipment just in time to beat it. Our only loss was a case of whisky, a choice malt which no doubt provided Christmas cheer to the striking dockers. At the end of November the boat arrived at Buenos Aires and it was suddenly time to quit work, give up my secure niche in the world, say goodbye and fly out to Argentina. It was a moment I had looked forward to with excitement and any misgivings were soon swallowed up in the thrill of departure and the anticipation of the coming adventure. It was a good time to be leaving Britain, in the middle of a cold and damp November at the onset of a foot-and-mouth epidemic, which would more or less stop climbing for months to come.

Even the long air flight was for me a new and exciting experience; to be transported within hours over the tropics and into the southern hemisphere, to fly over Rio de Janeiro and the jungles of Brazil and, finally, to circle the huge sprawl of Buenos Aires was an extraordinary experience in 1967. It was a journey from winter to summer and we emerged from the plane like butterflies from a cocoon, discarding coats and savouring the deliciously warm scented breeze and brilliant sunshine.

Gerhard Watzl met us off the plane. A stocky Tyrolean who had emigrated to Argentina, Gerhard was now president of Centro Andino de Buenos Aires. Thanks to him we walked straight through customs and into a waiting jeep. Driving us into the city, Gerhard told us the others were already underway to Patagonia by ship and lorry, loaned to us by Royal Dutch Shell under the kind auspices of the Everest and Kangchenjunga climber George Band, who worked for them. The road was bright with colour, lined with jacaranda trees dropping their blossoms like violet confetti. The city was huge and modern, a subtropical New York with skyscrapers packing the horizon. The city was alive, bursting with vitality, the pavements thronged with strollers and from the sidewalk cafes came the irresistible sound and smell of sizzling steaks.

We only had a few days to enjoy the fleshpots and for most of that time we were rushed off our feet making one hectic errand after another. We visited contacts, charged around vast cavernous government offices in quest of permits and were fortunately helped by an Argentinean climber Nestor and his fiancée Aida. He frightened me to screaming point with his lunatic Latin driving, and even Pete, a manic driver himself, was impressed.

Our final chore was to lick and stick several thousand stamps onto post-cards, something which kept us busy right up to the time when we could catch a plane to Rio Gallegos at the southernmost tip of the world.

We had barely accustomed ourselves to the heat of Buenos Aires before we were plunged into a wintry landscape of freezing windswept desert. As we arrived, Rio Gallegos was hidden in a sudden snow squall, a reminder that only the Antarctic lay beyond. Immediately we headed for Pinguino Electricidad, workshop and home of Pedro Kucharzewski, president of the local Andean club and someone used to helping itinerant climbers. The beat-up taxi rattled over pot-holed roads, through a corrugated iron suburb and stopped outside a decrepit shack with a weatherworn penguin and faded lettering that was barely discernible. Pedro greeted us, and asked us who we were and what we wanted, obviously relieved to discover that in German we had a language in common. We filed in through his tiny workshop, threading our way around piles of dynamos and generators and entered a hot little back room cluttered with more electric gadgets, half-stuffed penguins, books and Indian artefacts, all covered in a thick deposit of dust. A gas fire spluttered in the corner and on it sat a black kettle.

'Coffee? Sit down.' We stood awkwardly wondering exactly where we should sit until he impatiently kicked some rubbish off a bunk and waved us down.

Pedro was a Ukrainian by birth, a refugee who had been pushed around Europe first by the Nazis then the Russians, a dark passage in his life, which he was reluctant to discuss. He made his escape to South America as a young man, living first in Buenos Aires before moving south. Now in middle age, he was an eccentric divorcee who worked a little and pottered around a lot in pursuit of his many interests. He was cheerfully down at heel with three-day stubble and a shabby suit.

'You must excuse this,' he said, waving airily at the surrounding chaos. 'I am divorced; it needs a woman. But stay, make yourself comfortable, one of you can share my bed, and there's the bunk.' Pete and I accepted his offer but Peter Gillman retreated happily to a hotel courtesy of his expense account.

'You are lucky our club has been out on its crab-fishing trip,' Pedro said, showing us a couple of monster king crabs, which we soon demolished. Pedro knew everything and everyone connected with Patagonia and he promised he would easily fix us up with a lift to the newly declared Fitz Roy National Park.

Next morning he took us on a tour of inspection, although there was precious little to see. Poor little Rio Gallegos, unlovely and unlovable, swept continuously by scouring winds with a sullen grey Atlantic one side and a featureless shingle desert the other. It was an outpost, inhabited by exiles: Russians, Germans, Yugoslavs and Welsh. They had all come to seek a new life in this hard and hostile region. A few succeeded in making their fortunes but most, like Pedro, had not. Pedro, for all the intensity of his anti-Russian feeling, still yearned for his mother country. He welcomed a constant stream of expatriates and one night as I crept in late I found him with a friend, sitting in the dark reminiscing and sighing, head bent and close to tears. Perhaps the wide pampas, the space and empty skies evoked memories of home?

Pedro's efforts quickly secured a lift for us on a lorry with a load of building timbers. The flat-bed lorry called at four in the morning and woke us with a blast of its horn. We crept out of the house leaving Pedro muttering in Russian to himself in his sleep and climbed thankfully up onto the back. We nestled down in sleeping bags and the truck pulled out of the deserted streets and sped out across the pampas into the grey light of dawn. Away from the shabby town the desert country was strangely attractive in a wild and empty way. The ground was sparsely covered with low thorny bushes, and tufts of golden corion grass. The plains rose up in step-like mesas and on the western horizon was a distant gleam of snow on the sierras. There is only one product from the pampas: sheep, farmed in vast estancias visible for miles with their wind breaks of tall green poplars.

The country was full of wildlife. Hairy armadillos scuttled across the road like clockwork toys, rheas watched us warily before running off stiff necked on bouncing legs. Guanaco popped their heads over hummocks and stared stock still with curious eyes. We passed shallow salinas, pans of salty water crowded with waders. Where there was fresh water the land was lush and green and ducks and upland geese abounded.

By evening we reached a tiny village, tired and dusty and glad to flop down in the police post beside a rack of oiled and gleaming rifles. We were introduced to *yerba mate*, a bitter but stimulating drink sucked up from a gourd through a silver straw. The drinking of mate is a social ritual and after each suck the gourd is refilled with hot water from a small kettle and passed on until the infusion is spent. Little was said but at each suck the large sweating policeman would give a happy grunt.

Next morning the road became rougher and the ride more dusty but we were rewarded with an unforgettable view of Fitz Roy surging up out of the plains and riding a wave of storm clouds like a giant breaker. We were soon driving alongside a huge turquoise lake – Lago Viedma – fed by the continental ice cap, but by late afternoon were lost in a maze of rutted roads. We reached a river and sat perplexed until a gaucho rode lazily up and directed us to a newly built bridge. That night we slept in an estancia on piles of fleeces and emerged next morning to see the whole range revealed in perfect sunshine, jagged and stark against a brilliant blue sky. We crossed the Rio de los Vueltas and suddenly we were at a campsite. It was an idyllic spot on soft green grass among gnarled Magellan's beeches with a stream close by. The view was staggering; Fitz Roy dominanted with its huge but graceful bulk while Cerro Torre stood apart, an incredible crooked splinter of ice-encrusted rock. The two peaks lorded it over a cluster of satellite peaks like the king and queen of the range.

I felt too elated to just sit and wait for the others to return to camp and on the spur of the moment went dashing along an indistinct trail leading up a valley in the direction of Base Camp. I assumed I would meet the lads coming down, or at least find Base Camp. The walk started as a gentle stroll but soon I was trotting and then running flat out through dark and ancient forests of beech, leaping over rotten logs, crunching through dead leaves with green parrots screaming abuse and black woodpeckers appearing and disappearing mysteriously. I had little idea where I was going but didn't care; I was entranced. I reached a plain, gaily dotted with yellow calceolaria, and carried on running, over old moraines and around Lago Torre, until I was on the bare ice of the glacier. I slithered and leapt from boulder to boulder, but at last came to my senses and sat down to consider where I was going and why. A shadow passed over me and I looked up straight into the red and predatory eyes of a huge black condor circling low. I realised I was exhausted; I had eaten nothing. It was time to go.

The walk back was less euphoric. I was weak with hunger so gorged myself on berries and dandelions, trusting they weren't toxic. Finally, I stumbled into camp. The others were all back and beginning to wonder where the hell I had got to. It was good to see Mick and Dougal and interesting to meet José Luis Fonrouge but I was too tired to talk much and collapsed into bed.

Fonrouge was not typical of the Argentineans we had met so far. He was reserved with a slightly haughty manner and in appearance tall and blue-eyed with aquiline features; he resembled the stereotype of an old-world aristocrat. His family was certainly rich and Fonrouge, as far as one could gather, had never had to seriously earn a living. His English was excellent as was his German and French. He had made the 'grand tour' of Europe. His climbing record was impressive and he had made many first ascents in the Andes including a fine route on Fitz Roy. His knowledge of the area was proving to be useful; already he had acquired packhorses and most of the gear was already shifted to our Base Camp at the head of the valley below Lago Torre.

The camp was set in deep forest, a gloomy and enclosed site without views, but it was well protected from the ferocious winds we were soon to encounter. Straightaway we started carrying loads up the glacier, endlessly modifying our route through a huge and unstable moraine. We had barely settled on the best option when the weather changed. A mantle of grey cloud settled over Cerro Torre and the winds burst over the range with a fury that was difficult to believe. We found ourselves lifted off our feet, bundled over and deposited like bits of waste paper. Any forward progress was impossible; when the oncoming blasts announced their arrival with a roar like an express train leaving a tunnel, we would lie down flat and clasp a rock before sprinting for the cover of trees between gusts.

When the storms finally abated, Dougal, Mick and I set off from base to establish a site for a higher camp. We took a minimum of gear and for the first time approached the base of the peak via a long curling snow arête; it gave us time to examine the start of the route to the col on the South East Ridge. Our main concern was finding somewhere sheltered so we were extremely pleased to stumble on a large ice cave, which proved ideal. Feeling heartened, we dumped our loads and raced back down as the bad weather closed in once again.

Christmas came but we were ill-tempered and dispirited with enforced idleness. Fonrouge became restless and moody and suddenly departed in our lorry for Rio Gallegos while we sat it out. For the first time it rained heavily and this turned to snow. Our firewood became sodden, making cooking difficult; life was unpleasant. Pete volunteered to get a sheep and while he was away we drank one of our few bottles of Argentine whisky. It tasted awful but we swigged a glass down, and then another and soon it began to taste better.

I recovered consciousness sometime later, retching downstream when Pete came into view, manfully slogging up through the dripping forest, a huge carcass on his back. We had assumed he would spend a few days at the estancia and I now realised with a shock of guilt that the booze was finished. He swore at us with feeling but Dougal was still plastered and stony-faced while Mick was offensively good-humoured about it all. Pete's revenge was to cut and cook a choice slice of meat whilst we could only look on, hungover and feeling ill.

Two days later I awoke, immediately sensing that something was different.

It was strangely still and quiet; no trees creaked or groaned, a fly buzzed in the dappled sunlight and smoke rose from the embers in lazy blue curls. We had slept undisturbed and late. The morning was perfect. Leaping out of our pits, we packed up in a frenzy of activity and were soon charging up the glacier, happy at last to be on the move. For the first time we could fully appreciate the magnificent situation with the Torre on one side of the valley and Fitz Roy on the other. We reached the ice cave in the afternoon, hacked out a tent platform and prepared the first few pitches of the route to the col.

Next day Dougal and I set off to fix ropes. It was hard going up slabs of rock covered in deep snow. We climbed slowly until we had run out all our fixed rope, whilst the others were busily ferrying loads of rope and food up to the ice cave. We were determined to reach the col the day after so set out especially early with as much rope as we could carry. The weather was beautiful and the surroundings awe-inspiring. We were hemmed in and overhung by huge sweeps of granite capped by glinting cornices of ice. We stared in disbelief at one enormous hanging mass of ice and moments later heard an explosive crack as it began to drop. We ducked instinctively, then looked up and watched as millions of tons of ice cascaded down with slow-motion grace – right over the Maestri and Egger route.

'What about a photograph?' I blurted out after we had stood watching in horrid fascination for what seemed like minutes. Dougal fumbled in his sack and produced his camera, but too late to catch more than the last wisps of pulverised ice.

'Christ, I hope we don't see too many of those', I said unnecessarily; Dougal's face cracked into a wry smile. We were only too well aware of the summit ice 'mushroom'. In bad weather the howling westerly winds laden with moisture plastered the peaks, and the mushrooms grew. In good weather they dropped off. Subconsciously we had tried to ignore their menace but now we had been forced to acknowledge it.

The final section to the col went easily and with the last of the fixed rope we'd brought up, I climbed the final snow slope to the crest and whooped with joy. The view was sensational; 3,000 feet of air at my feet and then the graceful curling glacier, beyond which were the green forests of Base Camp, the huge lazy blue expanse of Lago Viedma and the tawny pampas. To our right the East Face of the Torre plunged in one clean vertical slice for 5,000 feet and beyond that the vast decrepit face of the Adela, rumbling in its constant state of decay. It was a moment to savour; we had arrived somewhere. Above, the South West Ridge rose clean and steep. We climbed the first few pitches and then ran out of equipment and time. We retreated in a light snow flurry, pleased with ourselves and happy to relinquish the lead for a few days.

Fonrouge had returned from his Christmas holiday and was now ready to climb with Mick. Pete would take over after a few days and in the meantime we would return to base and collect the last fixed rope. Fonrouge and Mick climbed up to the col next day but high winds prevented any progress. Then Pete and Fonrouge went up but once again, made no progress but this time they had brought bivouac gear so they cut out a grotto and camped. Next morning the weather was fine again; we could hardly believe our luck and felt uneasy that two days had drifted past without progress. Fonrouge led and Pete followed carrying a huge load of fixed rope. The climbing was superb at grade V and A1 and they made good progress to complete the first step in the ridge. While this was happening, Mick dug a snow hole big enough to accommodate everyone. The leads were rotated next day and, since everyone was to have two days out in front, Mick joined Pete in pushing up the next difficult section – a series of expanding flakes. Strangely, Pete the expert rock climber was reluctant to lead.

Above this point the ridge dropped back a little; it looked easy for a bit until the final crazy headwall encrusted in overhanging ice which seemed to defy the laws of gravity. But if this didn't look promising we were prepared to do a girdle of the mountain and climb the ice gullies on the West Face. Dougal followed up the rotation, replacing Pete, and on the ninth day of our climbing spell he reached a final steep step on the ridge. It was difficult to decide which route to take. Above it was hard and steep then easy-angled; to the right was a foul, iced-up chimney exposed to avalanches.

It was now my turn for some action and I found myself gripped with excitement. Would the weather hold? If it did we were surely in with a chance. I delayed my departure to collect mail brought up by Peter Gillman but as usual the letters were all for Mick. Pushing up the glacier, I reached the ice cave in good time so decided to push on up to the col. I was carrying a heavy load of food, the snow was soft and as the sun set I reached a particularly awkward section a few hundred feet from the col. It was a spectacularly beautiful evening; the Torre stood up like a flickering orange flame whose colour gradually changed to a dull reddish-purple. Fitz Roy and Aiguille Poincenot were the last summits picked out like two fiery beacons set in an indigo sky. Later, a full moon rose and dotted the Torre like a monstrous letter 'i'. I lay down in a state of rapture, intoxicated; in my imagination I was already stepping onto the summit.

I woke early and made short work of the final slope to arrive just as the lads were cooking breakfast. They were delighted to receive mail and told me about the route ahead. I decided to rest for the day but soon regretted my decision as I lazed around camp, frustrated at the slow rate of progress. So I busied myself enlarging the cave and cooking supper and then waited. By evening Dougal and Mick returned. It had been a hard day's climbing up overhanging cracks and up holdless walls that needed skyhooks and plenty of nerve. During the climbing Dougal had dropped our bolt kit; we could only hope they were superfluous.

Next morning we rose early and packed a complete set of bivouac gear; we were prepared to make a push for the summit. I set off first and felt full of energy as I swarmed up the fixed rope over the most tremendous exposure. Reaching the last ropes, I had time to appreciate the difficulties of the climbing before Dougal reached me. The next pitch was up a rib and it looked easy enough until I actually started up it. I was forced to traverse far to the right and then gain the crest by a crack, which petered out into a snow balcony. The crack was easy enough but the last few feet were desperate and I only just managed to claw my way up as the snow collapsed and left me holdless. I was left on a bare whaleback ridge. Three hours had passed. 'What's it like, Martin?'

'Well, easy-angled, but not much on it,' I replied.

How little there was I soon discovered teetering upwards on tiny holds to a miniscule ledge and belay. There was no anchor to speak of but it was time to take a risk.

'Come up Dougal, but take it carefully please.' He joined me, looked at the belay and smiled.

'Well, here goes. Looks like Etive slabs without PAs.'

The problem was short but tantalising. 30 feet above us was a well-defined crack; somehow we had to reach it or give in. We could not contemplate failure so soon, so Dougal examined the rock minutely, hoping to find a hold or two, which might just suffice. There were none, however, and in a last despairing gesture he hammered in a tiny RURP and swung up on it to stand there forlornly. I watched with horrid disbelief, half expecting to be plucked off my tiny stance at any moment. It was a place for one good bolt and, as if to remind us of the fact, Mick began to sing – to the tune of The Man who Broke the Bank at Monte Carlo.

'You can see him swinging up the ropes/with an independent air,/a man who doesn't care,/high up in the air./He's the man who dropped the bolts on Cerro Torre.'

Then Mick shouted, 'Hey, up there! Have you seen the weather coming in?'

We were too engrossed with our few square feet of rock to notice ominous plumes of high cirrus streaming in from the Pacific. It was time to retreat, obtain some bolts and have another go. We reached the col and then the cold damp wind hit us. Low cloud engulfed us and horizontal sleet stung our faces. The sickening realisation hit us; the fine weather had ended, we had had our fair chance and not taken it. Dougal and I stayed the night at the col. On the way down we tied off all the ropes and led one into the snow cave so we could find it later. By morning the weather was worse so we beat a retreat to the tent in the ice cave below. Here we met Pete who had rushed up with more bolts in vain. It was pointless staying so we all retired to base to sit it out.

It was in effect the end of the expedition, although we did not realise this. For 40 days the storm howled, the trees groaned with strain and our high hopes were blown away relentlessly with the wind. Time passed – a limbo world of sleep and reading, contemplation and cooking around a smoking fire. Occasionally we roused ourselves to action, cutting wood, rebuilding shelters or crystal hunting, but then there was nothing more to do. Eventually we slipped into a diurnal rhythm playing bridge all night and sleeping most of the day.

Eventually the storms subsided in their usual abrupt way and the Torre emerged like a ghost from its shroud. I had stupidly twisted a knee a day or so before and now had the double agony of watching everyone set off to see what remained of our route. The weather was finally set fair and for two days I had visions of a summit assault going on without me. Such selfish daydreams were soon shattered. Dougal came crashing through the undergrowth in long and angry strides. His face told me all I needed to know. The others trailed in, long-faced and exhausted. The ropes were ruined: cut, frayed and tattered. The ice cave had completely disappeared. It had taken a full day to reach the col, Mick was injured and blood-spattered, and Pete completely demoralised. A wet and cold bivouac had been the last straw. Our equipment was strewn all over the mountain. We could go home.

In the weeks that remained we evacuated all that we could salvage and I made a last mountain foray – an attempt at Cerro Adela which was defeated a few hundred feet from the top by another brief but violent storm. A few days later we were bumping across the wide pampas in an empty lorry on our long journey home.

We had failed. I didn't expect to climb Cerro Torre but I had allowed myself to hope. I was disappointed, inevitably, but I also felt we had woken from an enchanted dream, a dream which persists in my memory. The Cerro Torre will for me always be a symbol of impregnability, desolation and titanic natural forces too great to be diminished by man.

Boysen: *As Don and Dougal started back down the ridge, after helping Nick and me to install ourselves in the box at Camp 4, Don warned: 'Don't mess about lad, and don't let those ice towers stop you.' We felt very much alone that night, perched in our box on the crest of the ridge, full of wonder at the most incredible situation of our lives.*

We woke early. I felt like Jack the Giant Killer as we stepped into the shadow at the base of the first gigantic ice tower. A gangway led left to an obvious ice couloir, but this was covered by a mass of deep rotten snow, whose angle was such that the slightest movement started it sliding. I soon gave up trying to climb it, turning instead to an interesting hole on the right flank of the tower. I launched myself into this, headfirst, barely managing to contain my panic, wriggling and squirming until my head and shoulders popped out into the sun and air fifteen feet or so round the corner. Using an ice screw to give myself rope tension, I climbed out of the tunnel and surveyed my surroundings.

TWELVE

CRASH

The decision to give up on Cerro Torre was made with bewildering suddenness. One moment we were steeling ourselves for a final effort up the ridge with thoughts – nightmarish ones – of the summit mushroom, the next we had let it all go. Tension was replaced with resigned good humour blended with a pervasive sense of anti-climax. With Cerro Torre dismissed from our thoughts, all we wished now was to get home as fast as we could. A mad scramble ensued that saw us abandoning all manner of equipment we couldn't easily carry and within a couple of days we were on a truck, bound for the coastal town of Comodoro Rivadavia.

All planes back to Buenos Aires were full so we caught a slow bus that bounced and wallowed across the dusty pampas for two days. Back in Buenos Aires we basked in pleasant autumn sunshine, eating huge steaks, lounging around our cheap hotel and sorting out onward travel. Dougal was bound for Canada to meet up with his future wife Annie, who was working there as a nurse. Mick had decided to travel overland by rail and road to the United States. Pete and I were flying directly home to our wives.

We arrived at Heathrow on a cold overcast February day and slipped unnoticed back into England. There was no fuss or hint of the publicity that had marked our departure. There was no media interest in an unsuccessful expedition. Our failure no longer hurt so much; the disappointment soon faded and I clung on to the good memories. For me Cerro Torre was a beginning – the overture to many other adventures. For Pete there was less to ease the pain. He had done the lion's share of organisation and fund-raising yet had been oddly ill at ease on the mountain. His marriage was foundering, his future uncertain. Cerro Torre marked the end of his interest in climbing. Within a year he was divorced and with a typically abrupt change of direction had resumed his studies at university, this time in archaeology. He applied himself with his normal energy and intellect, made his mark and vanished as a climbing force.

Maggie and I were now living in a large unfurnished flat in a huge mouldering Edwardian mansion overlooking Alexandra Park in the once prosperous area of Whalley Range. Buena Vista, as our block of flats was grandly named, suited us just fine, and with its views of the park's trees and duck ponds there was little hint of the surrounding meanness. We lived above another climbing couple, Mike and Judy Yates, and shared many a weekend climbing with them. Nick and Carolyn Estcourt also arrived in the Manchester area, moving into a flat in Alderley Edge.

Shortly before we got home from Patagonia, the foot-and-mouth epidemic had ended. While we'd been away, climbers had been severely restricted in their access to the countryside. Now we were free to climb at will and Nick grabbed me to visit the hills of Wales, then plastered in snow and ice. Together we managed some notable climbs, including *Shallow Gully* on Lliwedd and several testing new lines on the Black Ladders. I was feeling lean and fit and looking forward to the climbing year to come.

As spring slowly approached I transferred from snow and ice to rock climbing. Mike Yates and I managed several first ascents on the gritstone of the Roaches area in Staffordshire. It was at the Roaches we arranged a fated visit to Don Whillans and his wife Audrey at Love Clough in the Rossendale Valley. A group of climbers, including Arthur Williams and Tony Lyons, had made occasional visits over the last few years. They were always jolly evenings with a few beers, a game of darts and much laughter. Tony particularly enjoyed the visits. Don, who enjoyed his reputation as a 'hard man', was soft hearted when it came to Tony. You couldn't help but feel affection towards him; he was tiny, entirely without means with half his lungs removed as a consequence of TB. He lived with his family in extreme poverty and yet was the most infectiously cheerful person one could imagine. The cheerfulness was not as deep-seated as it appeared; a few years later we were shocked to hear he had cut his own throat.

On this occasion Mike and Judy Yates, Tony Lyons, Maggie and I visited Don. After the usual evening out followed by a generous supper, made by Audrey, we set off home with Mike driving his Volkswagen Beetle. I was directing Mike through the dimly lit streets of Cheetham Hill, which I knew from my commute to and from Stand when I'd been teaching there. We overshot my usual junction so I directed him to take the next one. The following moments are obliterated from my memory – or perhaps mercifully suppressed since I still react with instinctive horror to any similar road configuration.

Mike failed to stop at the junction with the main road, which was poorly lit and unsigned. A police car, travelling fast, hit us broadside and we were smeared across the road. There was darkness and then I recovered a flickering consciousness. I was aware of a searing pain in my spine, lights flashed and there were voices.

'Here's another one. Watch him – looks like he's done his back in.'

I concentrated fiercely, wriggled one big toe then the other and passed out again into an all-embracing blackness.

Suddenly I was aware of bright green neon lights. A rubber mask was slapped on my face and I felt suddenly as if I was drowning, but from within. Desperate, I gasped tiny mouthfuls of air. Maggie's voice floated from somewhere. She was asking after me. A hard kernel of realisation hit me. I was fighting for survival and every breath I took was vital. Panting ferociously, I became aware of white figures floating around me. A tube was forced down my throat. Sucking and bubbling noises followed, and with relief I breathed more easily and once again heard Maggie's voice demanding to know what was happening to me. Then it went dark again.

I awoke next morning from drugged sleep and asked a nurse how Maggie and the others were.

'She's in the women's orthopaedic ward with a broken leg but she's fine.'

It was only later that the full extent of our injuries was made clear. Maggie had a broken femur ominously close to the knee joint, broken ribs, clavicle and pelvis. Typically her concern in the immediate aftermath of the accident had been for me, despite her own awful injuries. I realised perhaps for the first time her intense love for me. Perhaps it was the only good thing to emerge from the accident. The others were fortunately less injured; Judy had a cracked pelvis, Mike a damaged kidney, Tony a broken toe.

For my own part I had a compression fracture of the spine, several broken ribs and severe lacerations of my back. It appeared I had been tossed out of the car, and had skidded across the road into a slum clearance waste site. My clothes were ripped and shredded off my back, half my skin was removed and I was studded with glass shards and muck. My broken ribs had caused both lungs to collapse, there had been much internal bleeding and I was lucky that Salford Royal Hospital had been so close. I was now stuck to the sheets, lying prone on my suppurating back. Three times a day I was carefully rolled over. The sheets were peeled off my back and I was sprayed with antibiotic. All the while, I chewed my pillows to stifle my screams of pain.

After a fortnight I had made a good recovery; my wounds had healed over and the danger of blood poisoning was over. I was still immobile but feeling stronger by the day. Twice I was wheeled in my bed to Maggie's ward by giggling nurses and to the ribald amusement of the women's ward, the curtains were drawn around us. We just about managed to hold hands – a welcome point of contact – but we found it strangely difficult to speak.

There were too many conversational pitfalls, too many things best left unsaid. That Maggie was having a difficult time was obvious. Her leg was in traction, bone grafts had been performed to maintain her leg length but her other injuries were painful and prevented movement and this resulted in a large bedsore. She had never been a good patient.

After three weeks I was ready to leave hospital for bed rest at my new adopted home with Maggie's parents in Calder Vale. A few days before Easter I was driven north; lying backwards, barely able to move or see outside, I directed the ambulance through lanes bordered with freshly green hawthorn into the Bowland Fells. I scented the pungent peat and heather again, and was filled with hope and gladness. My recovery progressed wonderfully. Soon I was taking short walks and looking with longing at the distant Lake District.

It was not until the end of June that Maggie was allowed to leave hospital, her leg encased in an iron caliper. I met her as she was discharged. She was weak and pale, depressed and a little frightened of leaving the sanctuary of hospital. We visited our abandoned flat, struggled up the stairs and were overwhelmed with emotion as we saw the chaos within. Everything was as we had left it: books and papers lay opened where we had just finished reading, clothes lay waiting to be washed, a neglected plant had been toppled over by our cat and had struggled to regain the vertical. We burst into tears and hugged each other.

Maggie knew that all had not gone well with her leg. The bone had mended but when she came to try and flex her knee, she found it was impossible. The muscle of her thigh had grown into her new bone; her leg wouldn't be fixed until the muscle adhesion had been removed. This required the removal of most of her thigh muscle – the so-called quadriceps release operation. The outcome of such a procedure was worryingly uncertain.

It was a depressing time in our lives. I wondered if I would be able to climb well again with my aching back; Maggie wondered if she would ever be able to walk properly.

The summer passed slowly. I learnt to drive at last but we spent most of our time being looked after in Calder Vale and making regular visits to Manchester and Salford Royal. I visited Chris Bonington, now living in Cockermouth, and was briefly involved in his 24-hour marathon of climbing and driving from Ben Nevis to Scafell and Snowdon. I enviously watched Chris and Mike Thompson swarm up the Flake Crack of *Central Buttress* on Scafell before they sped south to Wales.

Both Maggie and I were in too much pain to do much so we were particularly grateful to our friends Colin and Ann Mortlock who put us up in their house in Pembrokeshire. All the time I could feel my strength and mobility returning but for Maggie there was little improvement possible. No amount of physiotherapy could move her knee joint; the operation would have to take place and the prospect hung over us. By the end of summer we had cheered up a little. Although Maggie was still confined to her caliper she had regained some of her old strength. She was ready to resume work at her school while I found a job at a college of further education.

When our friends returned from their Alpine holidays I was ready to start climbing again. Nick Estcourt and his wife Carolyn had moved house to Hale in south Manchester and he revelled in the opportunity to climb on gritstone. He was soon climbing better than he had ever done and I held his rope and struggled up behind him suffering acutely from dizziness and almost blacking out on a couple of occasions. I tried hard to forget how easily I had waltzed so recently up the same pieces of rock.

I was not particularly happy in my new job, teaching biology at an elementary level, largely to reluctant day-release students. Only two classes were stimulating, the first an adult group of mainly older women who worked with gratifying intensity and the second a class of mainly recent immigrants and school drop-outs intent on joining or re-joining the academic ladder.

In late December Maggie went for her quadriceps release operation. I awaited the result with trepidation but at last news came. The operation was successful, but to what extent would remain unknown for a month or so. At last there was a glimmer of hope. Maggie began to flex her knee and exercise with enormous perseverance. It paid off. Everyone was amazed how well the operation turned out, but it was mainly down to her own determination to walk again. The price she paid was a severely scarred and disfigured thigh.

I knocked on the door of Mike and Judy Yates's flat below ours, happy to report the success of Maggie's second operation. The news was received with stunning indifference and so ended a previously happy friendship. We blamed no one for the accident but it was agreed we would make a claim against Mike's insurance, since he was judged guilty of careless driving. Legal proceedings were briefly discussed and initiated by Maggie's father whilst we were still recovering. This news was badly received and the seeds of misunderstanding, guilt and distrust were sown. Mike and Judy soon moved out of their flat and out of our lives.

By New Year our lives had almost returned to normal and at last we could turn away from our ordeal and start to plan ahead. In the Whit holiday we made our way to Scotland with Dave and Toddy Alcock. I had climbed with Dave on and off for several years and together we had put up many new routes in Wales and Scotland. He was an engineer who later switched to be an outdoor instructor, rising to become director of Plas y Brenin. He was physically strong with a quiet sense of humour, utterly reliable and a superb climbing companion. Toddy was lovely and bright with a loving nature and enjoyed walking and the outdoors as much as Maggie.

We started off in Skye, camping on the foreshore of Elgol where we encountered Hamish MacInnes, his wife Cathy and Ian Clough. Hamish, already the *éminence grise* of Scottish climbing, was on the hunt for new routes and his normal playful and cagey self. Ian, amiable and friendly as ever, was not allowed to divulge their next location. It was not hard to guess; we had come to look at the Great Prow of Blaven so weren't surprised when we arrived at its foot to discover the others ready to tackle the obvious tricky crack system that bars the way. As the 'gritstone crack specialist', I was elected to lead a joint party in what proved to be a classic climb which we instantly named *Jib*. We followed this up with some other good routes, and expeditions traversing the local limestone sea cliffs, probing into the sea cave famously explored by James Boswell and Dr Johnson on their Scottish journey.

Hamish's party then 'disappeared' to another mystery location, but it just so happened that Tom Patey had mentioned to me that the cliffs of Fuar Tholl near Achnashellach and the Kyle of Lochalsh were huge and virtually unclimbed. I guessed this might be their next venue so we drove round to find their encampment on Platform One of Achnashellach station. We pitched our tents alongside theirs, causing them considerable surprise when they returned to camp from their day's climbing. No one seemed too bothered about our unusual campsite; the trains were infrequent and we received friendly waves from train drivers and passengers alike.

The crags were indeed large but made up of less than perfect quartzite. We managed a couple of decent routes while Maggie strengthened her leg walking the hills with Toddy and Cathy MacInnes.

That summer we returned to the Alps, and I climbed with Nick Estcourt. It was not a particularly successful season. The weather was very uncertain and I was still feeling weak and slightly giddy at times. I became short-tempered and mildly dissatisfied. Somehow the spontaneous joy I had previously enjoyed in the Alps had slipped away. The mountains were overcrowded and somehow diminished. Even so we managed a couple of good routes, climbing the Brown and Whillans route on the West Face of the Blaitière and the North Face of the Dru, where we were caught by Jack Street and Paul Nunn. We exited together and made haste to descend before a violent electrical storm hit us. Soon we were caught in icy rain as lightning flashed dangerously close. Once I was almost electrocuted as the charge travelled down our sodden abseil ropes. It was fortunate I knew the route down as the rain turned to snow, visibility vanished and I found myself leading a ragged army of retreating climbers to the safety of the Charpoua Hut.

The storm raged all night and when we emerged from our shelter it was obvious from the accumulation of new snow that there was little chance of climbing again for some time. Back in Chamonix we met up with Chris Bonington who was now working for the *Daily Telegraph* magazine as a photojournalist. Over beers and coffee in the Bar National we began to discuss possible expedition ideas – and learned that Chris was about to leave the Lake District and set up house in the Manchester area.

Nick and I had long mulled over the problems and prospects of initiating expeditions. We had each been on one, Nick to Greenland with a Cambridge University team and myself to Patagonia. We wanted to go again, preferably this time to the Himalaya. Unfortunately political upheavals had for several years closed the Himalaya from end to end. The Indians and Pakistanis were daggers drawn over Kashmir. The Chinese still disputed with India over the Tibetan frontier and tiny Nepal was anxious not to offend any of its quarrelling neighbours. There seemed no alternative but to go to the New World. Alaska was becoming the favourite.

As we were loosely formulating our ideas, Chris and Wendy arrived in Manchester. Chris had decided he was too far removed from his main source of income living in the Lake District. He was tempted to move to London but eventually compromised and they bought a house in Bowdon, a fashionable suburb on the southern edge of Manchester. While his house was being got ready they moved into Nick and Carolyn's small flat. In these cramped conditions it was natural that expedition plans were shared and it was even more natural that Chris should assume control of the venture. Chris was a seasoned expeditioner, with successful ascents of Annapurna II and Nuptse to his name. Moreover, he loved organising, so when unexpected news broke that Nepal was opening to climbers again, Chris immediately abandoned Alaska and began sifting through Himalayan peaks. The Nepalese government had limited his choice, and not surprisingly Chris plumped for a 'big one', by which he meant one of the 8,000-metre peaks. Although they had all been climbed at least once, no one had yet tried to climb them by one of their huge face or buttress routes. The stage was now set for this to happen. Almost simultaneously, the Germans were planning to climb the Rupal Flank of Nanga Parbat, the Japanese were getting ready for Everest's South West Face and the French for Makalu.

Exactly how we settled on Annapurna is now hard to recall. I had already heard tell of the South Face; Dennis Gray had talked of it in my presence, comparing it with the North Face of the Grandes Jorasses because it was similarly huge and divided into buttresses. It had appealed to me immediately and I mentioned it to Chris. Chris had subsequently thought of it and was in the process of gathering information from his Annapurna II companion, Jimmy Roberts. Jimmy was an ex-Gurkha officer living in Kathmandu and an expert on the Himalaya. Chris also sought the advice of David Cox and Roger Chorley who had been with Jimmy Roberts and Wilfred Noyce when they climbed Machapuchare, a lovely peak commanding a grandstand view of the South Face. Their comments were hardly encouraging. They talked of incessant avalanches and its awful size. Jimmy Roberts was more helpful; he had an exceedingly sharp eye for a route. He wrote to us with his assessment:

'The South Face of Annapurna is an exciting prospect – more difficult than Everest although its approach problems are easier. Certainly it will be very difficult indeed, and although I am not an oxygen fan, it seems to me that the exertion of severe climbing at over 24,000 feet may demand oxygen.'

A few days later, just after Chris had moved into his new home, Nick and I were summoned to have our first look at a slide of the mountain which had just arrived. Chris pointed his projector at the bare white wall of his sitting room and the picture flashed up, almost filling the wall. A thoughtful silence settled over us as we studied the face. I shuddered, both in anticipation and in fear; sitting in my armchair, my imagination took flight, transporting me to the chaos of cliffs, ice ridges and rock buttresses. It seemed hopelessly large but then I began to rationalise, to identify features, to divide the face into manageable slices and to link one section with the next by means of a tenuous line of possibility.

The face was larger than anything we had seen, 10,000 feet in vertical height and many miles wide. Like the Grandes Jorasses there were three main buttresses standing out proudly from the rest of the face. The left-hand one – equivalent to the *Walker Spur* – led directly to the summit. This was the best and most obvious route and it appeared to be the safest. The climb would be complex with icefalls at its base, followed by fluted snow ridges, serac walls and massive, steep rock bands. It was the equivalent of three hard Alpine routes stacked on top of each other with the added difficulty of high altitude.

'Well there's a line of sorts, but it looks bloody hard,' I said eventually, conscious that someone had to break the silence. Suddenly we were all talking in an excited buzz.

'Harder than Nuptse', declared Chris with emphasis.

'Harder than anything yet done,' Nick pointed out correctly. We peered and poked, sharpened up the focus and argued volubly – an easy matter if Nick was present – on the best hypothetical line and the most obvious dangers. We continued our discussion throughout that damp and gloomy day, ending up inevitably in the pub, where we sealed the fate of the expedition over several pints of beer. In a state of lubricated enthusiasm we agreed that this was going to be 'the expedition' – the first to tackle a major Himalayan mountain by its most challenging route. We would be making history. All we had to do now was climb it.

Chris shouldered the task of organisation with enthusiasm. He enjoyed the wheeler-dealer aspect of it and attacked the problem with the same zest he had for games of skill and cunning. Perhaps he was yearning for his days at Sandhurst, when he had dreamt of military success while studying strategy and tactics. As the expedition grew, Chris assumed more and more the role of leader, distancing himself from his friends. This was followed by a curious metamorphosis. His attitude changed; his eyes became glazed and narrow and his voice and inflection altered subtly so one felt one was being addressed by a senior officer rather than an old companion. He began to lecture us as though we were part of an audience rather than his friends.

The first and most important task Chris set himself was selecting the team. No longer were we a small expedition; the scope and scale of the challenge, combined with his success in raising money, dictated a larger personnel. It was natural that Chris should choose from his friends; they were more likely to be loyal and as they were all well-acquainted with each other would constitute a well-knit group. This was a lesson Chris had learnt on Nuptse, where weak leadership and selfish individualism had caused strife and argument at high altitude.

There were several obvious candidates, perhaps none more so than Dougal Haston. Chris had been involved with Dougal on the Eiger Direct climb and had witnessed at close hand Dougal's single-minded drive and fierce determination, which had seen him through to the summit. It was on the summit of the Eiger that Chris had waited for Dougal in a snow cave with Mick Burke. Mick was by no means a brilliant climber, nor did he share Dougal's joy in self-mortification, yet he was extremely tough and ambitious and when the chips were down he showed a dogged determination. One of his chief virtues was his cheerfulness and humour. Chris must have appreciated this, and, having survived several foodless days in a snow hole with Mick, had no doubts about selecting him.

Another obvious choice was Ian Clough. Chris and Ian had shared many adventures. Together they had climbed the Eiger's North Face and the *Walker Spur* on the Grandes Jorasses and been to the Towers of Paine in Patagonia. Ian was immediately likeable with an agreeably relaxed and smiling manner, which sometimes hid his deeper feelings. As a mountaineer, he was tremendously experienced, dependably safe and had demonstrated his ability at altitude on an expedition to Gauri Sankar with Don Whillans.

Perhaps the most difficult choice facing Chris was that of Don Whillans as deputy leader. Don was acknowledged as one of the greatest post-war British climbers. His record of routes in Britain, the Alps, Andes and Himalaya was formidable. In the Himalaya Don had had bad luck. On Masherbrum he had failed within reach of the summit due to the illness of his partner; on Trivor he had succumbed to a mysterious paralysis high on the mountain, which prevented him from going to the top. Subsequently he had narrowly failed, with Ian Clough, to climb a long and arduous route on Gauri Sankar in Nepal. Since then he had done very little, and a combination of soft living and hard drinking had made him less than fit and startlingly overweight. Despite the fact that Chris and Don had shared several notable ascents, including the Central Tower of Paine and the *Frêney Pillar* on Mont Blanc, their relationship was uneasy. They respected each other's abilities but they did not particularly like each other. Nevertheless, they did complement each other; Don's main contribution was that of down-to-earth common sense. He had a fine grasp of the practicalities of climbing and, perhaps most valuably, he was a sound judge of route difficulties and danger. Chris, brilliant as he was at getting the expedition off the ground, was not a good judge of a mountain. He needed Don's experience and wisdom, especially as this was his first expedition as leader.

I had known Don for several years and had a tremendous respect and fondness for him. We had climbed together in Wales and Derbyshire when he was still fit and keen and I was impressed with his ability. Although he was very short he was powerfully muscled; his movements were worked out with athletic precision. He had long shared the accolade with Joe Brown of being the finest of British rock climbers and had already secured his reputation with a collection of new routes – *Sentinel Crack, Forked Lightning Crack, Serth* and *Extol* – bearing his hallmark: boldness, difficulty and strenuousness. He was no longer the hard-climbing, hard-bitten man of legend; he had matured and mellowed fractionally, developing an ever-sharper wit that made him a marvellously entertaining companion. True, he was a man who did not change his opinion too readily; once he had taken a dislike to someone the dislike was permanent. He had very little time for Nick, and with Mick there was a constant mutual needling, which erupted occasionally into violent argument. But I liked Don enormously – enough to overcome the odd meanness of character, which could and often did cause offense.

Another choice, one that pleased everyone, was Mike Thompson – an able climber and a cultured and amusing companion. His task was to obtain food and plan a variety of food packs. This he did with flair and originality setting aside one or two horrible mistakes. Bearing in mind Napoleon's dictum that an army marches on its stomach, the food obviously did its job. We got to the top, but only just.

The expedition still needed a doctor, but the obvious choice of Tom Patey made himself unavailable for selection. I was there when he examined the slide of the face, and was alarmed when he pronounced the route a 'death trap'. In this prediction he was basically incorrect, an uncharacteristic error for so canny a reader of mountain topography. With appalling irony, Tom was killed abseiling off a Scottish sea stack called The Maiden two days before the South Face was climbed.

Our doctor when we finally got him was Dave Lambert, who came from the north-east of England, and was in many ways archetypal of the area, with a down-to-earth sense of humour, which augured well. The only worrying thing was a certain clumsiness combined with an eagerness for performing surgical operations in the field. He was particularly proud of his delivery forceps and fervently hoped to use them. As it turned out he was lucky to come with us at all after falling off a climb and breaking both wrists. They barely mended in time, but Dave was to prove a valuable part of the team, cheerfully slogging away carrying loads without complaint.

Raising a team of climbers is not that difficult, but raising money for them to go usually proves more awkward. Chris was extremely fortunate in having the services of George Greenfield, a well-known literary agent who dabbled in promoting various yachting and polar adventures; he represented Sir Francis Chichester and Ranulph Fiennes among others. George was my idea of a wicked uncle; dark, suave and mischievous, he oozed reassurance and confidence and his voice had the smooth purr of a cat anticipating its cream.

It was at George's suggestion – 'to open up the American market' – that Tom Frost was invited to join the expedition. Tom was one of the most famous American climbers at the time and had put up many new routes in Yosemite. He had climbed in the Himalaya and Andes as well as the Alps, where he climbed with John Harlin. He was at the forefront of technical developments with a masterly grasp of technical details and, with Yvon Chouinard, was in the process of revolutionising climbing equipment. I couldn't imagine a better choice, for Tom was a truly good man. He had the lean and loose-limbed appearance of an honest marshal and his face creased easily into a dazzling smile. Such saintly perfection can sometimes be hard to bear but not in Tom's case; he lightened it with a pleasant self-deprecating sense of humour. He was a Mormon and, therefore, denied common stimulants, but never once did he complain despite being exposed to our cigarettes, whisky and bad language. Altogether he was a wonderful advocate for Mormonism; he led by example and never tried to push his faith on us. Perhaps he realised he was on stony ground when it came to evangelising.

The expedition became financially secure when the Mount Everest Foundation and Royal Geographical Society decided to underwrite our costs. George Greenfield now had to recoup this money and this he did mainly through contracts with publishers and ITN and Thames Television. The television companies sent a four-man team to cover the climb to send in news items and make a documentary. We were very fortunate with our team. They were all marvellous characters, who coped easily with the hardships and discomforts of the trip. John Edwards, the producer for Thames, was an ebullient character, Alan Hankinson wrote the news items for ITN, while Jonathan Lane and John Soldini filmed and recorded sound. Alan turned out to be a mountain enthusiast who had long dreamt of climbing in Nepal. He worked at ITN on an obituary library and joked darkly that we were all on file. Somehow he had wangled his way out on the trip, but writing news items barely took any time and he much preferred to help on the mountain making useful carries. Despite being the oldest expedition member he showed a youthful enthusiasm that occasionally had to be restrained.

The final member of the team was Kelvin Kent, our Base Camp manager. He had recently been attached to the British Ghurkha headquarters in Nepal and as a fluent Nepali speaker was to prove invaluable for sorting out Kathmandu paperwork and recruiting porters. He had a deep love of the people and country and his energy was already legendary.

Equipment was boxed and parked at a mill building in the Lancashire Pennine country near Don's home in Rawtenstall. In early March it was shipped off to Bombay where Don and Dave were due to meet it. Everything was going to plan until we learned that the boat had broken down at Cape Town. We had no idea how long it would take to repair. Chris departed immediately to India to 'pull strings', which, as Don drily pointed out, would only be any use if they were attached to the boat. Fortunately the situation was not as desperate as we feared; the boat was repaired, and would only be a fortnight late. A British Army expedition was also preparing to climb Annapurna by the original route taken by Maurice Herzog and Louis Lachenal, and, by borrowing some of their food and some tents from Jimmy Roberts, and by taking out some of our own gear we would be able to manage until our supplies caught us up.

THIRTEEN
ANNAPURNA

We arrived in India and flew straight on to Kathmandu. I was aghast at the poverty, squalor and smells but gradually I learnt to accept and then to enjoy the city. Hiring great black Chinese bicycles, we set off ringing the bell to force a passage through streets crowded with people, cars, bikes and truculent cows. We threaded our way haphazardly through a maze of lanes overhung by balconies of delicately carved wood, popping out unexpectedly onto squares dominated by graceful pagodas and carvings of gods adorned with garlands and offerings of food.

The city was extremely colourful and always busy; Kathmandu is still the great meeting place for the diverse peoples and tribes of the Himalaya. The local people responsible for the fine craftsmanship were Newars. They were as neat and graceful as their art, farming the rich paddy fields of the valley, now largely built on, and transporting their produce in baskets slung on poles in the Chinese manner. The Tibetans were the most obvious ethnic group. They were tall, big-boned, and adorned with turquoise and coral; they had the jaunty wildness of pirates. Coming in from the hills was a constant stream of porters laden with huge loads of food, wood and other produce bound for the bazaars.

The city seemed preoccupied with religion; it was a local centre for both Hindus and Buddhists. There was a profusion of temples and even the scruffiest streets boasted marvellously sculptured statues of gods and animals that would grace any museum but were here taken for granted. Almost every week there was a festival of major or minor significance; it was Holi when we arrived and delighted children squirted us with coloured water and roared with good-natured amusement at the result.

Although the country was terribly poor and disease was everywhere to be seen, the people seemed cheerful and honest. One afternoon when Tom and I cycled out to the temple of Swayambhunath he discovered he'd lost his wallet containing all his money and passport. He naturally assumed the worst but it was returned to him within 24 hours.

While some of us enjoyed a few days' sightseeing, Chris and our Base Camp manager Kelvin Kent were furiously busy sorting supplies and transportation. At last we flew to Pokhara, on the lakeshore of Phewa Tal,

with the staggeringly beautiful backcloth of the Annapurna range, dominated by the nearest peak of Machapuchare – Fish Tail – a double-topped
mountain of flawless grace.

The morning we left, I woke to the subdued whispering of porters lined
up in orderly fashion to be allocated a number and load. We ate breakfast,
the gear was packed, Kelvin gave a quick pep talk and all of a sudden we
were moving off in the deliciously cool air.

Of all the mountain walks this one lives in my memory most clearly.
I found myself surrounded by so much beauty, so many new sights, new
flowers, birds and people; I could hardly contain my delighted enthusiasm.
We were fortunate to have the former Gurkha Jimmy Roberts walking
with us. He suffered greatly from an arthritic hip that slowed him down to
a painful limp but it was worth slowing down with him; he was a mine of
information, knowledgeable about the fauna and flora, religious customs
and mountains of the Himalaya.

These hills are the Ghurkha heartland, the region of the Gurung, Magars
and Pun tribes who make up the outstanding fighting troops that still
form parts of the British and Indian armies. Our porters were also from
the area and they were a tough and cheerful crew, living simply off the land
and fashioning themselves shelter or cutting wood with their wickedly
crooked knives. The head porters, the *sirdars*, had been in the British Army
and one old porter, barefoot and dressed in rags, had fought at El Alamein,
Monte Cassino and countless other battles in distant countries for a cause
that must have seemed equally remote.

At first the walk followed broad cultivated ridges following along the
Kali Gandaki river. Every so often we would plunge down through subtropical jungle, past trees with flaming red flowers on which parakeets
chattered noisily. Climbing higher we entered rhododendron forests full
of cream and pink flowers. The path was for the most part well-made of
great paving slabs and it was particularly good on the climb up to the
prosperous and well cared-for village of Ghandruk. Here we were royally
entertained; most of the porters lived or had relatives there, and were
proud to offer us hospitality.

From Ghandruk we dropped into the wild, steep gorge of the Modi
Khola, an area of virgin forest of bamboo and rhododendron. It was damp
and misty, festooned with mosses, epiphytes and orchids trailing from
every branch. Above us Machapuchare towered like a sentinel guarding
the approach to the sanctuary – the glacier basin in which Annapurna lay.
As we climbed up the gorge it became cooler, the forest thinned and great

winter snow banks and avalanche cones blocked the path. It was at this point that we met Don Whillans, who with Mike Thompson had gone ahead of the main team to recce for Base Camp. We spied Don's camp on the far side of an enormous and ominously new avalanche trail and hurried to hear his news while the porters, many barefoot, struggled to find footing in the hard snows.

Don met us with a familiar nod. He was slimmer and fitter and filled with a new eagerness. Having waited for his audience to gather and for silence to fall, he got straight to the point.

'It looks even steeper than the photograph.' Don paused for this to sink in, and then, with his usual genius for timing, restored our sinking spirits, adding, 'but after I sat down and looked at it for a couple of hours it leant back a bit. It's going to be hard, but it'll be alright.'

It was no more or less than expected but we were reassured that our route seemed reasonably safe. The bad news was that there was still an enormous amount of winter snow. This would make it difficult for the porters and so prevent us from establishing Base Camp as near to the mountain as we wished. Next day we made our way into the Annapurna Sanctuary until we were above the trees and wading through deep snow. The porters were incredibly strong, being constantly encouraged by Kelvin and the sirdars to keep going another half hour or so. I had to admire their stoic endurance of the hardships and discomfort they were suffering, especially as they were dressed in inadequate homespun cloaks, with bare legs and just sandals on their feet. To add to their misery, damp grey cloud enveloped us and it began to snow. A site was chosen, tents flung up at great speed and Tukten our cook, together with his cook boys, blew at damp, smoking fires while the porters waited to be paid before dashing off jubilantly back to the warm valleys. At last, we were together for the first time as an expedition, on our own in a cold uncomfortable world of snow and rock. The picnic was over.

We started with a chaotic sorting of equipment; most of it had yet to arrive so we improvised and adapted what we had. Fortunately we all had vapour barrier boots, a sort of glorified Wellington that was ideal for walking around our soggy temporary base. Our food was also yet to arrive, so we were fed a rather simple diet of rice and fish supplemented by marvellously substantial compo-rations provided by the British Army expedition on the north side. Nothing for the rest of the expedition tasted as good as the Army's tinned apple puddings and spotted dicks.

As soon as the weather cleared, we examined the mountain and decided where our permanent Base Camp should be sited. Nick was given the task of surveying the face, measuring the height and extent of various features. The television crew overhauled their equipment and began unobtrusively to record our activities. Kelvin as always was busy, trotting round camp like an eager terrier, being so industrious that it made everyone else seem lazy. Don and a few others walked up the glacier and discovered a safe site for Base Camp some three hours nearer the mountain. Slowly the business of ferrying gear up the mountain started.

Chris wanted the climbing to start, but we were greatly hindered in this until the main body of equipment arrived. Meanwhile, the first gentle jockeying for climbing partners had begun. Don and Dougal had already gravitated toward each other and it was assumed that Nick and I would climb together, as we had been doing for several years. This suited me, but it may have been a mistake. We were by this time ready for a change and there were signs of growing irritation between us. Chris as usual had not decided; he preferred to keep things loose so that he had as many options as possible.

By the time I was told to move up to Base Camp, the first camp on the mountain had already been established and for the next weeks I felt like one of the back-up team, a plodding foot soldier vainly trying to reach the ever-advancing front. Already a shortage of manpower was becoming obvious. Our Sherpas – the sirdar Pasang Kami, Pemba Tharkay, Ang Pema, Mingma Tsering, Kancha, and Nima Tsering – were too few so every member of the expedition, including Alan Hankinson, ostensibly part of the film team, was employed ferrying equipment.

As Chris, Nick, Don and Dougal sorted out a route through the next confused and contorted section of glacier which guarded the base of the spur, the Sherpas, Alan and I made carries to Camp One and the next day I stayed there and joined up with Nick. The pattern of the expedition strategy was now forming. Climbing pairs were emerging and after a spell of load carrying each pair would have its reward climbing. In this way the chore of load-carrying would be shared out equally.

This was the theory, but already it seemed to me that it was not being adhered to. Chris had a difficult job; it was his first expedition as leader, and he had to deal with powerfully motivated, not to say selfish individuals. He was as keen as anyone to have his turn working the route and never having been particularly sensitive to the feelings of others, he was certainly unaware of the niggling dissatisfaction among the rear guard – of whom I was one.

These frustrations bubbled over when Nick and I arrived to take over Chris's tent at Camp One, to find it an awful tip full of dirty pans and slops of congealed food. Chris came back glowing and hearty, but we soured his good mood rather by snapping at him like malcontent housewives. The real source of our frustration was that once again Don and Dougal were staying on at Camp Two, ready to push the route on; we felt it was time we were given a chance to be out in front.

Our chance came a day later. Don and Dougal climbed up from camp almost to the crest of the ridge and then came down. The equipment had arrived and there was an exodus back to base. We were given the task of completing the route to the site of Camp Three and then establishing it. It was a crumb of comfort, but it was really only load-carrying again.

We were the only occupants at Camp Two. It was an uncomfortable spot to the side of a great overhanging cliff and on the flanks of the first ice ridge, which we were avoiding by a long, easy-angled contour on its right. The camp was horribly noisy; the glacier groaned and grumbled all night. An express train of an avalanche swept past a few yards away from us as we huddled together in fear. Occasionally a stone or icicles whistled and clattered down from the cliffs above.

We set off early and climbed quickly up the frozen body of the avalanche that had nearly carried us away, until we turned the corner and were faced with a long and tedious treadmill up a couloir leading to a col. We plodded up silently at our own speed and then the angle steepened and the slope became icy. For the first time I wished I was in my proper climbing boots. Ahead a section of rope hung down which we were glad to grasp and so reach the high point. Another 20 feet of climbing landed us on the small flat col. We were the first persons to get there; a minor enough achievement but one which gave pleasure despite the nagging annoyance that Dougal and Don could have done what we were now doing – carrying a box tent and establishing the camp.

We dug out a slot, put up the tent and examined the way ahead. The first major obstacle was above us – a fantastically sculptured ice ridge, which looked very unstable and time-consuming to climb. It looked as if it could be outflanked on the left by a broad ramp system. We finished our task, zipped up the completed box and then slithered back down feeling well satisfied with ourselves for a change. Chris and Tom were already on their way up to take over the lead whilst we went back down to base to get at our equipment.

Base was now transformed; some six foot of snow had melted away leaving several empty tents ludicrously perched on snow mushrooms. Green grass and mauve primulas were pushing through the snow, blue mountain thrushes hopped and whistled around the camp and there was food, whisky, cigarettes and all manner of good things to enjoy. We idled away the next few days of perfect weather, lying in the sun, eating enormous and exotic lunches of oysters, pâté and cheese while keeping a critical eye on the goings-on up the mountain.

It is always the privilege of those doing nothing to criticise those on the sharp end but in this case our annoyance at what was going on had some justification; Chris and Tom seemed to be getting nowhere on a direct assault of the ice ridge.

'Why the hell don't they go round on the left?' we asked ourselves in the self-satisfied knowledge we could have done better if only we had been allowed to. After two days of perfect weather in which the advance practically came to a halt, it became ever more obvious that Chris and Tom were on a false line. So Don and Dougal went up and the attack was switched to the ice ridge bypass, which Nick and I had thought the most likely way. An easy plod outflanked the ridge but getting back on to it was a problem they solved after a few days of steep and exhilarating ice climbing up fluted ice overhung by all manner of ice confections – including a menacing 'layer cake' which threatened to collapse.

By the time Don, Dougal and Chris had gained the ridge it was time for us to move up to Camp Three. It would be our first night above 20,000 feet. At Camp Three we met Chris. He looked tired and his face had a new and drawn look about it. Nick, who could never refrain from voicing his feelings, immediately attacked.

'Why the hell did you waste the best two days on the ridge? I would have thought it was obvious to go round.' I remained silent, aware that the criticism was ill-timed. Chris was only too well-aware of his mistake and subsequently made up for it by driving himself hard. He explained that Tom was keen to try the ridge because it seemed a safer and more pleasing line. It was part of the paradox of Chris's character that he could be a firm leader and yet easily manipulated by those around him.

Our first night at Camp Three above the magic height of 20,000 feet was a landmark for us but not an enjoyable one. It was our first experience of prolonged high altitude and we were beset by intense headaches exacerbated by the smoking stove we were forced to cook on. We lay low for a day until the throbbing pain subsided and by next morning we had largely got over our acclimatisation problem, and resumed load carrying. We carried up to the site of Camp Four, a fine flat portion of ridge – the top of one of the wedding-cake structures seen from below. This was only a temporary let-up in the ridge's defences; above it reared up steeply in the next mad sequence of ice pinnacles.

Dumping our loads, Don prowled around, sniffing and probing the slope until he was happy. He straightened up and pointed at the snow.

'Okay, get off your arses. Get that shovel and start digging. Five minute shifts. You start Martin.'

We dug away furiously, cutting a slot deep enough to contain Don's pride and joy – his eponymous box tent. We tied and laced it up with reverent care in deference to its inventor. Able to withstand the worst storms without collapsing, it was a highly valued piece of equipment. It also had the highly welcome, if accidental, design feature of collecting a large pool of melt water during the heat of the day, which served the same function as drinking troughs did thirsty horses.

We all returned to the site of Camp Four next day heavily laden, but this time Nick and I were staying. At last it was our turn to be in the lead. It was a thrilling prospect to be left on our own with the task of finding a way through the ice towers ahead. Even so I was sorry to see Don descending. I had enjoyed being with him and felt reassured by his presence, for he was the most experienced climber and a fount of sensible advice. Although his and Dougal's hogging of the lead had annoyed me, his actual presence and acute sense of humour disarmed me of any resentment.

Don and Dougal were a highly effective team. Dougal provided energy and drive; Don brought canny knowhow. As Don remarked: 'He's like a greyhound straining at the leash. Slip the lead, and he's off.' Don was quite happy to plod along behind; he never rushed but all the time thought out the route, assessed the difficulty and any dangers and planned his strategy. In the light of recent events it was understandable that Don liked making his own decisions. Before he left, he eyed the challenge ahead, turned to me and smiled: 'Don't mess around lad.' Then he patted the box tent and toddled off.

We settled down to make ourselves comfortable, read our books and then followed our well-tried routine in which I cooked something tasty from our ration packs while Nick, who was always more lively than me in the mornings, did breakfast. There were basically four different food packs containing a variety of meats, chocolate, drinks and biscuits. Although in each pack there were favoured and less palatable items, one pack was universally shunned as it contained tinned lamb tongues as the main meal. The sight, smell and, above all, taste of these were all quite disgusting, defying even the Sherpa chilli treatment. Fortunately or not, the packages were labelled, which had the effect of diverting the lamb tongues ever upward. The higher up the mountain you got, the more likely you were to eat badly, a way the load-carriers had of taking revenge on those enjoying themselves at the front.

In the morning we were up early climbing the slope above our tent to the base of an extremely steep gully leading up the first ice tower. I plunged into it and was immediately disgorged along with a mass of unconsolidated snow. I attacked again, but could make no progress. Helplessly I looked around for alternatives but could see none until I spotted a hole leading into the ice. Peering into it for want of anything more positive to do, I was surprised to see that it continued. So I squeezed along this narrow sinuous passage until it emerged unexpectedly some 30 feet higher in the middle of a vertical ice wall. I wriggled out as though through a post-box and planted an ice piton. Then I began hacking at the ice. It was unsatisfactory stuff, rotten for the most part, filled with air and as soft as frozen foam. An occasional twisting band of ice gave it substance. I soon discovered there was no point in cutting snow away. The best policy was to push arms, legs and knees into it and advance as delicately as possible; any rash movement was likely to cause a total collapse.

After several hours of dangerous and exhausting effort I made it to the top of the first tower. I pulled the rope through and lobbed it straight down to Nick who jumared up to me, starting a small avalanche at every movement. By the time we were together he was puffing and panting like a played fish.

'You go on. I'm too buggered to do anything for a while.'

Normally I would have been delighted to retain the lead, but I was less happy now. The next tower looked worse than the first with an overhanging top. I hardly had any ice pitons and I was far from sure if they would be any use anyway. Once more I started climbing up the same awful snow and ice until I was on the vertical wall. Here I had a stroke of luck; a one-foot band of ice extended across the ice tower allowing me to place an ice screw and traverse right to a gap in its edge. By now I had run out of ice screws, but I bashed in a bunch of rock pegs and made my way tentatively rightwards. Finally the rope jammed. I was utterly spent and the shouts of Chris and Ian from camp reminded us it was time to pack it in for the day.

Nick completed the unfinished pitch next morning, hacking a trench through the final overhang to land us on a fragile crest of unstable snow. His anchor was purely psychological and he urged caution as I eased along the narrowest of ridges, which I did my best to kick down. When it rose steeply further progress became out of the question. Below me were some rocks and I headed for them. If I could find a solid belay I'd be a lot happier. I thrust the large metal plate of a 'Deadman' into the rotten snow and began to lower myself off it, ignoring Nick's pleas as he sat horrified: 'For Christ's sake, go easy. There's no way I could hold you.'

I told him to give me more rope. With a sudden lurch I felt the Deadman slice down through the snow. Expecting it to slip free, I braced myself but it held fast; I continued to lower myself down into a gully and then tensioned across some steep snow, making for the rock on the far side like a drowning man reaching for flotsam. As soon as I reached it, I banged in several pitons and collapsed into the snow.

Nick joined me and we managed another half pitch before we ran out of rope and energy. The regular afternoon cloud had rolled in and it was now snowing hard, so we retreated, happy to have got past the worst bit of ice on the ridge. Chris and Ian took over from us and we were well-pleased when they reported how impressed they were with our efforts.

After the physical hardship of days spent high on the mountain, load-carrying and leading, the prospect of idle days at Base Camp seemed luxurious. The only problem was that it was now a long way down and even further to get back up. The rich air and greening meadows were like a narcotic, making it difficult to rouse oneself and climb back up to the top camps again.

As we plunged downwards and rolled into camp, the smell of woodsmoke, grass and life itself was almost unbearably good. The television crew came out to meet us and fired off questions. 'How's it going? What are our chances? Will we ever get up the ice ridge?' Naturally, to those sitting at Base Camp, progress seemed ludicrously slow, measured in a few hundreds of feet a day on a face fully 10,000 feet high. We explained the difficulty but even we were not prepared for the ridge to hold us up quite so long. First of all Chris and Ian tackled it, then Ian came down for a rest and Dougal took over. Every day we listened anxiously to the radio call and it was the cause of some celebration when the ice ridge was finally breached after five weeks of effort.

The pace could once more speed up, but Chris, who once again had immersed himself in the action up front, was unaware of mumblings of discontent. Chris had decided he would not come down to Base again but would rest at Camp Three and so be close to the action from where he could best direct it. Unfortunately for those at Base Camp, it seemed sometimes as though Chris was passing them over and there were dark mutterings that Chris was losing his grasp; he was even nicknamed the 'Mad Mahdi' for a bit.

Mick Burke was foremost amongst the grumblers. It was true that earlier he had suffered from piles, but he was now eager to play his part; his only difficulty was catching Chris's ear. Radio calls became ever more chaotic as more and more camps listened in and everyone tried to push their own point of view. It seemed to us the gentleman's agreement that everyone should share the climbing and load-carrying was breaking down. Nick and I, fresh from our exertions in the lead did not feel hard done by, even though we had only had two days in front. I was still amazingly naive, unaware of the internal wrangling and manoeuvring. I supposed everyone was doing as I was and working as hard as possible for the common good. I had not given a thought to the summit, nor did I imagine anyone else had; the thought that anyone might be holding back and husbanding their strength was unthinkable.

Mick and Tom were now put together – a team of 'saint and sinner' – and they set off to take the lead. Meanwhile, Camp Five was being established at 6,900 metres, below an ice cliff some 500 feet below the Rock Band – the huge prow that barred access to the upper slopes. Then it was time for Nick and me to return and resume the task of load-carrying. From Camp Three Nick and I carried several times up to Camp Four and I expected to move up to Camp Four to make a few more carries before we moved up once again, eventually to take over the lead. I was taken aback when Chris told me he had decided to go up to Camp Four with Nick while I should remain at Camp Three.

I felt angry and abandoned. A change now could leave me without a partner, condemned to carry loads for the rest of the trip. But I concealed my unhappiness. That night it snowed heavily and in the morning Mike Thompson and I set off to plough the trail to the fixed ropes. As we reached steeper ground at the foot of the ridge we were confronted with enormous piles of drifted snow. Mike pushed on with manic energy to bulldoze a pathway, but the snow became chest deep and suddenly his energy faltered and he collapsed, utterly spent. I took over and began a more measured struggle. Nick and Chris had by now caught us up and while Nick plunged ahead for his share of breaking trail, Chris seemed preoccupied and quiet, his head lowered. He looked a beaten man. I was full of indignant energy and ploughed on until I reached the ropes. Having burned himself out, Mike was returning, so I shouldered his load on top of mine and allowed Nick to go ahead. Chris was obviously in a bad way and moving at a snail's pace. I had soon left him far behind to struggle by himself and when I dumped my load at Camp Four, I wondered if I would be back next day with my own personal gear to move back in with Nick. Sure enough, when I returned to Camp Three I found Chris had returned crestfallen and continued down for a decent rest.

I came up to Camp Four next day, resuming my previous niche, and waited for Nick to return from his carry to Camp Five. He arrived, grim-faced and tired. 'It's the worst yet, a real killer.' It was to get worse; Camp Five had been swamped continuously by falling spindrift and was shifted 500 feet higher. It was now a huge bergschrund below the Rock Band. Tom and Mick were to take up residence while Don and Dougal went down once more. It was now our unenviable task to support Camp Five. Thus began the most arduous week of my life.

I climbed up to Camp Five with Tom and Mick but Nick failed to make it all the way, feeling run down and somewhat depressed. To my amazement I found I was going very well. I enjoyed the acrobatics of the ice ridge, swinging round corners and bouncing from one rope to the next, and I was soon plodding up the final ice slope, up the ice cliff and onto the last interminable slope to the bergschrund. Here I disciplined myself, counting 50 steps before I hung back on the rope. The camp was inside an unwelcoming cleft, dark and shaded; inside the light was eerily blue. The tent stood rather forlornly. I didn't bother waiting long and was soon shooting down the ropes hell-for-leather to meet Mick and Tom still toiling upwards.

For the next six days, bar one rest day, I would make the same exhausting carry. It was a case of forcing myself to do it, for apart from Nick no one else seemed capable. Nick settled into a routine of one day on, one off, but our companions, like Mick and Ian, were unable to make the full run. Ian always tried to carry too much and consequently burnt himself out and would then shoot off down. Mike tried extremely hard but nearly died as a result. I was at Camp Five one day when Mike felt a fit of coughing start; he began to lose consciousness as Mick reached him. Since Mike seemed about to breathe his last, Mick thought he'd prise the bag of nuts he was holding: 'If you're dying, can I have your nuts?' This so shocked Mike that he recovered himself – but not his nuts – sufficiently until I came down to help. Such is the importance of food on an expedition.

When I reached Mike he was in a bad state of shock, mumbling to himself and barely able to handle the complexity of the fixed ropes on the descent. It was obviously his last trip above Camp Four; once more I would have to struggle up with my statutory load of rope and lamb tongues plus some extra.

It was on my return from this last carry that the most vituperative radio exchange took place. Chris had taken to thinking aloud on the radio and he outlined his plan. Dougal and Don as the strongest pair were to push straight to Camp Five and get on with establishing Camp Six. Nick and I were to continue the marvellous job we were doing. Nick exploded in well-justified exasperation.

'Doesn't he realise that the problem at this moment is getting loads up to Camp Five? There's no oxygen and not enough rope or food to keep Mick and Tom going, let alone anything else.' Nick managed to get his piece in and then it was Mick's turn to be angry. Don told him to get a move on with the route, and Mick was furious at this criticism. I listened as the arguments flew up and down the mountain but I was too tired and had little stomach for it. I lay back, holding on to my own thoughts, feeling an emptiness as the desperate energy and involvement that had sustained me drained away.

Of course I could understand Chris's reasons; Don and Dougal were rested and would obviously be fresh to push the route, while Nick and I were tired. Yet I had not felt tired up until this moment. I had been going marvellously well in fact; but I was not to be given my chance. For the first time I realised my assumptions had been wrong. We were not all equal; a caste system, as insidious and pervading as any, had predestined our activities and roles.

I now felt demoralised and my discontent was reinforced when Tom Frost, who until this moment had refrained from making comments about the expedition's politics, slapped me on the back, smiled and gently shook his head: 'You guys have been given one heck of a raw deal.' It was gratifying to know someone appreciated our efforts.

On their last day in the lead, Mick and Tom made a great advance. Mick, no doubt needled by Don's comments, had led out fixing a huge amount of rope over several steep steps until he reached an easy-angled snow rib that promised to lead around the upper section of the Rock Band. It helped open the way to the summit. As a result of Nick's arguments, Don and Dougal were doing a carry to Camp Five before they moved in. I did a half-carry with them and Don suggested I come up with them to give support. I jumped at the chance of some novelty, and next day took up my kit and camped in the tent inside the bergschrund, one of those given us by the military, before putting up a Whillans box tent. We left next day carrying rope and tent ready to reach the site of Camp Six.

It was an unpleasant day; the morning sun was soon extinguished and it began to snow fitfully. Dougal went off first and then Don but unfortunately I followed too soon behind, for after catching Don up I had to wait in discomfort until he cleared the overhanging pitches on the fixed ropes, by which time my feet were cold. I reached the snow ridge to see Dougal running out rope up it. I told Don about my cold feet and he told me to dump my load, get back down and put a brew on; they would be down shortly since Dougal had got to a suitable site. I set off, got into the tent and spent the next half an hour getting the circulation going in my feet. Nick climbed up to Camp Five later in the day and we moved into the tent while Don and Dougal occupied the box.

That night was one of the worst; snow fell and a cold wind drove the spindrift down the face so that it billowed and swirled into the bergschrund, forming a great mound over our tent. Suddenly it collapsed and we awoke with a horrifying sense of suffocation as the enormous weight of snow settled on us, pinning us down. We scratched for the entrance and as we found it a choking mass of powder blasted our faces. Nick inhaled a gulp of snow and practically passed out from asphyxiation before we were able to knock up Dougal and Don and creep into their box. We spent the following day digging out our tent and retrieving the sodden equipment inside, while Dougal and Nick dropped down to the dump and picked up the remaining food packs and other gear.

After we had completed our tent recovery I started to feel unwell. Various scratches on my hands had turned septic and one of the glands in my armpit was swollen and tender. I felt slightly feverish and lethargic. I was fed up and said as much to Don who seemed genuinely concerned about me. He even hinted I could come up to Camp Six with them, and then – who knew? But it was too late to bait the hook. I was tired and my resolve was already weakened. I was thinking of green meadows, flowers, warm feet and 'bed tea'. I began to pack and decided to go down. It was a decision I questioned and agonised over; I was well aware that if I went down I was unlikely to take any more significant part in the expedition. Could I hang on? Was I really ill? Was I suffering some degree of frostbite or was I just giving in to a general feeling of demoralisation? I suppose it was a product of them all, but once I had started downwards there was no changing the mind. I hardly stopped, pausing only to pass a few words with anyone I met; I was too full of remorse to say anything more.

I followed the course of action over the next week or so with detached interest. Nick followed me down after a few days; he had made two carries to Camp Six but had got to the stage where he was utterly spent. Chris continued the supply line, even using oxygen to enable himself to carry to Camp Six. As Don and Dougal pushed out the remaining fixed rope up a gully that cut through to the top of the Rock Band, Chris and Ian moved up to Camp Six, hoping that Don and Dougal would establish Camp Seven. This didn't happen, and after an awful night with four people in a two-man tent, Chris and Ian descended.

To make matters more tense the monsoon had definitely arrived; it was snowing harder and earlier each day as more and more grey clouds forced their way up the Modi Kola and spilled into the Sanctuary. I decided I ought to go back up the mountain to give support, but after spending two nights in empty camps I felt so lonely and such a sense of danger from avalanches that I decided to turn back. I reached base to hear the amazing news – Don and Dougal had made it to the top. They had gone in one push from Camp Six to the summit and back. We could start thinking of home, but not before Tom and Mick made a second attempt that ended prematurely.

These last days of the expedition were suddenly overshadowed by tragedy. First came the news that Tom Patey was dead, killed abseiling from a Scottish sea stack. I was deeply saddened and could hardly believe it; Tom had so much vitality it seemed impossible to wipe it out just like that. For years I kept expecting him to turn up; I kept spotting him in a crowd and had to constantly remind myself of the grim truth.

It was in the wake of this news that the second shocking blow fell. We were practically on the point of departing. Only Mike, Ian and a few Sherpas were still on the hill removing the last loads from Camp Two. We were lying in the sun; the television crew, after spotting someone coming down, had trained their cameras on him. It turned out to be Mike and he was running with a peculiar desperate carelessness. He stumbled into camp, hurled his ice-axe to the ground and said bitterly: 'Ian's dead.' The camp was stunned.

An ice avalanche had fallen as they came down from Camp Two; Ian was crushed a few feet away from Mike. The Sherpas went up and collected his body, which we buried in a flower-strewn corner of the camp. Tom read a few words at a simple and moving ceremony. Then we packed up and quietly left without any sense of triumph.

Capital Punishment   49m   E3 5c   ★★★

A great lead that is not for the faint-hearted. Sustained climbing and
well-spaced protection makes this high in the grade. Start below the
crescent-shaped scoop of Route 2. Climb up into the scoop. The triangular
slab on the left is delicate and bold. It steepens into a groove, which is
climbed with protection on the left. Then a good thread appears, and better
holds lead to the ledge crossed by The Garotte. Trend leftwards up the
wall above, to meet the finish of Route 1. This can be avoided by finishing
via the overlap on the right.
FA M. A. Boysen, D. E. Alcock, 11 September 1971

FOURTEEN
THE EIGER SANCTION

Returning from Annapurna was not the joyous occasion I had imagined. My general state of health was rundown, made worse by a serious bout of dysentery that I couldn't get over. It must have been a bitter disappointment for Maggie; she had made a huge effort for my homecoming but I felt so ill that I could barely show any appreciation. Thanks to the dysentery I developed a painful anal fissure. A minor operation soon sorted this out, but the surgeon turned out to be a member of the Rucksack Club, so my embarrassment was compounded. I lay there with my legs trussed up, as he chatted away about how he'd enjoyed a recent lecture I'd given.

Since quitting my last job at the college of further education it had become necessary to have a teaching certificate; if I was going to continue as a teacher I'd have to study. I applied to Didsbury College and enrolled in September; so began a largely tedious year in which I churned out essays on the theory of education that seemed to have surprisingly little bearing on its practice. I was, it must be admitted, an indifferent student. My heart was not in it, perhaps because I had already taught for so long. I found it irksome to write detailed lesson notes deemed essential to the task. The only pleasure I had was when we were allocated to our specialist subject departments. The biology lecturers were keen and cheerful, and the fieldwork and practical tutorials excellent.

My teaching practice was a mixture of good and very bad. The bad part required I take over teaching chemistry to the worst third year group. The chemistry master, although fantastically well-qualified, as he was keen to let me know, with a doctorate and degrees, was perhaps the worst teacher I have ever encountered. A short period of observation prepared me for my coming ordeal. He stood with his back to the class, muttering and scribbling notes and formulae on the blackboard as the class erupted behind him. Bunsen burners and tripods clattered across the ruin of a laboratory to loud guffaws and general merriment – punctuated by the occasional cry of pain. When I was abandoned to my fate, it took a lot of effort – both physical and mental – to quell the riot and maintain a tenuous degree of discipline.

As compensation, my other responsibility was a bright and charming group of second year pupils. Luckily for me, I was observed and assessed on my teaching skills with the latter group. I was rewarded with some gratifying praise on my performance until I was asked to present my lesson notes, which in this case was a scrap of notepaper with a few helpful jottings to help me along.

My lack of application was not helped when I discovered early on in the course that Maggie was pregnant. It was a shock, but not an unwelcome one, and we prepared for the great changes that would occur. Then things started to go wrong. Maggie became uneasy, and then one awful night she began to lose blood; she was rushed to hospital where our seven-month-old child was stillborn. It was a shattering blow, especially for Maggie, and it took some time to recover from it.

Meanwhile, I suffered a series of minor ailments that required surgery. Some varicose veins in my leg became infected and required stripping; then I had my tonsils removed. These had given me problems all my life, so my doctor, a wonderful old lady called Dr Willis, sent me to a very old-fashioned but 'excellent' consultant, appropriately named Mr Gill. I joined the back of a long queue outside his room, but it moved with surprising speed. Patients trotted in and out, often with long cotton wool buds poking out of various orifices. When my turn came I was commanded to sit down. I offered my throat for inspection, eager to maintain the rapid turnover, and was curtly told to shut my mouth. He was an ear, nose and throat man so I dutifully presented each in the correct sequence. I did not have to wait long for the diagnosis: 'Chronic. Operate. Next week.' Thus my tonsils were removed, an operation which left me weak with blood loss and infection. I spent a fortnight in hospital.

When summer arrived, Dave Little, an old climbing friend, and his girl-friend Janet Harper took over the flat below, formerly occupied by Mike and Judy Yates. I had climbed with Dave on odd occasions over many years, first meeting him in Wales shortly after he had left school. He was a keen, intelligent youth with a laidback attitude and a long shock of lank hair, which he was to lose with alarming speed. He was a good climber, known for his ability to climb all day and remain cheerful and utterly reliable. He was also a keen birdwatcher, an interest which was to take more and more of his time in later life.

Dave and Janet were limited to the usual short holidays so we decided to have a quick Alpine trip. We started in Chamonix, climbing the excellent West Face of the Petites Jorasses. The route enjoyed a reputation as a techni-cal rock climb, something that suited us well, and the ascent went smoothly, the chief excitement being the descent into the chaos of the steeply glaciated

Italian side of the mountain. We found shelter in a tiny empty hut perched on a rocky outcrop and next day savoured views of the secretive East Face of the Grandes Jorasses, scene of Gervasutti's most famous climb.

Maggie and Janet drove through the Mont Blanc tunnel to meet us and we then drove east into Switzerland to climb the beautiful Piz Badile's North Face. The Bregaglia peaks, just south of St Moritz, are one of the loveliest Alpine regions and we wasted no time driving our van as high as possible on forest track before setting off to reach the foot of the mountain. Dave and I decided we would bivouac at the bottom of the route to get ahead of other parties staying in the hut. It was a forlorn hope. Long before first light, torches were bobbing around us, but despite this we weren't held up much by other climbers. The route, a classic north wall first climbed by the great Riccardo Cassin, was an amiable sequence of granite slabs and grooves. We finished it quickly before making a long descent into the steamy Val di Mello, over the border in Italy. It was an impressive and beautiful place, full of dramatic crags and rich forests of beech and pine wrapped in swathes of mist – like an old Chinese landscape painting.

We returned home to a lovely autumn. I had by now secured a post as biology teacher at Altrincham Grammar School for Boys. The future was beginning to look more hopeful and Maggie was once again pregnant. This time we were much more hopeful. I also began one of my most enjoyable periods of rock climbing, with Dave Alcock. Together we climbed a number of routes on Suicide Wall in Cwm Idwal. They were hard and badly protected routes; our equipment was primitive and we climbed in the traditional manner from the ground up, without pre-inspection and cleaning the moss and soil out of pockets and cracks as we made our way up. This was before the development of micro-nuts; we didn't even use harnesses, just tied the rope round our waists with an old-fashioned bowline. *Capital Punishment* was the best of these new routes but the traverse of *The Garotte* was also exciting. I remember belaying Dave on the 'pocket ledge' of *Suicide Wall*, tied to a piton that wouldn't have held anything.

Soon after, Mick Burke invited me to make the first ascent of the Rock of Gibraltar. After Annapurna he had enrolled as a filmmaking student. Now fully qualified, he only needed a union card to further his career; climbing the Rock would be news and Mick would get his card. With typical inventiveness he set about the task. First he needed permission and that meant involving the Ministry of Defence. This was granted on the condition I climbed with Captain Henry Day, leader of the Army's Annapurna expedition. We had a great time in the sun, climbing a new route up the towering limestone pillar while being filmed by Mick and a small team from ITV, and all the time looked after in a luxury hotel. It wasn't like the Alps.

On the last day of the summer holidays, before I started teaching, Dave Little and I, together with Janet and a heavily pregnant Maggie, drove to Dovedale in the Staffordshire Peak District. We wanted to make the second ascent of *Adjudicator Wall*, recently climbed by Jack Street and Geoff Birtles. Geoff suggested it was hard and the route quickly gathered a reputation. I was eager to finish the holiday on a high and initially all went well. The initial diagonal traverse went to plan and I managed to place plenty of small runners before reaching the small overhang guarding the top wall. All I had to do, I hoped, was surmount the bulge to reach the safety of an *in situ* piton protecting the last hard moves.

I felt confident, moved quickly up without bothering to rest, reached the top wall and began to look for the piton just as my fingers began to tire. Suddenly the awful realisation hit me; there was no piton. I hesitated and, just to make things worse, burned up my remaining energy trying to place the only runner I had left – and failing. So I lunged for the top with my last strength, my fingers opened and I plunged downwards. At this moment, with brilliant timing, Maggie spotted me through binoculars rapidly disappearing from view. She wasn't the only one worried; I fell all the way to ground on the stretch of the rope, which tightened horribly around my chest, squeezing the breath out of me and crushing my ribs. It was the last time I would climb without a harness. I had one designed by Don Whillans sitting in a box at home.

As a result, my first days at Altrincham Grammar School were painful but thankfully not too energetic. I taught biology in a lively department run by Pete Marsh, who was animated and enthusiastic. The students were mostly keen and intelligent, the staff sympathetic and fun, so I soon settled down to the happiest time in my teaching life.

As the birth of our child grew nearer we felt it was time to move somewhere more appropriate. Our flat was becoming ever more rundown; our bedroom ceiling collapsed from water leaks and, more seriously, rats invaded the property. We could hear them scuttling behind the walls. The final straw came when they began to gnaw through the floorboards of our bedroom. I placed the heaviest – and most boring – biological tome over the hole but this didn't deter them. By the time they had almost nibbled their way through the top cover we had found ourselves a house to buy. Dave Pearce, a climbing acquaintance and friend of Nick Estcourt, suggested a house up for sale a few doors from him in Hale might be suitable. It was ideal – an Edwardian terrace with a neat garden, a short walk from my school. We moved in during a glorious Indian summer, a matter of weeks before the birth of our daughter Katie. Her birth prompted me to decline an invitation to attempt Everest with Chris Bonington, a decision I had no difficulty making; the birth was to be the most joyous moment of our lives.

Following Katie's arrival, I settled down to a period of contented domesticity. I was teaching biology in an excellent school a short walk from our new house, bought with the generous help of my mother. We got a small amount of compensation from our car crash and were able to buy our first new Ford Escort van. There was work to do on the house and garden and time to enjoy life transformed by a baby.

In the summer, Clive Rowlands and his wife Steph invited us to join them on a trip to Arctic Norway. Clive had come across a report from a university club of a visit to the Loppa Peninsula a short way south of North Cape. The report hinted there were some unclimbed peaks and fine rock faces to climb. It was an intriguing possibility for an adventure.

The van was loaded with baby food, disposable nappies were stuffed into every nook and cranny and we set off on the long drive north from Gothenburg to the Arctic, first traversing Sweden, sweeping past an endless procession of slow Volvos, their headlights on in the middle of the day. Leaving the Baltic we crossed the border into Finland and crossed Lapland plagued by clouds of mosquitoes. Finally we reached the small town of Alta far to the north on the Norwegian coast. At Øxfjord we met up with Clive and Steph and let little Katie out to graze the bilberries. A short trip on the ferry took us out onto the Loppa – or 'Flea' – Peninsula past some impressive coastal cliffs topped by an ice cap which still calved the occasional iceberg.

Clive had made arrangements to meet a young Norwegian who owned a small fishing fleet so we packed all our gear into a small boat and motored round to a sea loch where we set up camp. It was a wonderful site – remote and beautiful, visited by curious arctic foxes. Every evening two huge sea eagles sailed up the valley to a high eyrie. For supper we had fresh fish – cod, sea trout or coley, wrapped in foil and baked in the coals of an ample fire. Katie, with a discernment that proved typical for her, took offence at most of the tinned food. Apple purée, which usually formed a large part of her diet, was rejected entirely; I had bought the wrong brand. She thrived nevertheless, eating the fresh fish and was soon crawling for the first time.

The climbing was on spiky gabbro peaks not unlike the Black Cuillin of Skye. We made an ascent of the unclimbed peak – a rock climb of moderate standard – and were grateful to find no cairn or other signs of a previous ascent. The weather had turned from drought to downpour so further climbing was limited apart from one fine route up a 1,500-foot buttress emerging from the icefield. It proved a challenging climb with a dangerous pitch balancing around huge poised flakes. We were benighted in the final damp exit chimneys but the Arctic nights were mercifully short.

After the Loppa climbs we made the laborious but majestic journey south to Bergen, stopping briefly between torrential rain showers to climb on a lovely granite mountain near Narvik. We viewed the Troll Wall but had no desire to climb it, and then made our separate ways home. It had been a marvellous trip despite the generally awful wet weather. We had met some lovely people, been enchanted by the mountains and fjords and enjoyed our first adventure as a family.

Soon I was embarked on a more serious adventure. According to local legend, 'eat a Calafate berry and you will return to Patagonia.' I'm not sure if I ever ate the berry but it didn't take much to lure me back to Patagonia. Don Whillans was organising an expedition financed by a local businessman to Torre Egger, the neighbouring peak to Cerro Torre, and no less difficult. The team included a mixture of old and new friends: Leo Dickinson was in charge of filmmaking with his accomplice Eric Jones, Mick Coffey and Tut Braithwaite made up the English contingent and we were to meet up with an American doctor and special forces veteran, Dan Reid, and, a little later, Rick Sylvester in Patagonia.

It was the start of a bad period in Argentina's recent history; the military had taken over, radicals were being rounded up and the air of tension was palpable. Things were soon to get a lot worse with the terror of the 'disappeared'. We were delayed in Buenos Aires trying to arrange the passage of our equipment to Patagonia and while this was sorted we stayed in a flat owned by an Argentinean climber, Dr Eduardo, a plastic surgeon. We were not the only residents; also staying was an Anglo-American team comprising Al Rouse, Rab Carrington, Peter Minks, Mick Geddes and Jim Donini.

They had travelled overland through South America but when they finally reached Buenos Aires all their equipment was impounded by customs. Breaking the web of red tape proved difficult; there was insufficient money to 'lubricate' the transaction and, as usual, the British Embassy was uninterested in helping. Thus began a frustrating wait, which thankfully we shared only briefly, whiling away the hot nights with heavy drinking and extreme loafing.

Rab seemed fierce and angry, Mick Geddes rarely emerged from the bed he shared with the separated wife of Eduardo, while Minks threw himself into every situation with alarming energy. He would jump onto cafe tables to perform ribald ditties as often as not concluded with his *piéce de résistance*, a flaming-arse dance. How he avoided arrest is a mystery to me.

After a week of dissolute life it was a relief to finally head south to the mountains. Cerro Torre had become part of what is now called Los Glaciares National Park. Already there were signs of the tourist invasion that was about to overwhelm the quiet meadows at the base of the mountains. There was little to remind me of my previous visit except for the remains of our red plastic igloo, the mad brainchild of Pete Crew, now usefully employed as a hen house.

The various members of the expedition were finally assembled. Don arrived straight from a successful ascent of Roraima in British Guiana; Dan Reid had flown in from North America, recently demobbed from the army having served in Vietnam. We were an eclectic team. Leo was chirpy, Eric Jones strong and silent; Don was our rather overweight leader, Tut thin and emaciated, Mick handsome and charming with his slight stutter. Then there was 'Desperate Dan' the American dynamo. We made a strong, if disjointed team.

We quickly set up Base Camp near Lago Torre, the glacial lake I had first seen on our Cerro Torre trip although I noticed that the retreating glacier snout no longer carved icebergs into it. I teamed up with Tut and together we made good progress up the initial wall of the mountain. We suffered our first setback when Eric slipped and badly twisted his knee. Mick had a lucky escape when he fell down a crevasse and then, as expected, bad weather held up progress. I spent a few days wandering through the gloomy Magellan beech forests, spied a rare Huemul deer, watched the acrobatics of torrent ducks, and generally marvelled at the wildlife and dramatic scenery. With Mick, I made a long walk across the dry desert plain on a dirt road littered with bottles and lined with lovely yellow evening primroses to visit one of the region's earliest *estancias*, a faded remnant of another age, only just surviving along with its sad, alcoholic Norwegian owner.

When the weather improved our route on the mountain suddenly became a watercourse. At night the ropes froze and a vast icicle hung over us like the sword of Damocles. Tut and I retreated from under it and it proved to be our highpoint as the expedition lost momentum. Other teams arrived, including the stranded British team. An Argentinean climber called Rafael Juarez joined us briefly. I was astonished to see he was wearing my boots from Cerro Torre, which had never made it home. Tragically, he went off to climb a snow peak, Cerro Adela, and was lost – presumably overwhelmed in an avalanche. He and his companion were never found.

It was getting to be late in the season so to improve morale we decided to make the first ascent of a relatively minor rock peak known as the Innominata. We hoped to rename it Punta Rafael. It proved a delightful climb on perfect rock. Dan was in his element with a pitch of artificial climbing; I was thrown at the crux, an overhanging off width crack, and all the while Leo filmed manically. We were a large and cumbersome party and consequently were benighted without bivouac gear. Dan and I wrapped round each other to conserve heat and discovered a shared love of Thelonious Monk. We hummed 'Straight No Chaser' and 'Blue Monk' deep into the night to keep our spirits up.

It was the end. The expedition had fizzled out of energy. It was time to escape back home. It was a delight to get back to Maggie and Katie, who was proving herself to be a determined and intelligent little girl. I had had to leave my teaching job so I now took on the challenge of earning a living and going on expeditions. I thought I might be able to earn some money lecturing and in the meantime had an excellent opportunity to make some money working as a double on the Clint Eastwood film *The Eiger Sanction*, a rather unlikely thriller involving assassination plots on the Eiger's North Face. Dougal Haston, with his intimate knowledge of the mountain, had been signed up to organise the climbing team on the mountain. It was my job to double for the German actor and singer Reiner Schöne – a blonde but friendly giant, who played the part of Karl Freytag.

We drove to Grindelwald in the Bernese Oberland, caught the train up to Kleine Schiedegg and installed ourselves in its famous hotel. So began my first encounter with the frustrating, occasionally exciting, overpaid and strange world of Hollywood. Along with Dougal's assembled team of climbers, John Cleare was also involved as climbing cameraman. He was soon to lock horns with his American counterpart, a gifted and moody risk-taker called Mike Hoover. The remaining technical crew were mainly Italian – the Spaghetti Western team of Clint's early breakthrough films. They were a cheerful crowd, pleased to be working for Clint again; he was loyal to his old friends from the early years.

Filming started well. A location for a dramatic fall sequence was found on a spur on the edge of the Eiger's Mittellegi Ridge. The rock face was rigged, the scene was filmed successfully and we made our way up the ropes to a waiting helicopter. Then tragedy struck. One of the riggers accidentally kicked a stone off the cliff. It hit and killed Dave Knowles, a Scottish Guide working on the film. He was a lovely lad, was recently married and lived in Glencoe. Dougal was distraught. He was in charge of safety but could no longer face the task. The producers decided a more experienced safety officer should be brought in; Hamish MacInnes was the obvious choice with his background in mountain rescue and engineering.

It was some time before the filming of climbing sequences resumed, so in the meantime the crew focused on hotel shots and local colour. Katie now took the opportunity to drive her Tonka toy truck over Clint Eastwood's foot.

'What a cute little girl you've got,' he said. Katie looked up at him with icy disdain, as if to say: 'Go ahead, punk.'

With the mountain sequences up and running again, the boredom finally came to an end. The final phase was, more or less, a re-enactment of the tragic death of Tony Kurz during an early attempt on the North Face in 1936. Hamish rigged up a concoction of ropes and ladders extending like a gibbet out over a 3,000-foot drop looking straight down the face. Clint, trustful and very brave, had to cut one of his ropes and subsequently fall quite a way on to the other. We crossed our fingers and let the cameras roll, praying the ladders didn't fail, although it was all too well-organised for that to be a real threat.

To get the sequence we investigated a window onto the face leading from the mountain railway that burrows up inside it. It was surreal to stop the train in the middle of the mountain, unlock a great steel door and emerge blinking in the brilliant light of day in the middle of the Third Icefield. The whine of falling rocks soon underlined the inappropriateness of the location so a safer but less spectacular site was chosen.

The final scenes involved some ice climbing and I doubled briefly for Clint; he was becoming increasingly impatient of the delays and not a little fed up with the film in general. Yet it was fascinating to be around him. I enjoyed the work and had great respect for Clint. He was a fair and decent man prepared to take a risk. He proved to be no natural on rock but quickly learned what to do on ice.

It was also good to have made some money, which I hoped to top up with the odd lecture. Even more exciting was how my expedition climbing was about to take off. Chris Bonington had permission to attempt Changabang in the Garhwal Himalaya of India. After that there was the prospect of the Trango Tower in Pakistan and then Everest's South West Face. The future couldn't have been brighter.

Changabang (22,520ft.)

An eight-man Anglo-Indian expedition, led by Chris Bonington, made the first ascent of this fine peak in the Nanda Devi basin, via a route up the East Face and then along the East Arête. The summit was reached by Bonington, Dougal Haston, Doug Scott and Martin Boysen, accompanied by Balwant Sandhu and Tashi Sherpa.

'Are you interested in Changabang?' Chris Bonington asked me. I should say. Changabang was on my secret list of dream peaks, a spire of rock and ice in the Garhwal Himalaya that was extraordinarily beautiful. As with all the best dreams it was long cherished, nurtured by youthful readings of Tom Longstaff, Eric Shipton, H. W. Tilman and W. H. Murray. They had all made explorations around Nanda Devi, the region's highest mountain, trying to gain access to the meadows at the foot of its West Face. Known as the Nanda Devi Sanctuary, this hidden valley was protected by a formidable ring of mountains and breached only by the deep and difficult Rishi Gorge. During all these explorations the mountaineers had been astonished at the sight of Changabang; according to Longstaff it was 'the most amazing mountain I have ever seen'. For Bill Murray it was 'a vast eyetooth of milk white granite'. Although at 22,500 feet it wasn't high, at least not by Himalayan standards, it was a wonderful objective, as yet untried and in one of the most beautiful regions of the Himalaya.

Often one of the hardest parts of any expedition, certainly in the 1970s, was to secure permission to go there at all. This was especially true in the Indian Himalaya, which had been closed to foreigners since the 1962 border war with China. Restrictions had been eased a little in the early 1970s and Chris, who had attended a mountaineering get-together at Darjeeling, was offered the chance of a joint Anglo-Indian expedition for the spring of 1974. It was a chance not to be missed and Chris duly set about organising his team.

International expeditions have had a mixed history, often collapsing into bad feeling and conflict, so it was critical that the British contingent should be a cohesive group. Chris, Dougal Haston and myself had known each other a long time. Only Doug Scott, who was himself an experienced leader, was less well known to us. Chris already knew Balwant Sandhu, known as Balu, the Indian co-leader, and Tashi, a Sherpa instructor from the Darjeeling Mountain Institute. Ujagar Singh and Captain Kiran Kumar made up the rest of the Indian climbing team, while Captain D. J. Singh – a tall and impressive Sikh, was the team doctor. At the last moment Alan Hankinson, the ITN reporter on our Annapurna television team, came too.

His wit and intelligence were a welcome addition and he even volunteered to mastermind the writing of an expedition book.

After several days of heat and confusion in Delhi, we left the hotel to catch an evening bus. Arriving at the bus station, we expected to meet Kiran and were puzzled when he failed to appear. After an hour we dispatched D. J. Singh to see if he could make contact. Meanwhile, some miles away at the correct bus station, an increasingly desperate Kiran was using all his military authority to hold our bus, now full of rioting passengers, in the ultimately vain hope we might arrive. A short time later, a taxi screeched to a halt where we were still waiting at the wrong bus station and a distraught Kiran leapt out.

All was not lost. We still had our preferred option of riding on the back of the expedition flatbed lorry. We made ourselves comfortable, sprawled over our kit, and rumbled off into the night across the hot Indian plain. I watched the silhouetted mango trees stream past as we dodged ox carts, cows and nonchalantly naked holy men on our way to Haridwar and then up through cool pine-scented foothills to Rishikesh. We were following the famous pilgrim route along the upper Ganges to its main tributary, the Alaknanda.

We arrived in Joshimath, nestling high in the Himalaya, to be met by Balu. Usin his rank and tremendous charm, he had flown in directly after a parachute exercise; Balwant Sandhu was a colonel in the Parachute Regiment. What he didn't tell us until after the expedition was that his arm had only just been taken out of plaster. Balu, which means 'bear', was as tough as his name suggested.

We spent a couple of days in Joshimath, tying up odds and ends, buying fresh food and hiring extra porters. Ujagar was out already scouring the local villages for extra hands. The British contingent had delightfully little to do but scramble on the local boulders and lounge in the Nissen huts of the army camp where we were staying.

We left Joshimath, drove a few miles further to the village of Lata where we met out porters, a cheerful noisy crowd of local Garhwalis clad in thick woollen tweed jackets, many of them spinning yarn as they chatted. We also had a band of poorly clad Nepalis – immigrant road-workers – but we were still short of porters so hired over a hundred goats as well, each capable of carrying 10 kilogrammes.

This seemed a brilliant idea at first. Goats can feed themselves and aren't unionised but it meant breaking down the supplies into 200 small leather bags. We were rather dismayed starting the steep climb out of Lata when the goatherd stopped after a couple of hours. He claimed that was as far as his goats could go in a day. He was persuaded fairly forcibly they could go a little further and eventually we made the normal camp at the top of a ridge amongst birch and rhododendron forest. Our porter troubles weren't helped by a heavy fall of snow; the ill-clad Nepalis spend a freezing night huddled under a tarpaulin. Worst of all the porter carrying the entire cigarette ration had mysteriously not made it to camp.

The next few days were a wild and dramatic trek through flower-filled meadows, over rocky cols and finally a rock barrier that required a tricky ascent for the climbers, let alone the porters. After a recce to find the easiest way around this obstacle, some of the party were almost caught out descending after nightfall, as a light dusting of evening snow added considerably to the danger.

Next day, having broken through the rock barrier, we reached the valley of the Ramani Glacier. Here at last we could view our mountain and establish a temporary base. Changabang looked every bit as magnificent as I had imagined, its vast walls of creamy granite sweeping up to a bullet's head summit. We had come in hope of climbing the West Face, a rock route that looked inviting in our old and faded photographs. But we were now confronted with a huge smooth sweep of rock broken with overhangs and veneered with ice. It was obviously too formidable for our joint party. My heart sank; we were clearly on the wrong side of the mountain to climb it by any feasible route. To get to the other side we would either have to climb over a difficult ridge or walk back to the Rishi Gorge and penetrate this final barrier to the Nanda Devi Sanctuary. The latter possibility was ruled out as our porters had departed. That night was rather cheerless, as everyone huddled in their tents under a snow-filled sky, pondering the future.

Next morning in bright sun, Chris, the eternal optimist, snapped us out of our mild depression. We would keep up the momentum, establish a more convenient Base Camp nearer the mountain and force a route over the col. The direct route was problematical; the steep, iced-up rock would take some time to climb. However, it was possible to avoid this direct line by climbing an ice face about half a mile further down the ridge and then traversing back to the col. From this point we could drop ropes down to join up with others being fixed from the bottom of the first difficulties.

Doug and I were given the task of reaching the col and early next morning, as I showed a characteristic reluctance to move, Doug demonstrated exemplary keenness by wrestling with a reluctant Primus. Wearily we plodded off leaving the others to acclimatise, and were soon front-pointing up a surprisingly steep ice slope showing evidence of recent avalanches. It was clear we would have to get a move on before the sun hit our snow, so we soloed as fast as we could. I was delighted to feel that unexpected surge of energy that indicates good acclimatisation but it was a nervous race with the sun as we traversed under seracs, alarmed by their precarious angle.

Reaching the crest of the ridge we slumped in the snow. Doug fished out two tins of juice from his sack but when opened we discovered they contained mashed potato. I hurled mine away in disgust but Doug stoically munched through his; such were the hazards of our Indian food supply. By now it had started to snow again. Visibility diminished as we started the long traverse of the ridge. The climbing was dangerous; the cornice was often hidden and our progress was slow as we kicked lumps of snow off and watched them trigger avalanches hissing to the left and right of us.

The ridge went on and on. We could see very little, and tempers were becoming a little frayed. In thick mist we reached a col; Doug was of the opinion we should sit and wait for a gap in the cloud to see if we had arrived. I was convinced we had not yet reached the right col and should press on. A stupid row followed and then we continued only to be stopped by a couple of rock gendarmes blocking the ridge. Infuriated, we had to drop 300 feet to circumvent this barrier, and then climb back up a rotting snow gully to regain the ridge.

Having finally reached what seemed likely to be our col, we tied four ropes together, lobbed them off and, after a final argument as to who should be first to get the heck out, Doug won and disappeared into the misty void. An anxious few minutes passed. Were we on the right line to meet up with the lower ropes? A relieved shout from below confirmed our judgement and a few minutes later I was dropping earthwards.

A voice, surely Kiran's, drifted up the face. We wondered if he was waiting for us at the bottom but when we finally got to flat ground, exhausted after a 14-hour day, Kiran was nowhere to be seen. We began to stagger back as the light faded and the cloud dissipated.

Then, to our horror, we spied Kiran on the lower rocks of our col. What on earth was he doing there? Shouting at him to come down, he began to do so. We asked if he needed any help and were secretly relieved when he declined our offer; we felt far too tired to flog back up and render any assistance. Making our way to Base Camp, we glanced back anxiously to check on Kiran's progress and when we got back we sent Ujagar off to help while we brewed up, uneasy with ourselves and at what might happen as darkness fell. Inevitably we heard a cry for help. Wearily we stepped into our frozen boots and retraced our steps. A light back at camp indicated that Kiran and Ujagar had made it home. We had missed them and so turned round and an hour or so later were relieved to find them safe. Kiran had lost his ice-axe and slipped on the final ice slope, hurting his shoulder. It was a terrible blow for him. Kiran was such an engaging character, full of bounce and just a bit too much energy and daring for his own good. Quiet, shy Ujagar was suffering too. He had a stomach problem that effectively ended his participation in the climb. To add to the list of those too sick to participate, Tashi was suffering with piles.

With our ropes now in place for crossing the col, it was decided we could rest, acclimatise or do whatever we pleased. Dougal and Chris had their eye on a shapely unclimbed ice peak opposite our camp. Doug and I selected a less formidable but shapely little summit previously attempted by André Roch many years ago at the head of the Ramani Glacier. We enjoyed a fabulous day, climbing up a crisp and glistening snow arête to a tiny summit with views of twin-headed Nanda Devi and the formidable granite sweep of Changabang.

Over the next few days we made carries to the col and eventually made it down on to Changabang Glacier, a great icy bowl dominated by the East Face of the mountain. We could now examine our route at leisure. I did not much like what I saw; a complex face of snow and ice scarred by avalanche tracks. Just as one possible route was suggested a huge ice avalanche would break loose and change our opinion. A 'safe' line was picked out and Dougal and Chris made a recce. We decided to climb as much as possible at night. We now waited a few days for the weather to settle down. It was a frustrating rest; the only excitement was the discovery Doug was being attacked by lice. His sleeping bag was infested with them after loaning it, with typical generosity, to a shivering porter on the approach march.

After three nights, with food stocks diminishing, the six of us – the four Britons, Balu and Tashi – left our tents at 9 p.m. and set off through a complex maze of seracs and a basin of deep snow and scattered ice blocks. The day had been hot and steamy but the clouds had cleared towards evening and it was now much colder. We forced the pace, anxious to get beyond the obvious danger zone and it was lucky we did so, for a huge avalanche roared by, hidden by the night and only the gentle drizzle of ice dust to remind us of its awful power.

A 20-foot ice cliff barred our way and we waited silently, gazing at the panorama of Nanda Devi lit by the dying moon. The cold was intense and our feet began to freeze so the pink light colouring the rocks of Nanda Devi and heralding the dawn came as a relief. We climbed on, sweating now, round ice cliffs and up gullies until, weary and hot, we found a safe site for camp. We collapsed into our two tents, a tight squeeze with three men in each one.

At 2 a.m. next morning we were off again, initially on the wrong line, until we at last hit easy snow slopes leading to a col between Changabang and Kalanka. From the col a long and delicate ice ridge curled up to the summit. After a brief rest we began traversing the crest, a precarious and time-consuming process. Sometimes we would have to sit astride the ridge, a manoeuvre reluctantly undertaken by Tashi only just recovered from his ailment. We cut steps in the most awkward sections, conscious of our return journey. Having started climbing as two ropes of three, Doug and Dougal were sent off as an advance guard while Chris, Tashi, Balu and I followed behind as fast as we could. The sky clouded over a little, mist obscured the summit and doubts began to grow. Then Dougal disappeared in the mist but then a weary shout floated down: 'We're there!' The rest of us followed as quickly as we could and at 5 p.m. we were all on the summit.

It was not a particularly joyful occasion. The dangerous descent and the fast-fading sun weighed heavily. It was too soon to celebrate. The view was superb but we had too little time to admire the endless Tibetan plateau, green with new grass, or the distant summits of Kamet and holy Kailash. We descended slowly and carefully. I was preparing myself mentally for a bivouac. Then a moment of indecision halted our progress; should we rope off the ridge down to a snow shelf that seemed to offer an easier passage? Chris was lowered down, but the rope didn't reach so up he came again. This wasted valuable time and in a fury of impatience, I set off to solo down the ridge and prove it was safe. It was now freezing again so our footsteps were consolidating which made things much safer. Reaching the tents an hour or so before the others, I brewed tea and made supper. It was pitch dark by the time they arrived.

In the morning we slept late, making endless brews until we finally packed our gear and tried to identify our line of ascent. We were too tired to worry overmuch about the danger but we were nevertheless relieved to reach the safety of camp. That afternoon it snowed heavily and we realised how lucky we had been to summit on the one and only perfect day. We still had to face the hazard of climbing and descending our fixed ropes over the col, but finally we stumbled into Base Camp and the happy congratulations of Doctor D. J. and our cook Norbu.

What more could we do? We had planned to climb Kalanka and perhaps other peaks but in truth we were well-satisfied. It had been a superb mountain experience, we had enjoyed each other's company, made new friends, and it had been a well-organised and happy expedition.

Our return home was slow and punctuated by parties; this has clouded my memory somewhat. Doug had to rush off, I forget why, while Dougal, Chris and I allowed Balu to lead us from one officers' mess to another, enjoying generous hospitality in each. We made a visit to Agra and visited the Taj Mahal before the final drinks showdown. Early on, Dougal went into a catatonic state, for some reason sticking his arm up in the air. This acted as a signal to the alert servants that he needed a fresh ration of gin and tonic, which he duly downed, until finally he toppled over, still rigidly maintaining his Statue of Liberty pose. Next morning, we were driven, still reeling, back to Delhi and a few days later we were home and sober enough to consider our next adventures.

In 1957, Tom Patey had written: 'The main Trango Tower is the most extraordinary rock feature I have seen anywhere, cut off on all sides by walls as steep and long as the West Face of the Dru and attaining a height of over 20,000 feet. It poses a magnificent challenge in the new Golden Age of Himalayan climbing.' This followed the first ascent of nearby Muztagh Tower by Joe Brown and Ian McNaught-Davis. Unfortunately it was a false golden dawn, for the Karakoram was closed to climbers until the mid 1970s, by which time Joe and Mac were still keen while Tom Patey, sadly, was dead.

Chris Bonington with his usual thoroughness had been applying for Trango for several years so, when restrictions on climbing eased, his application was on top of a pile that included Joe Brown's party and, it was thought, a team of Americans led by Yvon Chouinard. Chris was immediately presented with a problem; as leader of the post-monsoon South West Face of Everest expedition he would struggle to find the time for Trango. His task of organisation was immense, and with the timing all wrong he reluctantly conceded that he could no longer go to both mountains.

I felt I could squeeze in both expeditions and so was passed on to join the jolly troops of Joe Brown, Ian McNaught-Davis, Mo Anthoine, Bill Barker and Dave 'Pod' Potts. It looked like a fun adventure before joining the more laborious Everest expedition. Mac, always ready with a bitingly witty insight, once observed that mountains came as two general types: the tit and the prick. In 1975 I would have the chance of attempting both – phallic Trango and the more mammary Everest.

Our expedition to Trango soon ran into problems. After a trouble-free and rapid overland journey by Mo and Pod, we flew out to join them in a cheap and seedy hotel in Rawalpindi. A huge American K2 expedition was already in action. It commandeered all transport to our common starting point in Skardu and thereafter enlisted just about every available porter to carry its tonnes of equipment and food up the Baltoro Glacier.

We kicked our heels for two weeks as bad weather stopped flights to Skardu. Time was running out and those of us with commitments began to feel uneasy. The Pakistan government finally made a DC10 military aircraft available, which didn't have the height restriction of the usual civilian Fokker and so we finally arrived at Skardu, capital of the remote and underdeveloped region of Baltistan. We immediately ran into our next problem of finding enough porters. Then it turned out there was no atta, the flour used for making chapatis. More days drifted past until finally, with the vigorous assistance of our liaison officer, we reached the road-head and the start of the trek into Trango.

Our porters soon revealed themselves to be a troublesome and inexperienced crew. They threatened strike action, demanding more than the statutory rate, and refused to carry to the agreed stages, remaining opportunistic and stony-faced throughout the trek. By the time we reached the Trango Glacier and established a base in heavy drizzle we were happy to pay them off, before arranging for some of them to return, and then watch them disappear into the mist.

Alone at last, that evening the cloud curtain was drawn back to reveal the dramatic granite shaft of Trango Tower. We were obviously going to have a tough time climbing it in the available time. The team was also not a happy one; Mac's business commitments were weighing on him, Joe Brown's wife Val had been ill when he left and Pod seemed to have lost his enthusiasm. It fell to Mo, Bill and myself to push the route, up a corner leading to a snow patch where a shelter was arranged below the start of the hard climbing.

Mo, Bill and I remained at this camp, laboriously forcing a route up difficult rock. Two of us climbed each day while the third rested. Support came in a trickle from below, and food and rope were soon in short supply. On the fourth day, after some exhilarating climbing on perfect red granite, Mo and I ran into an obvious crux – a steep and difficult off-width crack barring the way to easier climbing up to some ledges below a final chimney system.

I climbed that day with an energy born of desperation; our time was limited and this was our last chance of success. After two hard pitches, we landed below the leering crack. I set off, confident I could overcome it, armed with just one bong, a giant piton not unlike a Swiss cowbell. The start of the crack went, but with difficulty, and I placed my bong as high as I could to protect further progress. At 80 feet, the rock bulged, but above the angle eased a little. All I had to do was to climb the next 10 feet and life would become much easier. Shouting down to Mo to watch the rope, I eased my knee gently into the crack, flexed my leg and moved up a few feet. But then, as I attempted to repeat the manoeuvre, my knee slid down the crack a few inches further.

There it remained – completely stuck.

It was merely irritating at first. I had little enough energy to waste climbing, let alone wrestling my knee out of its enclosure. So I slumped down on it and felt the rock's grip tighten – and the first hint of panic began. I struggled furiously for a while, trying to tear the material of my climbing breeches but to no effect. I was rapidly running out of strength, and becoming more fearful as time sped past.

Mo shouted up; he had an emergency bolt kit and perhaps a loop of rope would reach him and he could tie it on? It did, but having got hold of the drill bit, I faced the problem of placing it from my painful position. I banged away with my hammer on the drill as best I could but my hand cramped up and the drill fell from my grasp and tinkled down the cliff.

I collapsed exhausted with fear and exhaustion and sank into a trance-like oblivion. My mind wandered aimlessly picking out memories and focusing on trivia until the anguish inside me welled up and forced me to face my unfortunate end. I choked out a single sob, a distillation of despair. I would never again see my daughter Katie, my wife Maggie, never escape this nightmare to experience once more the warmth of love and life. Everything would be taken from me forever, utterly.

The hours slipped by and the sun moved lower. I was now certain that I would die.

Mo shouted up again. I had completely forgotten about him. He was going down to get help. I roused myself out of my reverie to summon up my last strength and think of a way out. I remembered I had a knifeblade piton in my back pocket. I found it, sharpened its edge against the rock and began hacking at my breeches. The edge was not sharp enough so I pounded the blade with my piton hammer to produce a wicked saw-like edge. With this I laboriously shaved, cut and gouged at the thick material around my thigh. Blood began to ooze thickly through holes in the fabric and my fingers and knuckles became skinned and bloody from my frenzied cutting, but at last I felt the material give. I had cut right round my leg.

Now what?

All my hopes were pinned on the next few moves; I hardly dared to make a start to ease my knee. I tried, gently at first then harder. Nothing happened and my heart sank. I slumped back in despair again and then, I could hardly believe it, my knee slipped out and I half fell, half slid, down to the bong below me. I shouted out to Mo who was now many hundreds of feet below, having tied me off at the belay. With immense effort, I figured out how to descend while Mo waited. When I reached him, bloody and wrecked but alive, I burst into the sweetest tears and to his horror embraced him.

It was the end. By the time we got down to base the porters had arrived to bring us out. It was clear we had run out of time, energy and commitment. The expedition had failed. To add to my disappointment, on the walk back to Skardu I twisted my ankle badly and had to hobble along in great pain. It was not an auspicious start to my next adventure on Everest.

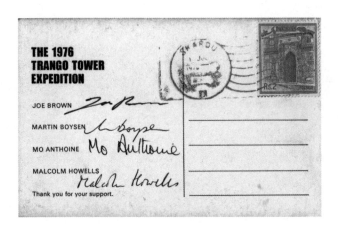

THE 1976 TRANGO TOWER EXPEDITION

JOE BROWN *Joe Brown*

MARTIN BOYSEN *M Boysen*

MO ANTHOINE *Mo Anthoine*

MALCOLM HOWELLS *Malcolm Howells*

Thank you for your support.

Afterwards one has time to reflect, to weigh up the achievement and put it into perspective. First and foremost, we went out to enjoy ourselves, and in this respect the trip was a brilliant success. We also went out to get up Trango Tower, of course. We did, and it was a tremendous route: 4,000 feet of difficult climbing all the way. It is difficult to grade pitches done at altitude, but certainly there were none less than VS, and many would be HVS at any altitude. It is without doubt the most technical and sustained climb to have been done so far in the Himalaya. Joe Brown summed it up adequately when he compared it to the Bonatti Pillar: Trango is twice as long and harder.

SIXTEEN

LOST ON EVEREST, FOUND ON TRANGO

By the time I arrived home after the inevitable delay at Skardu waiting for a plane out of Baltistan, the Everest expedition had already set out for Nepal. Chris Bonington had heard of our trials and suggested I have a short family holiday before joining the team at Base Camp a little later than planned. I was only too glad to take him up on the suggestion and enjoyed a week recuperating on a beach in the south of France. With my body healed and my state of mind restored I was ready to go to Everest. I flew out to Kathmandu, made contact with the delightful Mike Cheney, who ran the Sherpa Co-operative trekking agency, and after a short stay at the Yak and Yeti, met a young Sherpa called Nima, who was cook on Annapurna and would accompany me on the walk to Everest Base Camp.

It was a strenuous business. Nima was young and fit and eager to return home to Solu-Khumbu as quickly as possible. We started each day at our resthouse with a huge pile of rice and lentils. Then we walked all day steeply up and down, tearing off the leeches which waited on the wet jungle paths for a chance to insinuate themselves through our shoes and trousers. By nightfall we were at another lodge.

It was a lovely trek and I learned a great deal about the people and country from Nima, but I was pleased when we finally reached Sherpa country where we could enjoy the hospitality of his friends and relations, as well as chang, the local beer. On the last day we sped past the monastery at Tengpoche and on up to high yak meadows before finally reaching the Khumbu Glacier and Base Camp uncomfortably spread over the boulder-strewn surface below the vast and imposing icefall. The trek had taken an exhilarating 10 days.

I arrived on 25 August, just as the advance party of Dougal Haston and Doug Scott reached the site of Camp One on the upper edge of the icefall. It was a relief to meet up with the team but my delayed arrival caused me to feel the unease of the latecomer at a party in full swing. I had missed the pair bonding, which so often takes place on the walk-in. And after the relaxed informality of the Trango climb, Everest seemed a huge and ponderous siege. Base Camp was like a small untidy village. Yaks and porters arrived each day with produce to keep its population of Sherpas, climbers and filmmakers ploughing ever upwards.

After a few days of acclimatisation I made my way up the tottering mass of the icefall for the first time, skirting round leaning ice towers and over vast crevasses spanned by ladders, ingeniously strung together by Hamish MacInnes. The Western Cwm was a wonderful sight – an empty bowl of snow and ice, with Everest flanked by Lhotse and Nuptse. Afternoon snowfall added an air of mystery and solitude. Occasional avalanches hissed invisibly down the fluted slopes of Nuptse. It was a relief to join the bustle of activity at Camp Two with Pete Boardman, another Everest newcomer. Until this point, I had felt a little downhearted with my apparent lack of involvement in the climbing so it was a relief to be given a role in pushing the route forward; my mood cheered up immediately.

On 10 September I wrote in my diary: 'Amazing how one day's depression dissolves into happiness.' At Camp Two I had been at my lowest ebb, yet next day walking up the Western Cwm with Pete I felt, for the first time on the expedition, light-hearted and gloriously happy. The morning was so magically beautiful, the cwm swathed in boiling mists, Everest shrouded in dark blue shadow and Nuptse emerging diamond white, a hundred ice crests gleaming.

We spent the night at Camp Three, the first on the flank of the South West Face. Next day, Dougal, Hamish and Pete pushed on to the site of Camp Four. I waited for Chris to arrive with some heavily loaded Sherpas before moving to Camp Four. We arrived in the heat of afternoon sun and began digging into the slope deep enough so any powder avalanches would sweep over the box tents rather than pile up behind us. These were another technological masterwork of Hamish with plastic honeycomb bases and bulletproof fabric.

Pete and I were now a team of sorts. He was a likeable but reserved character, an English graduate, bright but impractical, and I was occasionally irritated by his helpless manner – like a demanding chick in the nest. Although he was local, living not far from Manchester, I had only climbed with him a couple of times, but I had no doubts about his ability and his quiet determination and ambition.

My first night in Hamish's 'super-box' was exciting; that evening's snowfall was a little heavier than normal, resulting in spindrift avalanches which swept over and around the boxes. Pete and I were relatively untroubled but Hamish, in the box above ours, took more of the force and was relieved next morning that he was still attached to the mountain rather than hurtling downhill in a canvas coffin.

Pete and I now took a turn in the lead. We jumared up fixed ropes left by Nick Estcourt and Tut Braithwaite and then set off up new ground. It was exhilarating to be in front, and although the climbing was of a low order of difficulty, it was satisfying to have to make decisions, think about the route and establish fixed ropes rather than simply jug up lines put in place by someone else.

Next day, Hamish and Dougal took over the lead. It was a dreary morning; after trying an oxygen set and finding it did not work, Hamish set out but was soon engulfed in a fine powder avalanche. He was swamped in snow and drew some down into his lungs, which almost suffocated him. He returned to camp grey-faced and shocked, injured to such an extent that he wouldn't recover in time to go back into the lead.

We were now using oxygen and, despite the encumbrance of a face mask and the heavy oxygen bottles, it made life easier on the upward plod. Chris and Ronnie Richards established Camp Five just below the Rock Band blocking our progress to the upper snowfield and beyond the South Summit. The expedition had now reached a critical position; no one had yet climbed the Rock Band. Previous expeditions had tried a route at its right-hand side, but we now investigated the left where there appeared to be a deep-set gully cutting through it. It was Nick and Tut's job to investigate this intriguing possibility.

The gully cut into the Rock Band like the Devil's Kitchen in Ogwen, and it left a route through the band that was remarkably easily. A tricky rake leading out to the right proved to be the one and only technical climbing challenge we'd encountered so far. Nick and Tut were jubilant to have made the breakthrough; the route was now open to the summit snowfield. We'd need to establish one more camp and then the summit would be within reach.

The momentum built quickly and we were all suddenly excited. Dougal and Doug, as expected, were chosen as the first summit pair. After climbing to Camp Six and fixing a short length of rope beyond it over a couple of rock steps, they set out for the summit, ploughing their way through tiresomely deep snow, up a shallow gully to the South Summit then along the ridge, over the Hillary Step and on to the summit, adorned with an aluminium tripod, like a maypole, left by a Chinese expedition that spring. It was late in the day, and as the sun disappeared behind the distant horizon, they enjoyed magnificent views in the sobering knowledge that it would soon be dark and they were far from camp. They chose to bivouac at a little col just before the South Summit rather than risk the descent, enduring a wild, hallucinatory night, desperate to avoid frostbite. Their oxygen ran out early that evening, and the stove they took at midnight. But they survived, and were back at Camp Six by 9 a.m. the following morning, having avoided frostbite, to share the news of their success.

Now it was time for the second summit team, gathered either to form a rescue party or to repeat Doug and Dougal's success. I was delighted to be part of it, along with Pete, the expedition sirdar Pertemba and my old friend Mick Burke, who was hoping to film the ascent. I was feeling healthy and fit and pushed up to Camp Five with a growing sense of excitement. Next day we climbed through the Rock Band and reached the two tents of Camp Six in good shape, with time to rest and prepare for the summit push. I shared a tent with Mick as we were the two smokers, and it felt like old times as he cracked jokes and prodded at his cameras with those shaking hands I had noticed when we first met. It was strange that so far on the trip we had hardly shared any time together, but such are the downsides of large expeditions. Mick was now well-established as a cameraman and working for TV companies. But at heart he was still a climber, just one determined to film on the summit.

We awoke very early, laboriously brewed up, donned our boots, crampons and oxygen kits and prepared to set out in the pale light of dawn. I struck out ahead and immediately knew something was wrong. The day previously I was going strongly and had been first to reach Camp Six. Now I was struggling to put one foot in front of the other. I waved the others past me and then struggled to climb the short rock step. I kicked feebly at the snow and a crampon dropped off. It was now that my befuddled brain worked out that my oxygen set was no longer working. I was carrying a heavy load of oxygen bottles but was being smothered by my mask. The whole thing was a useless weight slowing me down.

I retreated to the tent and fiddled with the set but to no avail. It was hopeless. So began what gradually turned out to be the most agonising vigil of my life. I howled with frustrated anguish and a degree of self-pity as I contemplated the cruel misfortune of my malfunctioning oxygen set. It occurred to me to try anyway, but Everest was as yet unclimbed without oxygen. It was very risky, even irresponsible, and likely to end in disaster.

I poked my head out of the tent every so often and observed Pertemba and Pete far ahead. Mick, with his extra load of camera and film, was slower but still advancing, some way back. I noticed with unease the wind pick up and cloud begin to move in. As evening came the weather was turning stormy and I began to stop feeling sorry for myself and to start worrying about the others.

Night fell and still no one returned. Then at last I heard a desperate shout from Pete, who was followed by an exhausted Pertemba. I ushered them into the other tent, and kept them supplied with brews as they told me about the perils of the summit ridge. They had reached the top just as the weather deteriorated, returning carefully in the buffeting wind to encounter, to their amazement, Mick still climbing upwards. He was just a hundred yards from the summit, and far too determined to give in now. He asked Pete if he would go back to the summit to film it, but quickly realised this wasn't on. They arranged to wait for him on the South Summit col, where Dougal and Doug had bivouacked on their descent.

As the wind howled and the light faded, their apprehension grew; if they stayed much longer they would freeze to death. Eventually, after an hour and a half, they had no choice but to set off down without Mick. Even then it was an immense struggle to make it back to Camp Six. They collapsed into their tent exhausted but uneasy with the decision they had been forced to make. No one else stumbled back from out of that bleak night and raging blizzard. Mick was gone.

The next two days and nights are a permanent scar on my memory. 48 hours doesn't seem a long time, yet each of those hours of waiting and struggle seemed to stretch to infinity. At first I couldn't accept Mick's death; we had so many shared experiences. He was such a survivor. Surely he must still be out there alive. There was no chance of going back up to look for him. The storm blew at full force, tearing at the tents and blowing gusts of stinging spindrift. It piled up around us, slowly crushing us. I roused myself to dig out both the tents from the fast-accumulating snow. It was only temporary respite. We were slowly being engulfed. Food was running out and the gas stove would barely light in the suffocating air. I was trying desperately to melt snow to take to Pete and Pertemba, who had suffered some snow-blindness; then I dug out the remaining oxygen bottle for them. In leaving the tent, my sleeping bag got more and more wet, and consequently I began to suffer from the cold. My fingers became damaged. Only the evening radio call raised our morale. If necessary we could hang on for another day or two, but our situation was becoming desperate.

I awoke next morning to an eerie calm. The wind had died; we were saved. A sudden wave of emotion overwhelmed me. I shed tears for Mick, for myself, for everything. I called to the others, dressed and began the laborious work of digging out the buried fixed ropes. It was not an easy task, and as I worked away I noticed my right hand had gone completely numb with cold. Anxious that I might suffer crippling frostbite, I pushed on down to meet Ronnie, Nick, Tut and Ang Phurba at Camp Five. At last I could drink hot tea, but we pressed on once more until we'd all reached the comparative safety of Camp Three. It was not a happy return. Chris greeted us at the end of the fixed ropes and we made our way down in sombre mood – a contrast to the earlier joy of Doug and Dougal's success.

Everest was not what I had hoped for. I was deeply upset at losing one of my oldest and best companions. No one was to blame. Climbing at high altitude is not much fun. One only has the strength, and barely that, to take care of yourself. It is the most selfish of all types of climbing. One is cocooned within one's own self. If things go wrong there is little chance of help. There is no 'fellowship of the rope' beloved by romantic idealists. It is a lonely and, all too often, tragic struggle.

It was a hollow experience, returning home from Everest that autumn, and our sponsor Barclays was eager to reap its publicity reward. The team was split up into lecture parties armed with a set of slides and an expedition film to be shown in all corners of the country. Then, towards the end of the winter, the shocking news broke that Dougal Haston was dead, over-whelmed by an avalanche while making a daring descent from one of the mountains near his home in Leysin in the Swiss Alps. He had been on the point of leaving for an extensive lecture tour in the American West, organised by one of his old friends Dick Dorworth. Dick was a one-time ski speed record-holder and had arranged lectures at almost every well-known resort from Idaho to southern Colorado. Chris rang me up and asked if I could take over Dougal's lectures. Annie, Dougal's widow, had asked if I was available and since I'd done all my UK lectures I was pleased to rescue the tour.

Getting to America was the hard part. I had to get a visa very quickly but in doing so made the fatal mistake of admitting the purpose of my visit. If I was earning a fee I needed a work permit and these were not easily granted. I pleaded that I was earning a pittance, which was unfortunately true, but it cut no ice with the hatchet-faced embassy official who dealt with me. A series of frantic transatlantic phone calls, interspersed with more embassy visits, yielded nothing. To make matters worse, on a trip to a London climbing wall with Ken Wilson following another fruitless trip to the embassy, I dislocated my shoulder. Dick was pulling strings as hard as he could at his end and even enlisted the aid of the Governor of California but I had already missed the first two lectures on the schedule and almost despaired of getting to America.

Once more I joined the embassy queue but this time was ushered into a booth manned by a cheery young man who smiled and, to my immense astonishment, stamped my passport and wished me a good trip. Exactly what went on to secure this change of heart I will never know, but I had two hours to catch the next flight to get to the Californian leg of my lecture tour in time. Luck was at last with me. I ran out of the embassy, hailed a cab and shortly after was sitting in a Pan Am jet gazing down as the icy Scottish Highlands gave way to Iceland, Greenland, Canada and finally Los Angeles.

The tour proved to be a financial disaster and barely paid for itself – perhaps not surprisingly in the circumstances. It was an infamous year of no snow, no skiers and consequently no audience. Despite the financial failure it was a great experience. I had the pleasure of making new friends and meeting quite a few old ones, often unexpectedly. Dick Dorworth and his partner looked after me well and at each new venue I was given superb backup and hospitality. In Los Angeles I stayed with a wonderful *Los Angeles Times* journalist and his family. In my free time he took me to an immigration office where my work permit problem was finally resolved and we even had time for a swim at Santa Monica, thanks to the unseasonal warm weather. At my lecture in Los Angeles my old Scouse friend Pete Minks showed up; he was an illegal alien working in California and as manic and good company as ever.

My main problem, once I left the big cities, was to get from one venue to the next. The sequence of lectures did not always follow in a logical geographical sequence and so involved zigzagging between often isolated destinations around the West by plane, Greyhound bus and private car. In a normal snowy year this would have been even more difficult. On the southern leg of my trip I stayed with Tom Frost and his family in Boulder and was sufficiently recovered from my shoulder injury to climb a classic route with Tom and Yvon Chouinard in Boulder Canyon. Tom saved me by driving me on the most difficult leg of the journey – to Telluride, an old-world mining town situated in a marvellous box canyon with a beautiful ice waterfall, known as the Bridal Veil, at its end. It was good to see him again and reminisce, remembering lost friends and mountain adventures on the long journey south. It was a typical act of kindness.

The final lecture was perhaps the most successful, given to a packed house in Seattle – a city of climbers surrounded by icy heights. It had been an arduous trip and I was happy to get back home and put my feet up awhile. Unfortunately I had plenty of opportunity to do so, having come down with chicken pox acquired in Colorado from Rusty Baillie's children. My recovery took some time.

After the trauma of Everest and the disappointment of our first Trango expedition, it seemed inconceivable that I might return. It had not been a happy expedition. Mac had not been able to recapture his old enthusiasm and Joe was not himself. Their long-held dream of attempting Trango had come too late. Only Mo, irrepressible as ever, was keen to return and he forged ahead in a relentless pursuit for permission in the summer of 1976. It was granted. Haunted by memories of the crack and those tantalising summit chimneys, I could not wait to return.

Joe, on the other hand, took a little persuading. He was too old, he said, he would miss the salmon run; but we all knew that Trango Tower was something special for him. He would do it and then hang his boots up. Malcolm Howells, an excellent and determined climber from Manchester, made the team up to four. Later, we decided to make a film of the ascent and were joined by Jim Curran and Tony Riley, good friends who could both climb and hopefully make an entertaining film that would pay for itself – or better.

In June, Mo and Tony set out for Pakistan in the expedition van. It was the start of a smooth-running expedition – in contrast to our previous trip. Six and a half days later they arrived in Rawalpindi and the rest of us flew out to join them. After the most tremendous hospitality from the British Embassy staff, we all flew out to Skardu and joined our cheerful and highly efficient liaison officer, Captain Zaffar. It took just a day to hire our porters and then we were off. This time our porters were excellent and we reached Base Camp in an enjoyable eight days.

We quickly retraced our route from the previous attempt, establishing a camp at the top of the couloir and got ready to retrace our steps. One fear haunted us: would our ropes from the year before still be usable? We fervently hoped so; we hadn't enough new ones to replace them all. As it transpired, they were mostly intact, though often buried under ice. The slow and precarious business of re-climbing the Tower could now begin. Often we needed to hack the ropes out, but sometimes they were buried too far and we had to re-climb pitches and leave fresh fixed ropes. It was a nerve-racking business, re-climbing the old ropes; in a year they might have abraded or been cut by falling stones.

Our aim was to stock the camp on the snow patch, inspect the old ropes and then make a push to the ledge below the chimneys. There we would bivouac with three days of food and hope to climb to the top. We were almost ready to carry this plan into action when the weather decided otherwise. A violent storm sprang up, it snowed hard all night and our tents were crushed, along with our summit hopes.

Next morning we descended all the way to Base Camp where a lonely Zaffar gladly welcomed us back. If anything, he was more disappointed at our delay than we were; he had got married only a fortnight before the expedition. We also faced the problem that our porters were due to return. Zaffar and Jim decided to intercept them while we stocked up on food and rest. Three days later the storms cleared and once more we picked our way up the tedious couloir. Next day we were determined to reach the ledge, so Mo and I set off early to do battle with the crack that had almost finished me off a year earlier.

It was strange, being back. The crack looked no easier but this time I was better prepared for it. Using my knee as a template, we had measured up an extra piton. I set off, shaking slightly with the rush of adrenalin in my blood, and, as I reached the fateful spot, hammered home the piton with relish. A step up and I was past it. The remaining crack was still hard; I recoiled from the prospect of jamming my knee, forcing myself to find any other means to climb it before reaching a tiny handhold. I pulled hard and rolled over the top. I was jubilant. As darkness fell we assembled on a snowy shelf hard under the final bulging wall. We dug out a ledge and collapsed into our sleeping bags as a brilliant moon rose. We were tired, but content.

Next day a weary Joe and Malcolm took over the lead. Our hopes for an easy pitch or two were rudely shattered. The chimneys were not chimneys at all, just a huge gash through the vast, overhanging walls. First Malcolm and then Joe climbed pitches as hard as any done so far. By late afternoon Joe returned, followed by Malcolm. They had climbed just over two rope lengths. Malcolm had stopped at a vicious ice-filled crack; he announced calmly that he was uncertain of its feasibility.

This was not news to make us sleep that night. We would be hard pressed to stay on our ledge much longer as we were fast running out of food and fuel – a day or perhaps two at the most. I was even more concerned when I woke to see the moon shrouded in a mist halo, always a bad sign. In the distance, lightning flashed over the plains; the monsoon was pressing in.

Mo and I set off early next morning and climbed up the ropes to examine what lay ahead. It was not as black as it had been painted. Hidden in the right wall of the slot lay a thin, overhanging iced-up crack which Mo attacked, well-armed with pitons. After two and a half hours he reached an icy niche and belayed. Frozen stiff and impatient for action, I threw myself at the next icy corner and nearly expired from exhaustion. We were now quite high, the air was thin and it was hard work climbing quickly. I pushed on but in my eagerness to get to grips with the pitch had underestimated the difficulty of the climbing. I found myself without pitons – these were still with Mo. Cursing the situation roundly, I descended to collect them.

Back at my highpoint, I hammered in a piton, stepped up and suddenly flew backwards as it shot out of the crack. I was now in a rage and hurled myself up, lunging for a snow shelf. As I shot off into space once more, I was thoroughly soaked; it was time to calm down and on the next attempt I addressed the rock with greater care. Looking up, I felt a little downcast. The chimneys seemed to carry on and on while clouds were already enveloping the summit rocks. I climbed a wet overhang, and suddenly a wide terrace revealed itself. Amazed, I struggled on to it. We were on a shoulder of the mountain; above looked easy and on the other side was the most fantastic view of the huge Baltoro Glacier flanked by the Karakoram giants, K2, Gasherbrum, Masherbrum and the black wedge of Muztagh Tower, first climbed by Joe and Mac 20 years before. It was late, though; I had wasted hours on the last pitch, the rope was covered in ice and Mo was having difficulty in climbing it. At last he arrived and marvelled at the view, then Tony arrived.

It was worth a try to get to the summit; the weather was breaking and it might be our last chance. I led off, up icy terrain in crampons, climbed an awkward corner, traversed left and shouted with glee. The route to the top was easy and only a few hundred feet high. We stormed up as the sun slipped towards the horizon, reached a tiny col and Mo stamped up the last 20 feet past me to the summit. It was hard to stop smiling. Like the very best adventures, we had made it – but only just!

We descended to the ledge just before nightfall. Joe was as pleased as we were. We could sleep happy. Next morning Joe and Malcolm set off up the ropes while we lay and luxuriated. But not for long, for soon snowflakes began drifting down. We began to descend the ropes for the last time.

That night we all met again at Base Camp. Joe and Malcolm had succeeded; we were all safe and happy. Our porters were waiting and we were ready to go home. It had been the climb of our lives, surely one of the most difficult and sustained yet done in the Himalaya. For Mo, Malcolm and myself it was a stimulus for other climbs; for Joe it marked a conclusion – his last major expedition, he said. I almost believed him.

After Trango I wondered about my next climb. Chris Bonington, I learned, had permission for K2, the world's second-highest mountain and a tough challenge for anyone. I confidently expected to form part of his team so when he phoned me and asked to pop in to see me on his way south I looked forward to seeing him and sharing his plans.

As soon as I opened the door I detected all was not well. Instead of striding in as he would normally, he lingered in the doorway and suggested we go for lunch in the local pub. It was in the bar that he delivered his news.

'Martin, I'm afraid I haven't picked you for K2. I know you will be disappointed; you have been a wonderful support, a loyal friend … '

Words of comfort continued to drift unheard and unheeded over my head as the essential message sank in: I was no longer part of Team Bonington.

This sudden rejection hit me hard. I felt a deep disappointment and the pain of a long friendship betrayed. I had always loved Chris; not uncritically, but we had shared a lot of adventures and I had given him my all when it really mattered. What caused my demise? I was too stunned and hurt to enquire why, and the lingering pain of the episode makes me loath to rake over old ground. Perhaps with the deaths of dear companions like Dougal and Mick I'd lost support. Whatever the reason, from now on I was going to have to seek out my true friends. Life was going to be more difficult but in a way it was good that I should rely on my own resources and plan my own future course.

It didn't take long to come up with a plan. On our first Trango trip Mo Anthoine, Bill Barker and I had gazed at the vast trapezoid of Gasherbrum IV at the head of the Baltoro Glacier. It was a formidable objective; the mountain had only been climbed once by no less than Walter Bonatti and Carlo Mauri by the easiest route, which was anything but easy. Our objective of the West Face would need a strong team so we invited two of the most outstanding young climbers to join our party. Joe Tasker and Dick Renshaw had recently impressed the climbing world with their audacious ascents in both the Alps and Himalaya. They had recently climbed the fine mountain Dunagiri close to Changabang where Dick had suffered some frostbite damage to his fingers. They seemed pleased to be invited but as our plans began to gather momentum Joe was offered a place with Chris Bonington on K2. He was unable to decline and shortly after Dick Renshaw followed him.

We were now down to three but at the last moment Pete Minks, temporarily ejected from America, resurfaced and was keen to make up the team to four. Unlike the lavish Bonington expeditions I'd experienced we were an impoverished expedition; unlike Chris, we'd been unable to attract the protective backing of the London Rubber Company, sponsors of the K2 expedition. To get to Pakistan we bought a cheap Transit van and packed it to overflowing with expedition kit and food. Then we set out on what was for Mo a familiar trip. It was a fast-changing journey, which foreshadowed the enormous political tumult about to take place in Iran and Afghanistan. The Black Cat, a watering-hole in Tehran for foreigners and a few guilty-looking Iranians, was now boarded up, a consequence of the growing power of the mullahs prior to the Shah's overthrow.

At the Afghan border the police were jumpy and became excited at the discovery of our two walkie-talkies. After a long delay, we had a policeman imposed on us and were directed to a higher police authority in Herat. From Herat we were sent on to the police headquarters in Kabul, all of which did little to improve our temper in our already overcrowded van. Fortunately, in Kabul the police chief in charge was an urbane and fluent English speaker. He dismissed our suspicious electronics as so much nonsense but he was keen that we cleared the border that same day. He hinted that trouble was imminent and there did seem to be an expectant air of unease everywhere we went.

We set off as fast as possible, still with our police liaison officer to help us through numerous roadblocks. It was a worrying journey; the army was on the alert and several times we screeched to a halt on failing brakes to come unnervingly close to the gun barrel of a tank blocking our way. The Afghan army did not inspire confidence; ill-clad, ignorant, nervous and nasty, a band of them set upon us as we attempted to fill up with fuel. As they attempted to bayonet our tyres, our nervous police escort fled into the night and we were left anxiously wondering if we would make our deadline, but we made the frontier and at last encountered an officer who could read our official pass. He was expecting us and we were directed into a safe enclosure for the night.

Pakistan seemed an oasis of calm by contrast. Our journey from Rawalpindi to Skardu went uncharacteristically smoothly, and our small party of climbers, porters and liaison officer were quickly assembled ready for the approach march, once more through the collapsing hell of the Braldu Gorge to reach the last village of Askole and then onwards past the Trango Towers, to Masherbrum, Muztagh Tower and Mitre Peak at the head of the vast Baltoro Glacier. Here we were at last – confronted with the West Face of Gasherbrum IV. It looked as formidable as we had feared.

We established Base Camp as close to the face as we dared, for it was a cramped and enclosed valley threatened by avalanche. Our liaison officer wisely departed to seek companionship with his own kind at the nearby K2 expedition Base Camp.

Early on in the expedition, after a heavy fall of snow, we heard from the K2 team that Nick Estcourt was dead, swept away in an avalanche.

Doug Scott, his partner, had miraculously survived. It was grim news, although Bill with his typically mordant wit pointed out how lucky I was to have been spared the Russian roulette of a Bonington expedition. It was dark humour, but I did feel the shadow of death pass ominously close.

With the threat of avalanches on our mind we decided against the obvious route up huge snowfields and gullies in favour of a safer but more difficult rocky buttress at the left side of the face. We made good progress at first but then Pete cracked his ankle and subsequently slumped into a narcotic haze. Bill and I pushed the route upwards and we felt a modest pride when we reached an icy crest high up on the mountain.

Hacking out a miniature platform for our tent, next day we climbed a mouldering marble gully above us. Gasherbrum IV may look magnificent but looks can be deceptive; on closer inspection we discovered the mountain is composed of the most awful and fragile rock imaginable – a striking contrast to the immaculate red granite of Trango Tower.

We waited next day for Mo to bring up more food, fuel and rope but he didn't arrive. At a loss to know what to do next, we eventually descended in bad humour to find him still at Base. It was out of character for Mo to let us down; our highpoint proved to be the last serious effort. The expedition fizzled out from lack of energy; we had lost enthusiasm for the attempt. The truth was we were under strength for our route. All that remained was to summon up a few porters on their way down from K2 Base Camp, pack up, retreat down our approach route and drive back home again, this time through a more scenic route. We drove over the Pontic Alps in northern Anatolia, now known as the Kaçkar Dag, and then, in the footsteps of Xenophon, steeply down through a thick rhododendron jungle – the infamously invasive *rhododendron ponticum* – then through hazel forests to Trebizond, the romantic last outpost of Byzantium, perched on rocks above the Black Sea. We bathed joyfully in the big surf before continuing on to Istanbul, the Balkans, Italy, over the Alps into France – and home.

SEVENTEEN
GOLD RUSH

It was good to be home and spending time with Maggie and Kate, who was growing up to be a delightful, bright and interesting child. She absorbed information, had a keen and observant interest in nature, and already exhibited a forceful and determined character.

The problem I faced was how to combine my climbing life with earning money. For a while I had managed to lecture on my exploits but the rewards were meagre and they had begun to dry up. Once more – and with some reluctance – I scanned the *Times Educational Supplement* for local teaching jobs, applying for the first available post. To my complete dismay I was appointed, on the spot, at a local secondary modern. It was not a happy choice; the school was efficiently run but in an old-fashioned way, which still included liberal use of corporal punishment. My teaching was intellectually unchallenging and I was horrified when one of my miscreants was brutally caned. I felt out of place and regretted accepting the first job I'd been offered.

In the middle of this rather depressing phase, during a dismal November, I answered the phone to hear the unhurried voice of Tom Frost inviting me to join his team for an ascent of Ama Dablam in Nepal, the stunning peak that guards the trekking route to Everest. To make it even more inviting the cost would be entirely paid for by a film company. I could hardly wait to hand in my notice.

Ama Dablam is a delectable mountain, shaped as everyone expects a mountain should be, its elegant beauty – in contrast with the dull outline of Everest – persuading lazy picture editors that this must be the highest mountain on Earth. In early 1979, when our expedition left, Ama Dablam had been climbed just once – in 1961. The ascent, by a mixed group of New Zealand, American and British climbers participating in the 'Silver Hut' research expedition, had been somewhat illegal, and the mountain had been promptly declared 'holy' and put off limits for almost two decades.

Tom Frost had gathered together a varied team, including most of the Lowe family – Jeff, Greg and parents Ralph and Jean. There was Doug Robinson and David Breashears as well as Tom's wife Dorene and their children, daughter Marna and son Ryan. Then there was Roger, a rather glum company-man directing film matters with several cameramen and various camp followers too numerous to recall.

I arrived early at Heathrow as snow was falling and flights were delayed. An agitated and athletic young man was stretching and standing on his toes near the check-in desk, so I took a guess and introduced myself. This was David Breashears who proved a marvellous companion. He was engagingly enthusiastic, had read every book and article on climbing and was about to become one of the best extreme cameramen around; he was already a superb climber.

David and I arrived at Kathmandu and, after the usual chaos and bureaucracy at the airport, caught up with some of the team at our hotel. Our first meeting was interesting; there was a great shake down of ideas. This was a far more democratic process than I'd experienced before. Tom had yet to arrive, but Jeff Lowe, the expedition's star alpinist, made it clear he was up for the unclimbed North Ridge even though we didn't have permission for that. Other team members were happy to climb the existing route. Some sort of consensus emerged; we would do the established route first and then see what happened.

It was refreshing making a whole new set of friends. Jeff with his white mane of hair and moustache looked like a reincarnation of Mark Twain and in fact he shared the same folksy humour. Dave, dark and intense, was bursting with energy and enthusiasm, forever cycling at speed through Kathmandu's labyrinth of narrow streets visiting temples and bazaars.

We spent a day filming in the city streets, shuffling around markets and temples and then Tom arrived with family. It was great to see him again and I hoped his calming influence would have an effect on our excitable team. The team was now complete and we were ready for the hair-raising flight to Khumbu; there would be no long walk-in this time. Gathered together at the airport early in the morning, we endured a couple of confused hours in the hurly-burly of the departure 'lounge'.

'How do they ever get anything done?' was the typical response from my new American friends watching this organised chaos.

In less than an hour we experienced what felt like a crash landing at the pocket airstrip of Lukla. A team of Sherpas quickly unloaded the plane before it quickly reversed the manoeuvre; clear flying conditions meant a fast turnaround. We set up camp and starting sorted equipment, all of which had arrived by the following morning. I marvelled at the variety of tents – every shape, colour and size imaginable. Everyone had his favourite specialised equipment and Greg was particularly proud of his inflatable sleeping pad, the first I had ever seen. It was unfortunate for him that the pad instantly sprang a leak and became an endless source of fun as Greg tried unsuccessfully to find the leak and seal it.

The Sherpas almost fell over laughing trying to put together the expedition's vast and complex geodesic dome tent, especially when it threatened to blow away with Sherpas still attached. There would be no wood fires however: 'the environmentalists will crucify us if they see smoke on film,' Roger told me. It took some adjustment to survive on a diet of peanut butter and 'jelly' washed down with highly iodised brown water and more vitamins and health nostrums than I could ever have imagined.

We moved off at last, dropping down to the Dudh Kosi River. It was still cold and there were few signs of spring; only the hardiest of the purple *primula denticulata* lit up the dull brown of the winter grass. In fact, it was so cold that next day we spied a huge frozen waterfall across the valley. The discovery prompted a break in the trek while we had another discussion, spending a rest day above Namche. I had a leisurely breakfast and then settled down to listen to the debate. Jeff was excited and wanted to climb it and Roger was keen to film the ascent, but how would we get there? Was the ice stable and would it be possible to shoot it? Could it be climbed or not? After talk had rumbled on for a bit, the subject was shelved in favour of the next tricky decision: whether we should stay where we were a few extra days to acclimatise. Roger's girlfriend was suffering a headache; we could not be too careful. I kept my own head below the parapet but warmed to this process of democracy in action. To my surprise, it seemed generally to work out well. While we rested I enjoyed competitive bouldering sessions with Dave and Jeff.

The film crew wanted familiar Khumbu images, the 'yeti' skull and so forth. At Tengboche Monastery I endured once again the gongs, trumpets, reedy oboes, clappers and droning incantations, delivered for the usual payment and concluded with yak-butter tea. It was a relief to finally leave the well-trodden tourist trail and head up steep grassy slopes to the foot of our mountain.

The ridge above looked interesting, rising easily at first then steepening to a thin icy crest where it was interrupted by steep rocky bands which led up to a hanging glacier – the *dablam* or prayer amulet for which the mountain is named. Unfortunately, because of the necessity to film the ascent, we were going to have to fix a good deal of rope, which would slow us down.

I climbed with Jeff and got on very well with him; gradually the film evolved to show us as the two-man team tackling the mountain. The route progressed well despite the absence of any orders from our leaders and we established a camp high on the ridge. Pushing on up mixed snow and rock, we reached the first of the rock steps and the first technical difficulties – 100 feet of rock climbing at a standard of around Very Severe. More ice runnels led up to the lower edge of the hanging glacier, which blocked us with an 80-foot wall of vertical ice. Jeff elegantly despatched it and when my turn came I realised my own crude Snowdon Mouldings ice-axe and crampons were somewhat rudimentary compared to the sophisticated tools of the Lowe brothers.

Above the ice cliff the angle relented briefly to a flat area perfect for siting tents. Our motley crew gathered and hatched a plan. Jeff and I would go ahead in advance of Tom, Doug and anyone else that fancied the trip. We set out early next morning. It was bitterly cold and my axe pick almost immediately snapped in the hard ice. Cloud soon enveloped us so the ascent was less exhilarating than it might have been. We climbed on and on, hidden in wreaths of white cloud, until suddenly we could go no higher – we were at the summit. Despite waiting hopefully for a clearance, it never came. After a while the others joined us and so we began the descent. This took us longer than anticipated; we were reluctant to leave the rest of the party behind so on several occasions waited, stamping our feet to maintain circulation. I had unwisely selected my light single-skin boots for the climb and now my feet began to freeze; I was still using my trusty old leather ones much worn in the Alps. Plastic boots were still in the future. I would suffer frost-nip in my toes but we made it back to camp by evening and next day descended to Base.

Over the next few days, several more ascents were made while I bathed my feet in hot water and watched the moving dots high on the mountain. Jeff was dissatisfied with our achievement and cast around for a partner to climb the mountain again by the mixed face to the right of our ridge. With my damaged feet, I was unable to accompany him and the other members were not quite as adventurous or as able as Jeff so he set off on his own and made a terrific one-day ascent using the remaining camp on our ridge for his descent.

The expedition ended on this high note. It had been a happy experience and just about everyone achieved some success. It was refreshing to see that large expeditions could run so smoothly without needing the heavy hand of leadership. The whole trip had been light-hearted and joyful and I returned home happy, still sporting a snazzy Zapata-style moustache inspired by my new American friends. Maggie and Kate thought it ridiculous.

Soon after I got back Ama Dablam, I came down with gold fever. I was visiting Joe Brown at his Llanberis home when I first heard of his trip to the Llanganati Mountains of Ecuador in search of lost Inca gold. Hamish MacInnes had stumbled on an intriguing mystery in a book written by Richard Spruce, a well-known, self-taught botanist who explored the Amazon and Andes during the 19th century. The story related back to an infamous series of events following the invasion of the Inca Empire by the conquistadors. Francisco Pizarro and his bold but avaricious band of desperadoes captured the Inca king Atahualpa and put him up for ransom – staking his life for a roomful of gold. Having received half the gold Pizarro reneged on his promise, and strangled Atahualpa for reasons unknown. The remaining gold was meanwhile being transported from the northern half of the empire when the news of the treachery reached the convoy. The gold was dumped, according to some in a deep lake called Yanacocha in the Llanganati. A letter written by a 17th-century Spanish official called Valverde contradicts the location of the gold; Valverde wrote to the King of Spain on his deathbed, giving directions to a vast treasure hidden in a cave in the mountains. No treasure hunt is complete without an ancient treasure map; such a map existed, drawn by an earlier treasure-hunter called Atanasio Guzman.

Joe and Hamish had earlier joined with Yvon Chouinard, then embarking on his successful and much more lucrative Patagonia clothing venture, and set off into the Llanganati Mountains to follow Guzman's map. They hacked through dense grass to reach high mountain ridges but, perhaps unsurprisingly, failed to find the golden breastplates promised by Valverde's letter. Hamish was not yet finished. Although he had failed to find gold in the mountains he was more successful in extracting pieces of eight from *The Observer* newspaper. These he intended to use for a further exploration of the fabled Llanganati.

Hamish had once again recruited Joe, this time for a watershed crossing into the Amazon basin; it was really an excuse for a spot of exploration disguised as a quest for hidden gold for the sake of our sponsor. Joe showed me the photocopied map and documentation and asked if I was interested in coming along. The answer was easy, especially as Mo was coming too. An expedition with Mo and Joe couldn't fail to be anything other than fun. Joining the party was a tall American anthropologist called Joe Reinhard, now better known as Johan Reinhard, who discovered the Inca mummies in the Andes. Joe had accompanied Hamish and Joe on a Nepalese adventure searching for another lost cause, the yeti. Hamish had made another valuable contact in Ecuador called Brian Warmington, an Englishman married to an Ecuadorian living in Baños not too far from our destination. In all probability he would be joining us on our trip through the jungle.

We flew to Quito with a long stopover at Miami. On their previous expedition, Joe and Hamish had arrived in Florida without a US visa and were subsequently imprisoned; this time we were armed with the necessary visas and paperwork. I even managed a short trip to a Miami liquor store with Joe. He was not such the trusty guide I expected; it had been years since he'd been home and the mean streets of Miami seemed more alien and dangerous than any of his recent adventures.

Quito, set at high altitude, was pleasantly cool in contrast to hot and sweaty Miami. For a backdrop, Quito has the giant volcano of Cotopaxi first climbed by German geologist Wilhelm Reiss and the Colombian Angel Escobar in 1872. Mo and I were delegated to top up our food rations. We'd brought a fair amount of freeze-dried stuff but needed the usual staples: oats, for Hamish's porridge, dried onions, absolutely not for Hamish, flour, salt and so forth. We made contact with Brian but, before we could leave our cheap hotel, were held at gunpoint by narcotics cops who found it difficult to believe anyone would willingly go wandering about mountains and jungle for the hell of it.

We climbed aboard the bus for Baños. Hamish, cradling a vast bag of pineapples, sat hunched between two cheerful Indian ladies, themselves clutching chickens, children and who knows what. From the high and treeless Altiplano we descended steeply into a deep valley flanked by huge organ-pipe cliffs of basalt before reaching the edge of the jungle at Baños. As the name suggests, this is a hot-water spa nestling under a high volcano. Huge torrents of piping-hot water gushed out of the rocks and into innumerable bathing booths and washing slopes thronged with women washing and pounding clothes. We stayed at the comfortable hotel owned by Brian's wife and gathered a few last-minute purchases, including the locally made sombreros. Having soaked up some last luxuries, we went back up to the high Altiplano city of Ambato, where we hired a flat bed lorry to take us on to the town of Pillaro, gateway to the Llanganati Mountains. Here Brian had arranged for us to pick up a number of porters to help transport our kit for a few days.

Our porters, once arranged, did not look a very likely lot. Geraldo, the headman, had bloodshot eyes and was swaying and reeling. He had clearly been on a monumental bender. His deputy, henceforth known as Deadeye Dick, was the proud owner of an antique firearm; he also sported a well-fed stomach hinting at a gargantuan appetite. The remaining crew, shod in green wellies, seemed a sullen lot, and were reluctant to make a move, saying it was too late and too hot to reach our first camp. It was only when Brian informed them, rather forcefully, that Joe Brown had been there before and that it was a mere two-hour stroll that the journey began.

We reached Lake Yanacocha after traversing a vast bog on a long causeway of logs. It was a black, marsh-fringed lake, framed by the high mountains that Joe and Hamish had previously traversed. Mo told Hamish he should dive into its inky depths and return with the fabled gold breastplates. Where gold breastplates came from never emerged; but it became a constant source of humour, particularly for Mo. He had the knack of immediately noticing any weakness or imperfection and would use it to barb his humour. As Bill Barker once said, if Mo was presented with the Mona Lisa, he would focus immediately on a blackhead on her nose.

We trekked initially through a great bog to reach eventually the Andean watershed where water trickled either side of the ridgeline to one or other of the great oceans. There was a dry spot for the tents and we enjoyed a clear and freezing night under a brilliant starlit sky before setting off next morning downhill through a great grass forest and then increasingly thick jungle. We passed a couple of forlorn clearances with the ruined remains of thatched huts but then left human habitation behind. The trail was now non-existent to our eyes; we were however following a clear plunging river, which we assumed to be the Parcayacu. From now on everything was an assumption; there were no maps that were definitively useful.

We made our way slowly, following what remained of the trail but this soon petered out. Stopping for lunch at a small clearing I dozed off and when I awoke discovered I was alone. For a short time I panicked, crashing this way and that through the undergrowth until I gave myself a good talking to.

'Calm down – use your powers of observation. Spot the footprints and broken twigs. They will show the path the others took.' After a frantic scramble through the jungle I caught up with the team but everyone seemed oblivious to my little trauma. The jungle had, for a short time, seemed a place of terrible loneliness.

We camped on the side of the river on a sandy bank deposited by a flood. It was fortunate we were in the dry season, otherwise there would have been very few dry spots to erect tents. To my ornithological horror, Deadeye Dick proceeded to shoot a brace of torrent ducks while Joe went fishing. The results were gratifying; he entered camp draped with a dozen decent-sized trout. Joe, with his carbon fibre rod, dry and wet flies, and sophisticated gear was rattled to be outdone in the hunter stakes by Geraldo who hooked a monster five-pounder on what appeared to be nothing more sophisticated than a stout stick and thick string.

A pattern of operation evolved over the next few days. Hamish the architect and engineer would build the communal shelter with sticks and tarpaulin while I would endeavour to light a fire and start cooking before the inevitable late afternoon rain began. Joe would be sent to fish while Mo and Joe Reinhard – dubbed Rhino to avoid confusion – would clear the site of boulders, fetch firewood and be generally useful. Brian, who as newcomer to our group was still a little withdrawn, was invariably washing something – either clothes or himself – sometimes both simultaneously. His cleanliness was, I noticed, close to obsessive. Perhaps his choice of Baños, Ecuador's Buxton, was not an accident after all.

After a couple of days it was time to send some of the porters back home before they ate all our sugar and porridge of which they were inordinately fond. It was only after they had gone for an hour that we discovered they had absconded with our best machetes and a goodly portion of bully beef. Geraldo and Deadeye were dispatched to retrieve these stolen items but by the time they caught them everything had mysteriously disappeared. Geraldo returned crestfallen and offered, no doubt in guilt, to make a rapid return to civilisation and buy us three more machetes. We would meanwhile push forward and establish a comfortable staging post, which became known as Fish Camp.

The trail grew ever more difficult. Sometimes we would hop and slide over algae-covered rocks at the side of the stream but then would meet a rock barrier too difficult to traverse and be forced up vertical mud banks and stinking bogs into the thickest canopy. This would take hours to cut into a manageable track. We were approaching a mountainous ridge where our river cut through a deep gorge and the going was worse than normal. Armed with nothing but Joe's old and damaged kukri and a small machete, contemptuously dismissed as 'the breadknife' by Mo, we would find it difficult to move further downstream. An alternative offered itself; if we could cross the river and pass over the mountain ridge we might circumnavigate the gorge and reach our next river – the Rio Mulatos. We hoped that our river flowed into this new one.

Mo and Rhino were sent off to see if there was any way through the gorge while Hamish and I, armed with the repaired kukri and breadknife, set across the river to search for a route over the ridge. It was of course impossible to see exactly where we were going in the deep canopy but our progress was straightforward, at least until the ground steepened. We returned to camp well-satisfied with our progress towards the col, while Mo reported his way was virtually impassable. While we waited for Geraldo and Deadeye Dick to return, we enlarged the camp and made it more comfortable. Joe fished until we told him we were sick of trout. When he returned from the river carrying yet another vast catch Mo upbraided him for his unnecessary slaughter. Even Joe conceded he had overdone it.

Still, Fish Camp was well-named and fish formed our staple diet until Geraldo returned. Deadeye shot another torrent duck and a few other nameless small birds to produce a surprisingly tasty bird stew. As chief cook and firelighter I spent a lot of time splitting wood to get to the dry inner core of the sodden fuel. I would then energetically fan the flames sending smoke unerringly straight into the main shelter. As cook, my main difficulty was disguising the dried onions and garlic, which formed an unvarying part of our diet. Hamish, annoyingly, claimed to have a serious aversion to all members of the onion family. He was, rightfully as it happens, suspicious of every meal I served him, picking through stews and curries in search of any allium. Luckily, no harm seems to have been done to his health.

With Geraldo and partner gone again we were now on our own and, after a couple more days of hacking and slashing with our shiny new machetes, we reached the col; it was exciting to have a view at last and the way ahead looked interesting. The col was named Observer Col in honour of our sponsors rather than Mo's suggested alternative of Crap Col in honour of a splendid evacuation.

Once we'd brought all our kit up to the col, Joe and Mo pushed the route down steep and tricky ground to a vast clearing. This proved to be an enormous and recent landslide that had engulfed the valley bottom with earth and rocks for what must have been several square miles. As yet there was virtually no vegetation to obscure the view and we felt like dogs on a beach, able to run around enjoying the space and the freedom it offered. Hamish as usual set off on a wild goose chase panning for gold with the largest plastic plate he could find in the kitchen. The odd speck of iron pyrites encouraged him despite Mo's constant mockery.

Joe, with his insatiable curiosity, was in his element catching and photographing giant insects, monster worms and anything else of interest. Despite Hamish's dire warning of deadly snakes, jaguars and biting insects we saw little wildlife to trouble us; blundering through the jungle, most animals were long gone apart from the odd hummingbird and vast clouds of butterflies which settled all over us seeking out the salt on our sweaty bodies. One of the most noticeable butterflies we named 'BP' due to the initials marked on its wings. This was inappropriate, Hamish informed us, since it was Shell that was busy despoiling huge tracts of Ecuadorian jungle in the quest for oil.

We now reached the point of no return; we had sufficient food, we calculated, to reach the first Indian village on the Rio Napo, one of the main tributaries of the Amazon. Having reluctantly left our landslide we plunged back into the undergrowth, eventually hitting the junction of the Mulatos with our previous river, the Parcayacu. This proved to be the first of several tricky river crossings. Mo was sent ahead to hop and eventually wade the stream before setting up a rope we could use to slide across above the fast-flowing water. Beyond this, the Parcayacu became tough going again. We progressed only slowly, alternately boulder-hopping – with the occasional slip and complete immersion – and jungle-hacking. Food grew scarce and we became ever more doubtful of our position on the map.

Before embarking on our trip, Brian had paid a few pence for a spot on local jungle radio offering a reward for a couple of Indians to come up river to meet us and assist our final few days. Mo and Brian, our only fluent Spanish speaker, were despatched with light loads to forge ahead and find out if any had taken up our offer. They set out early, crossed a dark and dirty tributary and, like Robinson Crusoe, found footprints in the sand. By the time we had made more lumbering approach, the dirty stream was a raging, black torrent, swollen by some distant cloud burst.

'This must be the Rio Negro', I announced and for this profound deduction I was rewarded with the task of crossing it, tied to two ropes and clutching a stout stave to steady myself. I was just able to reach the other bank without being swept off my feet, acutely aware of how dangerous the crossing was; many an explorer had been lost and drowned in similar situations, but we could not afford to be stranded on the wrong side of the river with our meagre rations. Once the crossing was made we secured a rope and the others carefully followed. It was not too difficult for tall Hamish and Rhino, but Joe, the shortest of us, only just kept his head above water and he emerged from his total immersion with a rather more fixed grin than normal.

We made contact later that day with Mo and Brian by following cairns and pointed sticks. They told us of the footprints so at least we knew we weren't completely lost and that our village could not be too far away.

As we descended, we entered a different type of jungle, more typical of the hot and steamy Amazon basin. The trees were huge with buttress roots, copious epiphytes and lianas. There were monkeys chattering and chucking down the odd nut from up high. Alongside the river we glimpsed flocks of brilliant macaws and frequently came across the tracks of tapirs. As the temperature rose, Hamish began casting aside his cold weather kit, sweaters at first, followed eventually by his thick sleeping bag. Joe Reinhard eagerly snatched each item, so as Hamish's load diminished, Joe's increased. His huge frame rucksack was already twice the size of any-one else's. Now it was enormous and Hamish christened it 'the pantechnicon'. Joe made good use of the extra warm weather kit. His next venture was to the high volcano tops of the Andes where he was to make his astounding discoveries of frozen child sacrifices made to the Inca gods.

Mo now suffered the only serious injury on the trip when his back seized up and he remained tent-bound in considerable pain. We debated staying another day but, with our fast-diminishing supplies, decided that the main party should push on. Lots were drawn as to who should remain as Mo's nursemaid. As Joe Reinhard was fetching water when the draw took place, Joe Brown was substituted for his namesake and immediately drew the short spaghetti. Rhino protested, suspecting a devious fix. To be fair, he had proved constantly unlucky on every previous spaghetti challenge, always conducted by Mo, usually with a malevolent grin. Joe, showing his usual kindness, chuckled and said he would stay behind and look after the invalid even though he was now down to his last packet of cigarettes.

The trail was easy for a while. We would see encouraging footprints alongside the river and then suddenly we would lose all trace of them. Then we stumbled on a good track and after a long uphill slog reached an encampment with a smouldering fire and a single occupant. He was a member of a party investigating the hydroelectric potential of the river system. He offered us a hot drink and presented me with a chunk of resin firelighter, which sadly was redundant. We were now on easy ground following a well-worn trail and by evening were pitching our tents on the only bare patch of ground we could find. Later that night a lithe, long-haired Indian dressed only in ragged trousers came silently into camp. He offered us bananas, a lemon and a gold nugget for sale and he gave me the most delectable hand-rolled cigar I have ever enjoyed. Even Hamish, who hates tobacco almost as much as he hates onions, was forced to admit it had a fine aroma.

Next day we arrived at a huge river and after searching around, an Indian ferried us across in his dugout. Beyond the river we reached Serena, the village from which our search party had recently departed. They had indeed done as we asked – picked up the news on the radio and come as requested, but they had left a day early on their way back. Nelson, the village headman, was in a state of severe intoxication, but his wife, with a pet monkey draped round her shoulders, directed us to a hut standing on stilts. Later that night we were fed a meal of unknown carbohydrate washed down by home-brewed yucca beer.

Next morning we were delighted to see a stiff-backed Anthoine and a grinning Brown walk into the village. Mo had, with the help of powerful painkillers, made a rapid recovery. Nelson had by now also recovered and was sufficiently sober to talk. Brian questioned him about the surrounding area. We asked him if he had been to the landslide; he had, and even more interestingly told us he knew of ancient stone structures not far from it. Hamish was intrigued, studied our documents again and ever the optimist postulated this was Valverde's gold-smelting site. Hamish, Joe and Mo would return next year without me, but having located the ruins were little the wiser for having done so.

The last day of the trek was made easy by hiring a horse to carry our heavy gear. We crossed another wide river, now flowing at a stately pace with our horse swimming alongside our dugout canoe, and passed our first substantial structure in weeks, a Catholic mission school full of lovely bare-foot boys and girls dressed in green smocks and tunics. Then we encountered the roar of a bulldozer forcing a road through the jungle. On either side of the rough track the trees had been felled and the understory burned in readiness for conversion to ranch land. It was a depressing sight.

Sitting by the roadside, a truck drew up and offered itself as a taxi to take us to the rough and ready frontier town of Tena. We were, apart from Brian, incredibly filthy, but after a meal, a beer or two and a cursory wash once more climbed aboard a bus and headed back to Baños. Valverde's gold mine and Atahualpa's treasure had eluded us – in all honesty we had never really bothered to look for it. But Hamish was not so easily diverted from his quest. The gleam in his eye was still undiminished and he would soon be back. For me the jungle had been a marvellous adventure, a botanical delight with the best and most amusing company I could possibly imagine.

EIGHTEEN
ENDGAME

That autumn I got a telephone summons from Hamish MacInnes to work with him on what he described as a 'huge film', provisionally titled 'Maiden Maiden'. It was set in the Alps and would be directed by no less a figure than Fred Zinnemann, Oscar-winning director of *A Man for All Seasons* and *From Here to Eternity*. This was exciting news; the prospect of interesting, well-paid work with a familiar gang of reprobates that included Mo Anthoine, Joe Brown, Tut Braithwaite, Rab Carrington, Paul Nunn and Ian Nicholson appealed to me greatly.

At an early meeting in the Bristol Hotel in London I was introduced to the producer Peter Beale and then to our director Fred Zinnemann. He appeared old and frail but also coolly authoritative, as he looked me over with his lizard-like eyes and a mischievous grin. His accent was still endearingly Viennese and I was happy to be told I was suitable as a double for the story's young Swiss Guide Johann Biari, to be played by French actor Lambert Wilson. Fred Zinnemann, Mr Zee in film parlance, had meticulously examined my previous film-double work and I was impressed he knew so much about my climbing. I learned that Sean Connery was to take the other main part as the more elderly Scottish climber, Dr Douglas Meredith. The story was set in the 1930s, involved a love triangle, and was going to involve a lot of climbing in period costume and equipment. As yet, the female love interest part had not been chosen. The location was to be the Bernina and Bregaglia peaks around St Moritz in the Engadine region of Switzerland. Filming would start in early summer the following year.

In early spring I was asked to fly out to Chamonix to meet my other self, Lambert Wilson, and climb with him to assess his ability and suitability to act as a Guide. It was a treat to experience the magic carpet of money and organisation that came as standard on a Hollywood project. Air tickets, hotels and chauffeur awaited me as I was whisked effortlessly to Chamonix for a weekend visit.

I met up with Lambert who was a likeable if highly strung actor very conscious of his big chance. He was roughly my size, his hair colour was similar and it seemed clear I could pass as his double. Next morning we embarked on a small training climb, with a French Guide, on one of the minor peaks of the Brévent on the south side of the valley; the high mountains were still deep in winter snow. I had never been to the Alps in spring before and it was a delight to see early flowers, particularly the soldanella, or snowbells, emerging from the melting drifts.

The climb was easy but it was soon obvious that Lambert was not a climber. It was not entirely discouraging. I was sure with a bit of training he could pass muster, but unfortunately acting commitments would keep him fully occupied until filming started. When I got home I told Hamish what I thought.

'Bloody hell, his agent said he was an experienced alpinist,' Hamish replied. Peter Beale was not happy with the agent's hype, but it was too late to change actors, and with my assurance that Wilson could learn quickly and be convincing as a Swiss Guide, the decision to cast him was confirmed. His inexperience, allied to his fragile ego, was to prove problematical later.

Early in June, Mo and Joe picked me up in Joe's car for the long drive out to Pontresina where the advance guard of the film were assembling. It was a formidable array of up to three separate camera crews. There were costume departments, hairdressers, make-up artists, set designers and builders, and the obligatory complement of unionised electricians or 'sparks', required and otherwise. Diplomatically, local Swiss Guides had been involved and we were lucky that the chief Guide Andrea Florineth was both helpful and friendly for it was inevitable that some conflict of interests would arise during a long period of filming in high season.

We were installed initially in an old-fashioned Edwardian hotel once much favoured by rich English visitors. Here we made friends with the Italian first camera crew led by Peppino de Filippo and his assistant, 'Bene the Gate' as he was quickly nicknamed. Peppino was a lovely man with a gentle sense of humour. He had filmed with Italian greats like Fellini and it seemed nothing would perturb him. The hotel soon proved to be irksome however, constantly locking up at 10 p.m. as though it was a Swiss bank vault rather than a hotel. Our team of climbers, nicknamed 'the Mafia', later 'the Scottish Mafia' due to the number of Scottish accents, were locked out on successive nights and only reluctantly let in after several minutes of hollering and banging on doors and windows.

For the first few weeks we explored suitable locations. Paul Nunn and I were dressed up and equipped with ancient ice-axes and nailed boots and encouraged to familiarise ourselves with the ancient art of step cutting and tiptoeing up rock with tricouni nails. My boots had been specially made for me at vast expense by the last boot-maker in Switzerland capable of doing so. I was so excited to try them on. Walking to the nearest rock, I stepped up on my tricouni edges and to my horror felt the boot's sole snap cleanly in two like a rotten stick. It was impossible to mend them so I was condemned to climb in a dreadful pair of bendy, ex-Swiss army boots which were useless for climbing anything much harder than a staircase. I protested vigorously and as a result a pair of old rope-soled scarpetti like those used in the early days was secured from the depths of the Malenco Valley. These proved much more useful for climbing, although their oddest feature was soaking the rope soles to get the best grip on rock.

Betsy Brantley now arrived to complete the casting as Kate, the climbing partner and illicit lover of her uncle Dr Meredith. She was a charming American girl from the Deep South, currently working in London. Athletic and keen to learn to climb, after taking her up a couple of practice climbs on local crags it was obvious she would do well. It was a pity that Lambert didn't also get in some early practice; acting as a Guide he, more than anyone, needed to look at home on rock, snow and ice, and be thoroughly familiar with handling rope.

While we were practising, fake hotels and huts were temporarily constructed and Hamish, as safety officer and general adviser, was dashing about in helicopters surveying glacier ice crests and rocky summits for the perfect locations. Fred Zinnemann was not an easy man to please; he had an exact vision of what he wanted and it wasn't always possible to provide the exact location he had envisaged. We had two outstanding pilots at our disposal. The elder was Ueli Baerfuss, who was steady and calm and had worked for years for Swiss mountain rescue; the younger was Jörg 'Capito' Wiesmann who delighted in showing off his aerobatic skills, swooping over cols and initially frightening us to death. After the first excitement had worn off I secretly hoped that Ueli would do most of the piloting on the basis that an old pilot must, by the law of survival of the fittest, be the safest. (Capito is, happily, still flying in his sixties.)

After what seemed an age, filming began. Paul and I, suitably dressed, climbed aboard Capito's chopper, which with breath-taking speed was soon hovering over an ice ridge halfway up the North Face of Piz Palü. Capito moved in until the skid nudged the ice crest and the blades scudded a mere metre or so from the mountainside. Hamish was as nervous as I had seen him and whispered: 'For God's sake step out gently or you'll tip us into eternity.' I did as I was told, creeping stealthily out and away from the blades. Perhaps Hamish's plea was directed more at Paul than me, for Paul was a big man and notoriously clumsy; tales of his unwitting destruction of art works, furniture and crockery were legion. Oddly, once on rock, he was as delicate a mover as one could imagine.

Once this manoeuvre was successfully achieved and the helicopter had wheeled away, we were left in sudden silence and faced with a climb to the summit. It was my task as Guide to lead the way up the narrow ice crest, which was fortunately not too difficult even encumbered by our ancient equipment and clothes. The ridge led up to a giant summit cornice below which nestled the second camera crew. This team comprised the hyperactive Austrian, Herbie Raditschnig, once a climber of renown who had worked with Heinrich Harrer, and my more laidback old friend Tony Riley.

Other scenes required me to trip lightly along a knife-edged ridge, no easy task in bendy hobnailed boots. I also had to abseil in classic style quickly down vertical rock, something only possible in lederhosen underpants to prevent serious rope burns. I had to restrain my irritation with the plump and pompous little dictator Raditschnig who was always pressing me to go faster and risk my life a little more. Most fun of all was dodging a huge 'rockfall' of painted polystyrene blocks, so well-disguised that it took an entire party of onlooking school children to retrieve them from the surrounding scree.

At this early stage in the filming bad weather slowed progress and Paul had an unfortunate accident. The Mafia had been sitting on a roadside terrace cafe enjoying an after-work beer when Mo, followed nonchalantly by Joe, leapt over the road's retaining wall as a short cut to the toilet. A short time later Paul attempted the same manoeuvre. There was a sickening crunch. Paul hadn't realised there was a three-metre drop on the other side, and that Mo and Joe had jumped precisely where they knew there were sandbags piled up to break their fall.

Paul missed them completely and hit the pavement, cracking all his front teeth, splitting his chin and doing considerable harm to his sturdy knees. He quickly departed bleeding profusely, pretending unsuccessfully to be only slightly damaged. That evening Rab was called to administer first aid and stem the bleeding as his wounds burst open and blood spattered everywhere. Next day Paul was due to take Sean for a glacier walk. He appeared, walking with difficulty, in a bright yellow jumpsuit, which looked for all the world like a giant Babygro. If he was hoping to deflect attention from his battered face, it didn't work. Fred Zee took one look at him and sent him home for treatment.

It was now that Ian Nicholson, 'Big Ian' as he was known in Glencoe, took over as Sean Connery's double. In theory this was fine but Ian was taking full advantage of our generous expense account and was carousing each night to quite a degree. The Mafia, fed up with hotel living, had moved into a comfortable house in St Moritz. While Paul was away we carefully made it Nunn-proof by stowing away every item that looked fragile. On his return, Paul was given the bedroom adorned with not one but two crucifixes – one to remind him of his lapsed faith, the other to protect him from harm, Mo suggested.

We were issued with a VW Transporter and every morning Rab, a most ruthless early riser, would usher us into the van for our morning assignments. For me it was make-up and wardrobe at 6 a.m. While Ian was acting as double, he would frequently fail to make it back home and we would pick him up staggering slightly on the road to film headquarters in Pontresina.

By the time we were made up, dressed and had our first breakfast of black coffee and heavenly bacon rolls, Ian was just about compos mentis. I was actually quite concerned; we were about to do the most difficult and dangerous film sequence, climbing on iron-hard steep ice leading up to a col – the Porta da Roseg – which, according to Andrea Florineth, had only been climbed once in over a hundred years. Capito dropped us on the narrow col along with the film crew and we roped down about 200 metres and then began the laborious task of step cutting a zigzag path towards the col. I was allowed to wear an ancient and heavy pair of crampons and I protected myself to some extent by driving ring pitons into the ice. Ian, just about sober, passed the test and belayed me with care; he was after all an ice climber of great skill in his native Highlands. When I offered him the chance to take over the lead – as a skilled client might occasionally do – he gracefully declined.

'Och no, Martin, you're doin' fine as you are.'

Our next scene was on the huge Morteratsch Glacier, which was no longer the pristine white desired by Mr Zee. A huge crevasse was chosen as the site where a frozen corpse would be discovered in the film. Mo, Rab and others had constructed elaborate internal scaffolding from which Mr Zee could direct operations, and the edge of the crevasse had been reinforced where I was to leap across it. Fred, as only the Mafia were allowed to call him, was in his element being hoisted up and down the crevasse. As double, I acted as best I could and was relieved to pass his exacting standard. The body, a not terribly convincing dummy, was brought to the surface and Big Ian, as Sean's double, was asked to gently brush snow from the frozen face. Ian, no doubt inspired by Paul's reputation, proceeded to knock the dummy's head off its shoulders.

'Och, I'm sorry Fred. I'll try to be a bit more gentle next time.'

This was the moment when Lambert had to show his paces as Sean Connery's Guide, moving over the ice and handling the rope. He was nervous and unconvincing in his movement. Yet instead of encouraging his fellow actor, who was after all in his first major film and understandably nervous, Connery was cruel and held him up to ridicule, completely undermining Lambert's confidence. True, Lambert's rope handling was cack-handed, and he strode over the glacier as if on a stage rather than a sheet of ice, but he didn't deserve to be embarrassed. I wasn't impressed by his bullying and watched wryly when later he sidled up to Rab Carrington and started a hail-all-things-Caledonian conversation. He had picked the wrong Scot to charm. Rab answered: 'If you love Scotland so much why don't you try living there?' Connery stalked off offended.

I was given the job of acting as special tutor to Lambert, something I greatly enjoyed. I had him endlessly coiling ropes and walking in a slow deliberate manner so that he gained confidence. I learned about his acting family, as famous in France as the Redgraves are in England. He was genuinely grateful to me, rewarding me with a fantastically expensive cognac, which Paul eagerly downed in a couple of glasses, and it was in his company that I was introduced to the delightful Anna Massey, who was enjoying her Alpine holiday acting a minor part as a fussy English dame.

My task as Alpine tutor was just about done when disaster struck; Lambert developed an unsightly boil on his nose. He was devastated to suffer such damage to his good looks. Filming was put on hold and Lambert dispatched to a skin specialist in Paris. When he got back, the Cockney electricians, who had more time than most to amuse themselves inventing names, started calling him 'Bert the Icer'.

'What does it mean, Martin?' he asked me.

I explained Cockney rhyming slang as best I could; 'I suppose' meant nose, and, when shortened, like Lambert to Bert, gave I-sup ... i-cer. Hence, Bert the Icer.

For the final scenes we were whisked off to the Disgrazia in the nearby Bregaglia where we bivouacked for a night; I was then dropped onto a sharp rock spire where I had to throw the rope down in a graceful loop before abseiling off. It was starting to feel like the task of Sisyphus, endlessly undertaking filming here and there but rarely to the satisfaction of Mr Zee. Fred was meticulous in selecting the best footage and in a quest to get some shots showing me back-and-footing – as I had done for *The Eiger Sanction* – I was flown to Piz Badile in search of a likely location.

We were allowed hardly any free time and when our wives and children visited to remind us of our other lives, we scarcely had time to give them the attention they deserved. We were of course very well paid and each week we queued up to receive our two crisp blue Swiss banknotes as running expenses. These accumulated and eventually I had enough to repay Mo a considerable debt I owed him from past expeditions.

On the rare free weekends when we were given time off, the keenest of us, including Rab, Tut and John Yates – a late recruit to the Mafia – would trundle off over the Maloja Pass towards Italy and climb in the Albigna Valley or a little further to the fabulous Val di Mello. This instantly became one of my most favourite climbing locations with its immaculate granite crags rising out of beech forests, with the distant snows of the Disgrazia as a backcloth. We had little time to explore but managed a most beautiful climb called *Luna Nascente* and some hard slabs including *Nuova Dimensione*. I greatly enjoyed climbing with Rab. He was equally keen and a fantastic slab climber while I excelled in cracks. It was a case of Jack Sprat and partner for we made an effective team capable of climbing most things the rock could throw at us.

By autumn the film was just about done but Fred still lusted for the pure white glacier shots he could only get in winter. Yet it was now hunting season and the film crew were suddenly unwelcome since helicopters disturbed the game. The producers decided to pack up and perhaps return in winter for the remaining shots.

I headed home to England with Rab and John Yates, who had recently moved to Altrincham. John was an outstandingly talented climber, particularly on boulder problems, and while he had worked as an art teacher he was about to become an outdoor instructor and Guide. We drove home in his van, which stuttered to a halt on numerous occasions, and it was dark by the time we reached the boulders at Fontainebleau and camped. Next day we discovered just how unfit we were for hard climbing. Airdrops each morning of bacon rolls, followed by three-course lunches and thick wedges of *Engadiner Nusstorte* every afternoon had clearly done their damage. Yet we arrived home with lots of film booty, allowing Rab to start his company making down clothing and sleeping bags, which built up gradually to become a highly successful enterprise. The money also gave me breathing space to plan my future. As we drove home from the Alps, there were already ideas about our next expedition.

Later that winter I was summoned again to Pontresina to secure Mr Zee's missing shots. The weather was perfect and we were whisked up high on Piz Palü and Piz Roseg. Fred was in a buoyant mood, and requested shyly if it would be possible to climb to the summit. Next day Hamish, Fred and I were landed on the Silver Saddle in Ueli's helicopter. Fred was as excited as a young lad on his first adventure and with him roped between us we made our stately progress to the top. Although Fred was well into his eighties he skipped along and it was a genuine pleasure to see how much he enjoyed himself. His love of the Alps was rooted in his youthful memories. As a young man he had climbed a little before he escaped the horrors of Nazism in Vienna to achieve fame in America. His list of films shows a surprising variety, from *High Noon* to *The Nun's Story*. I couldn't resist finding out a little more about some of my favourite movies and asked Fred if *High Noon* had been a dig at the McCarthy era. He smiled with his familiar tight-lipped grin.

'No, Martin, it was just a good story.' I got the message that the great film director did not wish to elucidate.

For our final winter outing he kept me on when the others had all departed to repeat a climb he had done in his youth. Fortunately a cable car took us most of the way to the top of a now popular ski destination but it was a privilege to guide him and he was deeply moved on reaching the summit. Those last few days in his company were such a pleasure.

Five Days One Summer, as it was eventually titled, was a lovely old-fashioned film with the most beautiful mountain photography. It was also Fred's last. The movie flopped commercially and was savaged by the critics; fashion had moved on and we were now in the era of gimmicks, special effects and fast-paced action. Who cares? It pleased Fred and it still pleases me to have been a significant part of it.

If Fred was done with films, then I was almost done with expeditions, although I had no awareness of this when we were planning our expedition to climb Latok in the Karakoram. Our objective was its formidable North East Ridge and this would turn out to be my last big mountain venture. Back from Switzerland, I had sufficient funds to be able to afford my own small expedition. We were ambitious to try something difficult and the Latok ridge was an obvious choice.

It's an incredible mountain, one of a group of granite towers and spires that includes The Ogre. The route had been attempted once before by a team that included some old friends from America: Jim Donini, Jeff Lowe, George Lowe and Michael Kennedy. They had climbed a large portion of the ridge in excellent conditions and were within striking distance of the summit when a vicious storm hit them. They were marooned in their tiny tents for several days, running low on food and fuel when things went from bad to worse. Jeff Lowe began to sicken, perhaps suffering some form of oedema brought on by high altitude. When the weather cleared their only option was retreat, something they only accomplished with great difficulty and effort. A friend of mine happened to meet the climbers as they reached the Panmah Glacier, describing them as exhausted ghosts. Their attempt remains one of the most epic near misses in climbing history.

The route was very long, involving both difficult rock and ice-encrusted ridges. One of the main difficulties would be logistical. How many days should one plan for? How much food and fuel would we need? Then there were the factors one could do nothing about; how would snow conditions and weather affect the route?

John Yates, Rab Carrington and I had climbed with each other for some time. John was an outstanding boulderer with a splendid Alpine record including most of the great north faces. Rab was an outstanding rock and ice climber and his record of daring and difficult peaks in the Alps and Andes, most often climbed with Al Rouse, was also well known. Perhaps the most audacious ascent was that of Jannu, the spiky neighbour of Kangchenjunga, which he had done in alpine style as a team of four.

We were faced with the problem of the missing fourth member. It was quite possible to climb as a threesome but it made more sense to have the possibility of climbing as two ropes of two. Late in our deliberations a climber from Oldham called Choe Brooks approached us. He was a tall, good-looking chap with a dark mane of curly hair. He was a talented rock climber with a good Alpine record, had a calm and easy-going temperament, all of which made us think he would slot in with us three despite being given the nickname 'the three grumps' by one of our climbing friends.

There was thankfully little to do in preparation. We had all the kit we needed, we were not fixing any rope and we had a small tent for the climb so our only big outlay was buying sufficient amounts of the latest American freeze-dried foods. Gas and fuel we would have to obtain in Pakistan. By June we were ready, flying to Islamabad and then trying to fly on to Skardu. As usual this proved to be the bottleneck. We decided that rather than wait an indeterminate period for a flight we would drive there on the recently opened Karakoram Highway. It was certainly high but not much of a way. We set off in the evening through the aromatic smoke of a thousand cooking fires; our driver was fast and nimble despite a slightly doped appearance. He drove relentlessly, hardly stopping or sleeping for two days on the most exiguous road carved out of the side of the Indus gorge. There were landslides every few miles as the unstable mud and boulder cliffs collapsed into the vast, churning river. Finally we escaped the riverbank to reach Skardu at the confluence of the Shigar and Indus rivers, at over 8,000 feet.

Skardu, the starting point for most Karakoram trips, was now much better set up for expeditions. The once dilapidated rest house had been enlarged, porters were now available and the terms of employment were clearly stipulated. Transport had also improved; there was a fleet of jeeps and tractors that could transport our team and all its kit further than was previously possible. The Pakistan government were at last putting some money into the otherwise neglected region of Baltistan and there were plans to push the road all the way to Askole, only possible by crossing the Braldu River and forcing a route on its far bank. We, unfortunately, were still required to walk through the Braldu Gorge as it had not yet been bypassed. My familiarity with this evil place did not increase its appeal by one jot.

The Braldu is a violent river forever undercutting its soft sand banks that are flanked by mountainsides of boulders and mud that are ready to avalanche at the slightest hint of rain. Luckily the weather was dry but the porters were rightfully wary and before entering the gorge they prayed with an understandable fervour. The gorge had already caused the death of an acquaintance of mine; in 1978 Pat Fearnehough had slipped into the river when the bank collapsed, was trapped by a boulder and drowned. Another death was that of a highly experienced kayaker. I attended a lecture he gave and mentioned the horror of the Braldu, one river he should avoid, which instead of putting him off only encouraged him to have a look. His fatal accident, while helping another paddler, happened in one of its calmest stretches.

From Askole, after the usual greeting and supply of eggs and chickens from wily headman Hajimedi, we set off into the now familiar hinterland to reach the Panmah River, which drained its eponymous glacier. This was the starting point for the spectacular glacier system known as Snow Lake, extensively explored by Eric Shipton and Bill Tilman. It was now becoming an adventurous trek through the Karakoram peaks and we were lucky to encounter an Italian party who had just completed it. They had some surplus food and, to our delight, donated two smoked hams. We were amazed they had managed to bring in such decidedly *haram* meat. We kept quiet about its provenance and ate with relish.

Our liaison officer, having received his stipulated clothing and equipment, wisely decided he preferred to stay in the relative comfort of Askole. This suited us but left us in a weak position to persuade the porters up the last stage onto the glacier. They deserted us at a pleasant ablation valley with grass, stream and a useful cave above the huge glacier. We wasted time and energy transporting kit and food several miles further to a gravelled area on the glacier. On the way there we passed a sizeable clump of dwarf willow scrub and by diligent effort we gathered several loads of dry firewood for cooking. This was useful as well as cheering; we had little fuel to spare. It also allowed John to perfect the subtle art of chapati making.

Once we had assembled all our equipment it was time to examine our objective and plan our attack. We set out before first light heavily laden and reached the base of our ridge. A short snow slope brought us to the rock and it was comforting to spy the first piton with its tattered rope loop used for descent by the previous party. The climbing was good, not desperately hard, but difficult enough with our heavy loads. By evening we had climbed a good section of buttress. Ahead the ridge levelled out a bit before it rose again into an ice and snow crest. We dug out a ledge, nestled down, cooked and brewed up, and wondered what the next day would bring.

It was an uneasy night; the air was too warm, which we knew was bad news. Sure enough, next day we encountered melting snow and caps of ice dribbling like giant ice creams off the top of the ridge. At one stage we had to pass under a huge overhanging cornice, which might collapse at any moment. We held our breath, said a silent prayer and tiptoed past. Having survived one dicey situation we now faced another, a steep long snow slope to the top of an ice ridge. Rab set off with his usual fortitude, ploughing his way up the unstable mass, thrusting his arms and ice-axes deep into the unconsolidated snow. He ran out of rope, so we tied on another and watched with fearful fascination as he slowly punched his way up the ever-steepening slope to finally reach the top. At this point Choe hinted at his growing unease. I dismissed this unsympathetically and after reaching the top of the ridge went down again, fuelled by anger, to bring up Rab's sack.

We were now situated in an airy spot on a narrow snow ridge that dropped alarmingly on all sides. Carving out a ledge just sufficient for our tent, we squashed inside. Once again the omens were bad; it was still far too warm. We had made good time, being ahead of the previous team, but they encountered consolidated ice, which was hard technically but at least moderately safe. By contrast, we were confronted by very unsafe snow. Next day Rab and John pushed on a couple of rope lengths and came back so we could consider our strategy. If the weather became a little cooler we would be fine. It was then that Choe produced his bombshell; he was unwilling to go on. Rab looked furious. John and I were less angry but nevertheless greatly disappointed. Rab grabbed the empty tent and hurled it over the edge with the comment: 'Well that's it then.'

We retreated in silence, each filled with his own thoughts. I did not blame Choe; it was indeed a dangerous route in the conditions we found it and he had been brave to express his misgivings. The thing we didn't know was whether it would have improved had we waited. We would never find out now, and it seemed a hollow and unsatisfactory end to what could have been a great adventure.

Once we reached the glacier Choe decided to get home as quickly as he could. The rest of us packed up as much kit as we could carry and staggered slowly towards Askole. The weather was still unbearably hot and the melting ice and snow was turning small rivulets into fast and dangerous crossings through deep water. We managed the first *nullah* but the second was worse and we only managed to cross by forming a triangle and advancing one at a time. Relieved, we finally reached the main track and were delighted to see a couple of porters coming down who were happy to burden themselves with most of our loads for the usual remuneration. If we thought our troubles were nearly over we were sadly mistaken. In the extreme heat, the Braldu River had risen to an unprece-dented height. It had cut away large chunks of the path and with a growing sense of horror we watched the path ahead of us collapse into the raging torrent. At one stage we were trapped, as the path behind us sank into the river as we were confronted with a vertical sand bank. The porters began shouting prayers; our sand bank was relentlessly undermined. But with some skill and daring, one of the porters managed to climb the bank, and by clinging on to his useful T-shaped stick we clambered up as the whole bank on which we had stood collapsed and disappeared into the river. We could no longer follow the usual track. Instead we climbed arduously for several thousand feet and traversed the steep mud and boulder cliffs by a path more suited to ibex than humans.

From Skardu, we made the road trip back to Islamabad and a few days later were flying home in subdued mood each of us sunk in his own thoughts but reluctant to talk about them. Latok proved to be a turning point, and not just for me. Our failure forced me to examine and evaluate my life as a mountaineer. Expedition climbing was certainly proving to be dangerous; I had been lucky and dodged death several times but how long would my luck last? As an absent father pursuing my own selfish ambitions I was aware that I was putting an unfair burden on Maggie and I was missing the childhood of my daughter Katie. I was certainly not pulling my weight financially.

It seemed more and more unjustifiable to take such risks and remove myself from family responsibilities for such lengths of time. Perhaps I was at last facing up my long neglected responsibilities after a protracted youth? In any case, I no longer felt the desperate urge to tackle big mountains. Instead I was happy to settle for domestic contentment and the more immediate joy of rock climbing without everyone having to suffer. At around the same time, Rab Carrington, for his own set of reasons, was also forgoing mountaineering. As climbers we were of a like mind and fell into a successful rock climbing partnership. It's a friendship that has lasted many years.

THE ROCK CLIMBING YEARS

It seems impossible that the last 30 years of my life have passed so swiftly. Perhaps it's a measure of how much I have enjoyed myself rock climbing after giving up serious mountaineering.

Having turned my back on the all-consuming life of a mountaineer, it was essential to earn a living and teaching was the obvious choice. Maggie had resumed her career after having Katie, and once more starting from the bottom had risen to become head of science at Fairfield High School for Girls. It was an old established grammar school, soon to become a comprehensive for 11 to 16-year-olds, situated on the edge of Droylsden, a rather dreary suburb of Manchester.

To our surprise, when we took our first look at the school we found it was situated in a delightful hidden green enclave with a cobbled square surrounded by modest Georgian houses set alongside an ancient cemetery and church. It formed part of a Moravian settlement, founded in the 18th century, and the school, much enlarged, still occupied its original site.

A temporary post soon cropped up in Maggie's department and for a short while we caused much amusement teaching O and A-level biology in tandem. Maggie was an outstanding teacher and for the first time I could witness the devotion she inspired and her uncanny ability to maintain a friendly discipline without apparent effort. Her skill did not go unnoticed and she rapidly rose up the career ladder to become deputy head at two nearby schools, and then head of Buxton Girls School; it was her bad luck to end a successful career less happily, as head of a large local comprehensive.

As Maggie departed from Fairfield I obtained a permanent post. It must be said I was a less skilled teacher than Maggie but I was enthusiastic and I hope my love of the subject was passed on to my pupils. The school had its advantages for biological studies; it contained a seasonal pond in the grounds with spawning frogs, and millions of dancing water fleas which provided food for hydra, the tentacle-waving freshwater jellyfish. Nearby was a canal and in summer I would take the class pond-dipping behind the factory wall of Robertson's, savouring the fruity aromas of jam-making while the girls squealed in surprise at the fierce dragonfly nymphs, newts and leeches they gathered in their nets.

Our daughter Kate was growing to be a lovely girl, intelligent and determined. She passed her 11-plus and went to Altrincham Grammar School for Girls. Despite the best efforts of her parents she resisted all offers of help with her favoured science subjects. After breezing through O-levels without apparent effort, she surprised me by wanting to study A-level sciences elsewhere. She had seemed happy enough but had not been sufficiently stretched academically. Maggie had taught at Loreto College in Hulme after returning to work after having Katie, and knew the science staff there to be excellent. Kate enjoyed the two years she spent there, became head girl, and worked her way to a place at Christchurch, Oxford – to read biology.

While Maggie and Kate went on to ever-higher achievement, I was happy to settle for being a low-profile classroom teacher. I still worked hard and gave it my all but it allowed me the time and energy to climb, as well as teach. Maggie, by contrast, worked hard and long, spending many evenings in meetings of one sort or another.

Throughout my life as a climber I always maintained my passion for rock climbing. It started early when I first touched rock and has been sustained between expeditions and long after I gave up the excitement and perils of the high mountains.

One of the great pleasures of climbing is making new friends, even as I got older, mixing and meeting so many characters from every walk of life. Over the years I have climbed with innumerable companions and I've rarely been anything but delighted with their company.

In the early days, living in Manchester, I had climbed mainly with the Alpha Club, often with Arthur Williams and Dave Little. Dave was laid back, happy to do what anyone wanted and with his great ornithological interest and quiet intelligence he was a perfect companion on the rope. Arthur, anticipating his future in America, would arrive in his vast two-tone Zephyr Zodiac and we would wallow along through Chester, Ruthin and Capel Curig to Snowdonia. We invariably headed for Llanberis and the social scene centred on the slightly seedy Padarn Lake Hotel. I loved catching up with friends and hearing the gossip, playing darts tournaments officiated by Joe Brown and Pete Crew. I loved our days on Dinas Mot, and climbing *The Skull* on the overhanging prow of Cyrn Las with Jud Jordan.

Climbing partnerships evolved and often ended. For several years there was no pattern to it at all. One weekend, I would be climbing with Richard McHardy, the next I'd be dragging Chris Bonington away from writing his memoirs to climb on Esk Buttress. There were great days out with the notoriously unreliable Paul Nunn or Clive Rowlands and the odd Lakeland encounter with 'Little Mick' Burke. In the early seventies, I made a more lasting partnership with Dave Alcock who lived in Colwyn Bay. He was a stalwart climber, strong, sure and reliable. We pioneered a good number of routes, like those I've written about in this book on Suicide Wall and Clogwyn Ddu, and our fine winter days putting up ice climbs on the Black Ladders, Ogwen and Cader Idris.

Over the course of many expeditions and changes in work, I met all sorts of new friends but Alan Hubbard has been the most enduring. With his black beard and twinkling eyes he was an argumentative but always amusing companion. We shared a love for climbing in the south-west and had many exciting adventures, repeating hard routes, most often those of Pat Littlejohn: *America* on Carn Gowla, *Darkinbad the Brightdayler* on Pentire Head and *West Face* in the Great Zawn of Bosigran.

Another lasting friendship was with John Yates and his first wife Linda, a lovely lady, whose hospitality we still enjoy, with her husband Mal. I met John at Frodsham, where he was skulking under an unpromising and mossy overhang. He was sweating and looked slightly the worse for wear, in the process of making a comeback after a prolonged break from climbing. He was small in stature with a solemn face but was obviously tough. John had been brought up by his granny in Leek, close to the Roaches, and was an early and notable pioneer on his local rocks. He was also an exceptionally talented boulderer, one of those people who are annoyingly accomplished at whatever they take up, in John's case as an artist and guitar player.

When John and Linda moved close to us in Hale we naturally teamed up; I was initiated into the delights of the Churnet Valley and we pioneered some fine routes elsewhere, including *The Slash* on Ogwen's Milestone Buttress, later notorious after the sturdy oak at its base was felled. Another unjustly neglected crag where we did some new routes was the Pillar of Elidir. John had been guiding in the Alps when I was working on *Five Days One Summer*, and we managed to find work for him in the later stages of the film. It was then that Rab, John and I first really got to know one another. John and Linda later moved to Wales, and Rab, his wife Sue, Maggie and I often stayed with them.

Tom Leppert is another character that has played a big part in my life. He also lives in Hale and became – in fact, still is – a regular midweek companion. He's a colourful and talented climber, living frugally, turning his hand to just about anything, his main love being carpentry. With his mane of curly locks and drooping Zapata moustache, he is conspicuous yet has the uncanny ability to mysteriously disappear. Together we amused ourselves digging out and re-cleaning lost quarries and various bouldering venues in deepest Cheshire. He is a keen naturalist and lover of the more esoteric climbing arts with a rare ability to sniff out unclimbed routes. He delights in being secretive and is always reluctant to reveal his discoveries. Like the proverbial grasshopper, as soon as the sun shines, he drops his tools and heads off in his beloved VW van to the next secret venue, most often in Wales.

Although climbing with so many different people offers variety and is often stimulating, it can also be frustrating. The problem of having no one to climb with had been a major setback in my youth and plans were often thwarted as a result. After our Latok expedition, when I formed a strong friendship with Rab, it was a tremendous relief to have a partner who was utterly reliable and equally keen. We enjoyed each other's company, were roughly the same ability and complemented each other's strengths. Over the years we have learned from one another; Rab has improved enormously at cracks and I have become a decent slab climber. Amazingly, we still get on well, our taste in rock climbing is catholic and we can enjoy just about any location.

A useful by-product of climbing with the same person is that we share all our equipment; at the end of a day we stuff whatever we have draped round ourselves into our sacks, ready for our next meeting. It is an extra good fortune that Rab's wife Sue is a keen walker and with Maggie has walked all over the world as we climbed.

In the early years of our climbing partnership we spent many weekends camped in Mo Anthoine's garden in Snowdonia between the holy well of St Peris and the less holy septic tank. When Kate was quite young she would disappear for hours making dens and scrambling among the jumble of rocks behind Mo's cottage. She was often 'forced' to go on walks with Maggie; she would be seen loitering behind with a sour expression vowing never to put any of her own offspring through the same torture. Fortunately, as is so often the case, the vow seems to have been forgotten. She is now a keen walker and we've had many walking trips and holidays with Katie, her husband JC, and her two children, Poppy and Arne, who are a delight and seem much more amenable to walking than Katie was.

It was on these weekends with Rab, Sue and family that we enjoyed some of our most memorable days out climbing. We were happy most of the time to repeat existing routes. Rab was not too bothered with the tedium of cleaning new lines but we climbed a few on various crags, including Craig yr Ysfa. On one typical weekend we walked up to Dinas Cromlech and climbed *Foil*, *Right Wall* and *Resurrection* in quick succession. The climber ahead of us on *Resurrection* had struggled on the crux and watched Rab cruise up it in respectful silence.

'How does he manage to make it look so easy?' he finally asked.

I could only think of one answer: 'Because he is a much better climber than you are.'

The holidays gave us more time to travel further, and in summer we normally headed to Europe. Rab, Sue, Lizzie, Jack, Maggie, Kate and I would set off in our two vehicles to camp and climb from the Pfalz in Germany to the Verdon Gorge in southern France. One of our early trips was a visit behind the Iron Curtain to the Bohemian sandstone towers of communist Czechoslovakia. Sue had very recently given birth to her son Jack, so Rab was alone in his Minivan while Maggie, Kate and I were in our car. The holiday started badly. I had casually assumed the climbing was near the city of Teplice close to the East German border. Only later did we realise that there are many Teplices, but an arduous drive through the night eventually got us to the right destination.

The bureaucracy in those days was tedious. We were obliged to exchange the equivalent of 10 dollars a day for local currency but found it impossible to spend our daily allocation despite our best efforts, buying beer for all and sundry and eating out on all possible occasions. The beer was exceptionally good and unbelievably cheap and this, according to one of the more cynical Czech climbers, was the secret of the inefficient, repressive Communist regime's survival. 'Keep the beer cheap and just about everyone is half-cut and cheerful.'

We made many good friends and were dragged away from our official campground to pitch our tents in a local climber's garden. We had to troop off to police headquarters to inform them of our relocation and leave our passports and visas. In our new campsite we met Bernd Arnold, the *Wunderkind* of East German climbing. Like his Czech counterparts he was confined to climbing behind the Iron Curtain and the frustration they endured was palpable. Bernd was a brilliant climber, seeking out new routes and enjoying the company of us 'outsiders'. His dearest wish was to visit the fabled climbing grounds in the West. It was many years before the fall of the Berlin Wall allowed him to fulfil his dream. In the meantime he kindly invited us to visit his home territory, the Elbsandsteingebirge, famous sandstone towers near Dresden in Saxony, home to many of the most famous German climbers such as Lothar Brandler and Dietrich Hasse.

It was an interesting holiday, and we enjoyed great hospitality and climbed many slightly scary routes, including some impressive cracks. These were all done without chalk and minimal protection, which was mostly knotted slings and the occasional ring bolt. Rab had to leave promptly to get back to Sue, but his rush home was soon stymied. He eventually managed to overtake a long convoy of combined harvesters blocking the narrow road but was immediately flagged down for speeding; while paying a hefty on-the-spot 'fine', which took the last of his money, the combines lumbered past. Then, at the Austrian border, he discovered to his horror he'd mis-placed his visa. While collecting our passports from the police he had failed to separate his own visa from ours. He would have to wait at the border until we passed through, which turned out to be a good while later since we spent a leisurely day sightseeing in Prague. We actually chose a different border crossing to Rab but the border guards were obviously expecting us and after I had the shock of opening the wrong visa, and being confronted with Rab's stern stare, the information was passed on to the other post by the border guards, who found the whole thing hilarious. He was finally released from limbo.

The following year we visited the Verdon Gorge in Provence and follow-ed this up with a trip to the Picos de Europa in north-west Spain where we climbed on the mist-shrouded Naranjo de Bulnes. It was on the way home that we heard the news that Al Rouse and Julie Tullis had died in tragic circumstances high on K2. Al had for many years been Rab's mountain-eering partner and together they had done many notable routes in the Alps, Andes and Himalaya. I had known Julie Tullis for many years and had fond memories of her from my first days on southern sandstone. This was the first time but alas not the last that our holidays would be punctuated by the sad news of a lost companion.

Our promised trip to East Germany to climb on the sandstone towers near Dresden was less happy than our Czech visit. Applying for a visa through bulletproof glass at an unfriendly embassy should have warned us. If the Czech Republic had seemed repressive, East Germany was 10 times worse. We nervously approached the border and endured minute scrutiny of our vehicles before it was finally discovered I was missing some document or other. We waited for several hours while the guards consulted officials in Berlin and we were allowed to go on. We drove along the original concrete autobahn now crumbling and almost empty of traffic to Dresden. It was shocking to see the city, still half in ruins 40 years after the war ended. The famous Frauenkirche was like a rotten tooth standing beside the River Elbe.

The city was blackened by brown coal and exhaust fumes from the belching Trabants; I couldn't escape the thought that we had bombed a city once known as the Florence of the North into this pitiable state.

To add to this general air of dolefulness, the weather was cold and wet. We met up with Bernd who invited us to camp in his garden and then showed us around his local crag. He pointed us up one of the more testing climbs. Rab clipped the first ringbolt and then faced a long run-out to the next one. He tried to place a knotted sling to bridge the gap but they had to be poked in using a wooden peg, and not being familiar with the technique began to struggle. Unwisely he decided to press on. He fell unexpectedly, his sling popped out of the crack and, partly thanks to my less than attentive belaying, he hit the ground, injuring his ankle. To compound the agony, Rab's young son Jack became ill with pneumonia and the weather turned from bad to worse. The famous sandstone towers of the Saxon Switzerland were most often shrouded in drizzly mist, set among dark pine forests.

We did manage some good routes, and were impressed to discover hard climbs – by modern standards E1 5b – pioneered by the American Oliver Perry-Smith in the early 1900s. There were routes by Dietrich Hasse climbed in the 1950s that were probably the hardest in the world at that time. We actually ran into Hasse while we there, on his annual visit to his old stomping ground. He was now elderly and a little stiff with old injuries and a rather crusty character. We were quite grateful to leave East Germany, although I'm glad we managed to witness it in all its repressive glory before the fall of the Iron Curtain.

Rab and I avoided police states in the following years, concentrating on the fine granite slabs of the Grimsel Pass on the edge of the Oberland and then the Arco Valley in the Gran Paradiso of Italy. We squeezed into a crowded campsite and enjoyed two terrific days' climbing before a cloud burst in the night caused an earth avalanche that nearly engulfed us. We fled in near panic. Katie's tent was washed away in a flood with her rolling around inside screaming. Next morning, with our tent under two metres of mud and stone, we decided to regroup in the glorious Val di Mello south of the Piz Badile. Here we met up with old friends Dave Alcock, Toddy and their son Jamie. It was the last year when wild camping was permitted so we made the most of it, sitting around a campfire each evening and climbing to our heart's content on the immaculate granite cliffs fringing the valley, most memorably the *Flauto Magico* on the huge Precipizio degli Asteroidi.

There were trips to the Catalan Pyrenees and the lovely crags of Taüll and also to Corsica. Despite the intense heat of high summer we enjoyed a few great climbs on the strange sculptured granite formations characteristic of the island. A route called *Jeef* at Bavella, 400 metres long and an absolute masterpiece at 7a+, was perhaps our best outing on a rare cool day although the wind nearly whipped Rab off the delicate final moves up an exposed arête. Maggie and I walked the GR20 over Corsica's mounainous spine, which made a fine end to the holiday.

A year later we headed once more to Switzerland, this time to the Rätikon, which boasts some of the finest long limestone routes in the Alps. Bad weather curtailed our activities, forcing us to lower venues in France. It was here that we received the terrible news that Paul Nunn had died in the Karakoram. Paul had been climbing as long as I had, he was a dear companion, we had both shared many adventures and he seemed to be a sturdy fixture in the climbing world. I remembered seeing his red hair bobbing above the crowds pouring off the ferry as Maggie and I waited for him in France, all those years ago. Now suddenly he was gone.

With Katie grown up and free to go off by herself it was possible to plan some more ambitious holidays. An obvious choice was America, particularly the famous granite of the Yosemite Valley. Rab had already spent some time there in his youth hanging out at Camp Four; he advised it would be too hot and crowded in Yosemite itself so we chose instead to go high and climb on the domes of Tuolumne. I loved it. The alpine flowers were a delight, and the climbing no less so. The best route of the trip was the horribly named *Shipoopi* – a 5.12 vertical wall studded with innumerable small 'chicken heads'. We completed the trip with a drive to the Needles, a remote and beautiful series of towers set high in the southernmost Sierras, climbing absolute classics like *Thin Ice* and its neighbour the five-pitch *Don Juan Wall*, including its final hideous overhanging off-width.

We returned to America in the summer of 1999, meeting up with old friend Jim Donini and climbing Petit Grepon in Colorado's Rocky Mountain National Park. In Wyoming we visited the strange crack-climbing paradise of Vedauwoo and then climbed the even stranger Devil's Tower that rises out of the level Wyoming plain. We were back in Boulder in time for bird-nesting restrictions in Eldorado Canyon to be lifted and finally got the chance to climb *Naked Edge*, ending the holiday on a high note.

By the summer of 2001, both Maggie and I had retired from teaching. At last we could plan holidays outside the limits of school terms. However, shortly before leaving for America, Maggie slipped on a pile of slippery magazines and broke her leg badly. She endured a summer of being pushed around in a chair, but by late autumn her leg was sufficiently mended for us to have our belated holiday starting out in Salt Lake City and ending up at the City of Rocks in Idaho. Once again we threw ourselves on the hospitality of Jim Donini and his wife Angela, who were now living in southern Colorado in the fine old mining town of Ouray. Despite Maggie's disability we had a great time. Jim took me to Indian Creek where I met up with Paul Ross, an old friend and legendary climber from the Lake District. We climbed with a bunch of Cubans eager to learn the mysterious art of hand jamming. I climbed Six Shooter Peak with Jim, and a vast number of cracks of every type before setting off on a fantastic drive with Maggie down Route 191 through the canyon lands of Arizona, ending up in the enchanting Cochise Stronghold. Back in Ouray, I ended the holiday by climbing with Jim in the dark and forbidding Black Canyon. He chose the 5.10d route *Scenic Cruise*, perhaps one of the finest long rock climbs I have ever done and we were hard pressed to finish before night fell in the short days of late November.

When Rab sold his business and also retired we planned a mammoth celebratory trip around America in the autumn. Starting off in Red Rocks outside the city of Las Vegas we suffered in the heat, with temperatures pushing into the mid-30s. Yet a few weeks later we climbed a nine-pitch 5.11c called *Levitation 29* in driving snow flurries, a route Lynn Hill described as one of her favourites in the whole of America. Our trip took us south with a visit to the Grand Canyon, the strange inverted wedge of the Enchanted Tower and the majestic canyon of Zion National Park. We ended up in late November at Joshua Tree, braced against a freezing wind, climbed out, and ready once more for the comforts of home.

On our next big trip, we headed to Canada and the huge granite cliffs of Squamish Chief, towering over the fjords of British Columbia. We were blessed with perfect weather and took advantage of it. Camped at the base of the cliff, in the evenings we wandered around talking to other climbers, who seemed happy to share information with two old-timers. They obviously didn't expect too much from us; the routes they recommended were often too easy and each evening we caused some surprise by the standard of our achievements.

One of our best climbs happened by chance. We had settled on a delicate slab climb at the base of the cliff and consequently dumped all our large nuts and Friends to climb unencumbered. I had already spotted a stunning cracked pillar high above us and when we finished our slab just below it,

I suggested we give it a go. The wide crack was the only problem – we had no protection for it – but I weighed it up and set off confidently up the first moves. As I pointed out to Rab, if I could do the first moves comfortably I could in theory do the same for the next hundred feet or so. And so we bagged *The Grand*, perhaps the best route of all at Squamish. It leads to the summit, so we had a long and agonising shuffle back down in painful climbing shoes.

Later on we climbed more classics including the 5.11d *Freeway* before finishing with *Cerberus*, another 5.11d on the Chief's Tantalus Wall – and one of the best slab climbs in North America. This had just proved too hard for one of the young hotshots we'd met at the campsite and we couldn't resist returning him several quickdraws he'd been forced to leave on the crucial diagonal traverse.

With Rab and I both retired it was possible to escape the dreary early winter months and visit Australia. We had long read of the Arapiles and the Blue Mountains so to arrive in Melbourne was incredibly exciting. We enjoyed a couple of days meeting up with our old friend Andy Pollitt but the Arapiles were rather less than we expected and armed with perhaps the worst guidebook ever printed we spent several days trying to sort out the geography of the crag and climbing a few undistinguished routes. Such was our early frustration that Rab unexpectedly bellowed to whoever was in earshot: 'The Arapiles are rubbish!' It was, I suppose, a case of the emperor's new clothes; everyone kept insisting how marvellous the Arapiles were when to us they seemed a fairly minor collection of slick, sun-baked rocks poking out of the desert.

There was no such disappointment with our next venue – the Grampians. Here we met up with Jim Donini and his friends Bob and Ruth who had just visited New Zealand. The rock climbing on the golden sculptured sandstone was exceptional and Taipan Wall must be one of the world's great crags. We enjoyed another outing to a hidden gem called Eureka Wall, where we climbed two immaculate face routes. Camping in the Grampians brought us into close contact with the wildlife. Every morning kookaburra, emus and kangaroos would run and hop alongside our cars. In camp we had our own 'sandwich wallaby', which loitered expectantly and joined us round the evening campfire. At night the opossums rattled the cooking gear and one even squeezed through the partly open window of Bob's car, consumed a two-kilo fruitcake, and was consequently too fat to make its escape.

Jim, in his characteristically disorganised manner, managed to lose all his clothes. Having packed up camp we headed to the town of Hamilton to celebrate Rab and Sue's 30th wedding anniversary in style. Spotting some bins at the roadside, we thankfully dumped all our camping garbage packed up in black bin bags. It was only when we passed the laundry that Jim demanded to know where his clothes were. He'd placed them in an identical black bag, which we had unceremoniously deposited in the bin. He managed to retrieve it just before the bin lorry arrived.

Despite our warnings, Jim and Bob insisted on visiting the fabled Arapiles, so we dutifully tagged along and I must say, with a little more knowledge, we found a few half-decent routes including a difficult over-hanging crack put up by 'Hot' Henry Barber some years previously.

Our final destination was the Blue Mountains near Sydney. On the way we stopped at a strange granite lump called Mount Buffalo. Here we were handicapped by not having sufficient rope to abseil blindly into unknown territory to start the best climbs. It was also unfortunate that Australia was enduring one of its droughts; wild fires were an ever-present danger. Already in the Grampians we had been denied several of the best crags due to burn-outs and in the Blue Mountains danger loomed. Driving along a high ridgeline overlooking the vast forested plain below, we spotted a tiny puff of smoke in the distance. A couple of days later black cinders and grey ash were falling on our tents and soon Blackheath was thronging with cheerful and burly fire crews cutting swathes of forest to protect the neigh-bourhood. Despite the fires there was still plenty to climb in the Blue Mountains; the walking and climbing everywhere apart from Arapiles had been terrific.

Our Australian trip was a great success but it was the last time we would enjoy our best health. Rab was the first to suffer when he was diagnosed with early bowel cancer. Fortunately his operation was timely and successful. My own health also suffered a decline with a persistent if mild case of Crohn's disease, and an increasingly arthritic shoulder. Having made a swift reco-very, Rab was climbing harder than ever and as if to make up for lost time we engaged in a burst of short holidays to Turkey, Morocco and Mallorca. These were a prelude to our next big trip, this time to South Africa.

South Africa, despite its new freedom and the ending of apartheid, still seemed an uneasy place with the startling contrast between very rich and poor only too apparent. To match our own unease the weather was extremely unsettled and we only managed one route on Table Mountain before thick mist swallowed us up, denying us a view. We had looked forward to climbing and walking in the Cederbergs but it lashed with rain, forcing us to move on to the lesser delights of Montagu. Our efforts to climb in the northern Drakensberg around the rather bleak town of Harrismith were thwarted by icy rain and I suffered an episode of Crohn's. Once more we were forced north to the subtropical Waterval Boven. Once again we were lashed with heavy rain and for several days we remained marooned in our chalet with the dirt access road made impassable. Eventually the crag dried out enough for us to enjoy some good routes but the highlight of the holiday, it was generally agreed, was the final few days driving through the immense Kruger Park, watching the so-called big five African game animals.

Although I had to acknowledge that old age and growing decrepitude were catching up with me, I was still as keen as ever to experience climbing in far-off destinations and we planned a grand finale to the fabulous granite domes in the highlands of Madagascar. Then, a few months before departure, I started to feel unwell with what appeared to be a random set of symptoms. At first I had persistent laryngitis, then I was briefly deaf in one ear. The usual antibiotics proved useless and I began to feel strangely weak and to experience heavy night sweats. Blood tests once more proved negative but my decline continued with frightening speed. We obviously had to cancel our trip and wished Rab and Sue good luck.

My condition worsened. I began to have excruciating pain in my joints and peculiar blisters on my hands, and at this point I was packed off to hospital for more tests. Within a few days I was fighting for my life. Luckily a diagnosis was reached in the nick of time; I had a rather rare autoimmune disease called Wegener's granulomatosis. This formerly fatal condition can now be controlled by a heavy regime of steroids, immuno-suppressants and other drugs, but considerable damage to my kidneys and lungs had already been done. The disease left me so weak that on my first trip to the hospital bath I found myself too feeble to climb out of it without calling for assistance. I returned home grateful but still unwell and then underwent a course of chemotherapy. Slowly I began to recover and from being unable to walk more than a few yards I built up to a few miles a day. My 70th birthday was more a celebration that I was still alive than anything else. One of my first ventures on rock was a visit to the bouldering paradise of Fontainebleau. This time I was happy to be on the children's circuits.

I am now, after two years, in good health and pray that I do not have a recurrence of the disease. I am climbing again – a little shakily but I am getting better and stronger all the time. Rab has been very understanding leading me up climbs we would once have dismissed as too easy or would have casually soloed in our youth. My recovery has been hard won and once more I can look to the future with hope. I am immensely grateful to still be alive; I savour each moment of joy with special appreciation and in particular I cherish the love and support of my family and friends.

My illness has given me a great deal of time to reflect on my life and complete this book. I have had a marvellously interesting and happy life. Climbing has given me rich and intense experiences. Through climbing I have met a vast number of people from all walks of life, made lasting friends and learned many life lessons. I still have the same passion for it. My decline may not have been as graceful as I would have wished but I have enough good memories to sustain me.

'Could I have achieved more?' I sometimes ask myself. Of course I could, but although I had talent and a level of determination, I lacked the ruthless drive and physical strength necessary to achieve greatness. I have never sought fame or fortune and was able to step back when it seemed right to do so. Perhaps I should be thankful for my failings. I have, after all, survived and am enjoying my old age with my wife, family and grandchildren, digging my allotment and hanging on to the last.

CHAPTER INTRODUCTION
ILLUSTRATIONS AND EXCERPTS

Chapter 1   pvi
Me as a child in Alsdorf, Germany. Photo: Boysen collection.

Chapter 2   p8
Excerpt from *Southern Sandstone*, by Mike Vetterlein and Robin Mazinke. Published in 2008 by The Climbers' Club and reproduced with permission from the publisher.

Chapter 3   p24
Terry and Julie Tullis at High Rocks. Photo: Terry Tullis.

Chapter 4   p40
Route description from *Southern Sandstone*, by Mike Vetterlein and Robin Mazinke. Published in 2008 by The Climbers' Club. Topo from *Southern Sandstone*, by Dave Turner. Published in 1989 by The Climbers' Club and reproduced with permission from the publisher.

Chapter 5   p50
Topo from *Classic Dolomite Climbs*, by Anette Köhler and Norbert Memmel. Published in 2008 by Bâton Wicks Publications and reproduced with permission from the publisher.

Chapter 6   p68
Maggie and me at the short-lived Alpha hut below Millstone Edge. Photo: Alpha Club members.

Chapter 7   p82
Excerpt from *Llanberis South*, by P. Crew. Published in 1966 by The Climbers' Club and reproduced with permission from the publisher.

Chapter 8   p96
Excerpt from *Gogarth*, by Andy Newton, Andy Pollitt, Steve Haston, Paul Williams, Mike Gresham and Ian Smith, edited by Geoff Milburn. Published in 1990 by The Climbers' Club and reproduced with permission from the publisher.

Chapter 9   p112
The North Face of the Grandes Jorasses from the ruined Leschaux Hut. Photo: Chris Bonington Picture Library.

Chapter 10   p126
Excerpt from *Eastern Crags*, by A. Davis and N. Wharton, edited by S. J. H. Reid. Published in 2011 by the Fell and Rock Climbing Club and reproduced with permission from the publisher.

Chapter 11   p142
The 1967/1968 British Cerro Torre Expedition postcards, signed by Pete Crew, Mick Burke, Dougal Haston and myself.

Chapter 12   p156
Excerpt from my account of the Annapurna climb in *Mountain* 12, November 1970.

Chapter 13   p170
Nick Estcourt and me (smoking) at Camp IV on the South Face of Annapurna. Photo: Chris Bonington Picture Library.

Chapter 14   p186
Route description from *Ogwen*, by Mike Bailey. Published in 2010 by The Climbers' Club and reproduced with permission from the publisher.

Chapter 15   p196
Excerpt from *Mountain* 37, July 1974.

Chapter 16   p208
The 1976 Trango Tower expedition postcards, signed by Joe Brown, Mo Anthoine, Malcolm Howells and myself, and excerpt from my account of the climb in *Mountain* 52, November/December 1976.

Chapter 17   p222
Stocking up in Quito. Photo: Joe Brown.

Chapter 18   p236
Taking a break to read the royal wedding edition of *Newsweek* during filming for *Five Days One Summer*. Photo: Joe Brown.

Epilogue   p250
Joe Brown playing darts in the Padarn Lake Hotel. Photo: Terry Tullis.